A GUARDIAN OF *Slaves*

BOOK TWO

NAOMI FINLEY

ISBN: 978-1-7750676-6-5

Cover designer: Victoria Cooper Art
Website: www.facebook.com / VictoriaCooperArt

Editor: Scripta Word Services
Website: scripta-word-services.com

For my husband

Prologue

Livingston Plantation, 1851

ON SCHEDULE, CHARLES HENDRICKS'S PRIVATE CARRIAGE rolled down the lane and through the gates of Livingston Plantation a few hours after sunset.

The man on the ridge leaned forward, arms resting on the neck of his mount, awaiting the outcome of his earlier sabotage of the carriage. If all played out as planned, Hendricks would take his last breath tonight.

He'd cleanse the earth of the Hendricks and Shaw bloodlines once and for all, breaking the curse Olivia Shaw had placed on his family all those years ago. Even the hangman's noose hadn't snuffed out her witchery.

He inhaled deeply of the cigar clutched between his teeth, the hot, sweet smoke slithering down his throat to circle in his lungs. Removing the cigar with a gloved hand, he puffed out billowy gray rings of smoke. The rings floated into the starless darkness above, shifting form before vanishing into the autumn night.

Below, the carriage began to sway violently from side to side. A warmth radiated through his chest as he watched Hendricks fight to regain control. Before his hungry eyes, the moment he'd waited for played out. The watcher lurched forward as the carriage rolled over, eager to see its demise.

The piercing squeals of the horse shattered the quiet of the night as it went down thrashing. In the wreckage, the carriage lantern set fire to the surrounding grass and brushwood. The man sat mesmerized by the beauty of the flames as the fire took life, the drumming in his chest elevating to a roar in his ears. Squinting past the glow of the blaze, he located the form of Hendricks, pinned beneath the carriage.

The watcher released a long, slow breath of satisfaction. He'd put his plan in motion; he would become master of everything the Hendrickses owned, and he'd incinerate anything or anyone standing in the way.

His brother would delight in his achievement. Revenge would be theirs.

With a jerk of the reins and a kick of his heels, he dug his spurs into the sides of the horse, and it leaped forward, bound for home.

Sometime later, the man veered his mount off the main road and bent low under the hanging vines of the cypress trees. He guided the horse onto the serpentine path on the other side.

The trail ended at an untamed, moon-drenched meadow. The gray, weather-beaten barn's shadow devoured the smaller building next to it—a windowless, one-room cabin suffocating in the entanglement of evergreen vines. Dismounting at the barn, he lifted the board barring the doors. Groaning in protest, the doors swung open. He lit the lantern hanging on a beam near the entrance, the jagged yellow glow the lantern cast elongating his dark silhouette across the barn floor.

Whimpering to the right made him spin on his worn heels to face the handful of slaves he'd taken from the freed Negro's plantation a few miles over. A sinister smile crept over his unshaven face. The man reveled in the sight of the slaves' bulging eyes as they sat huddled together with their hands chained above their heads.

Filthy animals! Damn Negroes, going around thinking they can sow the same ground as the white men. The rich Negro got what he deserved.

The drunken singing of his father floated in from outside.

Grumbling to himself, the man urged the horse into a stall. He shoved at the horse's hindquarters to get by the animal and removed the saddle. The horse nudged him from behind as he slung the saddle over the side of the stall. Cursing, he drove a fist against the side of the creature's head, then kicked the gate to the stall closed and left the barn, barring the doors shut behind him.

He found his half-naked father riding his horse up to the cabin. A bottle of whiskey swung in his hand as he continued to belt out a tune. "Useless bastard," the man said, storming toward him.

He pulled his father off the horse and slung him over his shoulder, grimacing at the overpowering stench of body odor, whiskey, and jasmine. Women and gambling were his religion. Kicking the cabin door open, he carried the unconscious man to the far corner of the room and deposited him in a heap on the bed there. Straightening, he peered down at his pathetic excuse of a father.

One quick slash of his throat and the burden of him would be gone, the constant gibbering in his head slowed to say. *End his life. Make him pay for what they did to you.*

"Silence!" He cuffed his own ears with his hands as he moved away. He slammed the door, and it shook on its rusted hinges. His father's weakness for women sickened him. Had his mother taught him nothing? Women were the demise of all men.

He lowered himself into a chair in front of the fireplace.

Pulling off his boots, he stretched his legs out in front of him. The throbbing in his right foot grew worse with each passing year. Damn Virginia and that blizzard! It had claimed three of his toes.

Turning to the warmth of the crackling fire, he slid his hat down over his eyes and tried to shut out the grating of his father's drunken snores.

❦ CHAPTER ❧
One

S HIVERS RACKED MY BODY. MY SHOULDERS ACHED WITH THE tension from my white-knuckled grip on the reins that bit through my brown leather gloves. Bile scorched the back of my throat. Beside me, my friend Whitney clung to the side of the wagon, jaw tense with worry and yes, fear.

We must make it! We must! Squinting through the relentless rain blinding my vision, I scanned the horizon for the edge of town. *He can't die. Please let him make it alive.* I winced with each jaw-rattling jolt of the wagon, worrying for the gravely wounded slave hidden behind the false plank under the wagon seat.

We pushed through the rain-filled ruts suctioning at the wheels with each rotation. Droplets of cold muck splattered our clothing and faces.

Last evening, the slave had shown up at Livingston, pounding on the front door as blood pooled on the veranda from the gaping wound in his midsection. Leaning on the frame, he gasped for air, his eyes wild with fear. He cried out repeatedly, "I come seekin' de Guardian."

The risk of keeping him at Livingston past morning had been too high. He'd killed the overseer over at the Thames Plantation. Art Thames would be out for Negro blood, and that of anyone harboring him. Despite his condition, we had to try to get him out on the afternoon ship leaving for Baltimore. The dark, early morning skies had held the promise of a downpour, but we'd hoped to reach town before they unleashed their torrent.

The edge of town stretched out before us, but as we rounded the bend, my breath caught at the sight of four riders galloping toward us. Rain glistened on the coats of the charging beasts. The horses' hooves kicked up the wet ground and surrounded them and their riders in a cloud of black liquid.

Whitney's hand moved to the rifle leaning on the seat between us.

Deafened by the thrashing of my heart as they drew near, I focused my line of vision straight ahead.

The horsemen pulled their mounts to a stop in the middle of the road. One held up his hand. "Halt!"

I eased the wagon to a stop.

The speaker moved his horse to my side, and I gulped back the lump forming in my throat as I locked eyes with Art Thames. Out of the corner of my eye, I glimpsed another man taking up a position alongside Whitney. He was none other than Richard Carter, the father of the town gossip, Lucille. The other two men circling the wagon were strangers.

"Is there something we can help you with?" I cocked my head in Art's direction.

"We're looking for one of my niggers who ran off last eve. He was injured and couldn't have gotten far. You didn't happen to see a stray nigger, did you, Miss Hendricks?"

Holding his yellow-tinged eyes with mine, I said, "No, but if I do, I'll certainly let you know."

The men at the rear threw back the oilskin tarp covering the goods in the bed of the wagon.

Forcing myself to breathe evenly, I asked, "What does the man look like?"

"Average height; really ugly. The slave's a problem and has been since I bought him. He's got a well-deserved scar running from the top of his forehead down to his belly."

A gnarly scar, I recalled all too well. I'd gotten an up-close view of the scar when Mammy had cut off the man's blood-drenched shirt to sew him up. Someone had found pleasure in torturing the slave, and that someone sat in front of me.

My throat tightened. The desire to hang the slave's master by his thick, hairy neck surged through me. But a lynching would be too easy for the brutality he'd dealt out.

The man's eyes drifted to Whitney.

"So he's recognizable," I said, lifting my hand to my chin as if pondering. "As I've said, I haven't seen him, but I'll be on the lookout for a slave matching your description."

"You do that," he said. "All right, let's go." He pulled his reins and kicked his heels into the sides of his horse.

We sat still until the thundering of the horses' hooves faded, leaving only the pelting of the rain on the wagon.

"Bastards!" Whitney cursed as she jumped down to secure the canvas. "No respect for any persons or their goods."

I gave the removable plank under the seat a light kick with my heel.

"You all right?"

A weak, muffled noise came from within.

"We're almost to town, and soon you'll be far away from that madman."

No reply came.

Whitney boosted herself onto the seat. I whipped the reins, and the horses lurched forward.

CHAPTER
Two

ADGER'S FOLLY WAS BURSTING WITH ACTIVITY. BRICK WAREHOUSES cast shadows over the granite bridge. The harbor was congested with steam engines, and further out, the dots of sailing vessels threaded toward the open sea. Endless piles of cotton and rice ready for shipping lined the wharf.

We located Captain Gillies out in front of Hendricks Enterprises' warehouse, shouting orders to the dockworkers loading wooden crates and bales of cotton onto a flatbed wagon.

He turned to face us as I pulled alongside him. He stood with his shoulders curved forward against the cold and the rain. "Miss Willow, Miss Whitney, I wasn't expecting you until the end of the week."

"We came to make a delivery to the general store, and I thought I'd stop by to check on things here."

His bushy copper brows lifted, and his keen blue eyes studied us intently. Several seconds ticked by before he shrugged and said, "It's always a pleasure to see you ladies. Days on end filled with these grimy sailors can get to a man after a while." The captain clapped the shoulder of a black sailor as he passed. The sailor grinned up at us and nodded.

My eyes flitted from the captain to him. "Afternoon."

"Afternoon," he said and continued on down the dock.

"Can I talk to you privately?" I asked, loosening my grip on the reins as the horses jerked against them.

Captain Gillies's expression grew serious. "Let me get this last load of supplies tended to for Captain Phillips so he can depart on schedule."

"Hurry. It may already be too late," I said.

He stiffened before he whirled and started barking orders to the men with heightened urgency.

As Whitney and I climbed down, a whistle from a steam engine startled me, and I fell backward, crashing onto the dock with a brain-shaking thud. Whitney hurried to help me to my feet. Frowning, she said in a hushed tone, "What are we going to do? We need to get him on the ship today."

"We will. I need to get Captain Gillies alone to inform him we have cargo."

Captain Gillies, my father's confidant in all matters to do with Hendricks Enterprises, had schooled Ben and me on how my father had run his ships. The captain had shown us the trapdoor under the pile of nets and ropes that gave access to a hidden room. Father had concealed fugitives there until he could deliver them to the next station along their journey to freedom. Captain Gillies's desire to aid my father, and now us, in our cause derived from his family's years as indentured servants.

Soon the captain's loaded wagon made its way toward the ship, and he joined us.

"We have cargo, and it needs to be on that ship." Whitney nodded at the *Olivia I.*

"What?" He tipped his face up to address her. "We hadn't planned on—"

"The cargo arrived late."

He took a wide scan of the dock. "Bring the wagon inside," he said, and disappeared into the warehouse.

I led the horses inside, and Captain Gillies closed the doors behind us and dropped the board into place to bar it closed. Whitney hurried to slide open the plank under the seat. The slave tumbled out onto the floor of the driver's seat.

He lay unmoving.

No! I lifted his wrist to take his pulse. Nothing. "Whitney…"

Whitney pushed me aside and took his wrist between her fingers. Moments later, she lowered his arm to his chest. Sadness permeated her green eyes. "He's gone."

Tears itched at the corners of my eyes. As I'd feared, the man's wounds were too severe. Each loss of a human life entrusted to my care etched a little more out of my heart.

A year had passed since my father's death, but it felt like forever. Ben Hendricks—my father's brother and my birth father—and I had spent countless hours discussing Hendricks Enterprises with Sam, my father's lawyer, and Captain Gillies. Collectively, we'd decided that with the help of Jones I'd tend to the matters at the plantation and Ben would see to the importing and exporting.

Before Whitney, her twin siblings, and I returned from Rhode Island at the end of summer, Ben had left for England on business.

"What do we do now?" Whitney rubbed a slender hand over the nape of her neck.

"We can't chance taking him back with us to bury."

Captain Gillies removed a canvas draped over some crates and dropped it on the floor. He lifted the body of the slave and gently laid it on the canvas. "I'll get rid of the body. You ladies head on out of here before someone grows suspicious of you delivering goods on a day like today."

"It's our Christian duty to at least offer a prayer for the man," I said, and held out a hand to Whitney.

Captain Gillies stood and removed his rain-drenched hat. Heads bowed, we said a prayer for the dead man.

Minutes later, heavy of heart, Whitney and I left the warehouse.

❦ CHAPTER ❦
Three

B Y THE TIME WE PULLED UP IN FRONT OF THE GENERAL STORE, the rain had lightened to a drizzle. Silver puddles glistened on the cobblestones with the reflections of shops and passersby. Horses clip-clopped down the street, pulling wagons and carriages. A freckle-faced newspaper boy splattered his gray trousers with water as he stomped through a puddle. Unfazed, he bellowed, "Read all about it! Get your paper!"

As I was climbing down from the wagon, a woman's saccharine voice called out, "Is that you, Willow Hendricks?"

Every muscle in my body melded into stone. Her voice stopped the flowing of rivers and drove mother birds to abandon their nests. I squeezed my eyes shut and whispered, "Give me patience."

Lucille Carter stood across the street on the boardwalk outside the dressmaker's shop. In one lace-gloved hand, she clutched a cream-colored parasol. The other she waved frantically at us. Tucked under her arm was a brown paper-wrapped package. She threaded through carriages and wagons to cross the street.

"Have we not endured enough for one day?" Whitney's expression soured unbecomingly, and she beat her foot on the ground with displeasure.

Relaxing my clenched jaw, I swung to face Lucille. With grace and composure, I feigned a smile of delight. There was a time when I'd have been troubled by the façade I displayed to folks, but the complexity of my life left no room for me to pause and ponder on these matters. When the troublesome thoughts entered my mind in moments alone, and when my mind settled at night, I pushed them away.

Lucille lifted the bottom of her pale yellow skirt and shook off the beads of rain. She turned her nose up in disgust at the mud spotting our faces and clothing and lost no time in intruding into our affairs. "What are you two doing out in this weather?"

"Delivering supplies to Miss Smith." My fingers flexing at my sides, I countered with her own question. "Why are *you* out shopping on a day like today?"

She continued as if I hadn't spoken, inspecting the back of the wagon. "Surely a delivery can wait for a more pleasant day."

"How about you mind your own business and stay out of ours?" Whitney said as she circled the wagon to join us. Her shoulders were thrown back as if she were an archer taking aim, taut and ready. She pinned Lucille with a lethal glare.

Lucille's heart-shaped mouth gaped open, and her hand slid up to her ivory throat. She swiftly recovered from her shock at Whitney's bluntness and turned her highfalutin attitude on me. "For a girl from proper Southern society such as yourself, I'd think you'd surround yourself with more reputable company. Your first mistake was moving this obnoxious Northern girl into your home. My pa says you may as well be sleeping under the same roof as the enemy." She gestured to Whitney as if she were an object. "If you keep up with your poor choice of company, it'll surely lead to your fall from grace."

I bristled at her words. "If you find the company I choose to keep so offensive to your sensitive taste, why do you go out of your way to seek me out?"

"I see she has already tainted your manners." She clucked her tongue in disgust.

"Enough! I'm not in the mood for your intrusive ways, and I'll not stand here and be ridiculed by you."

Her eyes widened in disbelief at my bluntness, but she brushed it off. "Please forgive me if I offended you. I assure you it wasn't my intent. On a more pleasant note," she said without hesitation, "Julia's coming to town next month, and I came to ask you about arranging a luncheon at your home for all of us, if need be." She flicked a hand at Whitney as she would a pesky hornet, her eyes never leaving me.

"And why would we do something like that?" Whitney responded with a blistering chuckle.

Lucille's face flinched ever so slightly.

If it wasn't a sin to bet, I would've bet my prized Arabian mare that Whitney had Lucille's knees knocking in her petticoats. I restrained the wicked smile that fought to broadcast itself across my face.

She ignored Whitney and pressed forward with her insistence on tea. "I know it's rude to invite oneself, but with the remodeling at our plantation in preparation for the social season still finishing up, Mother says we can't entertain guests." Without taking a breath, she said, "Josephine has been acting rather strange lately, and for her sake, I thought maybe being around some other ladies might dispel the melancholy which appears to have overtaken her."

Lucille wasn't one to be underestimated for her cleverness. Compassion didn't flow through her veins, but she aimed to play on our hearts by pretending Josephine might be in need. However, as self-centered as Lucille was, it was the hopefulness in her face that confused me.

What was she up to? Not only was it rude to invite oneself to another's home, but it was a bizarre request after what had just transpired. It had to be another ploy to nose around for information. But what information? My heart sped up. Had her father put her up to this?

Though my instincts told me not to allow her anywhere near Livingston, she left me with no choice. My family's social status amongst the Southern planters allowed me to pass crucial information to the leaders of the Underground Railroad. I had to extend an invitation if I expected to keep up the image of Livingston being a thriving slave-labor plantation.

I felt as if Whitney's eyes were carving a groove in the side of my head. She was staring an intense warning at me. Ignoring her, I turned back to Lucille, smiled, and said, "We'd be more than happy to have you. I'll send an invitation."

CHAPTER
Four

THE CHIME OVER THE DOOR ALERTED THE SHOPKEEPER, MISS Caroline Smith, to our arrival. We found her balancing on a ladder, stocking shelves.

"Good afternoon, ladies; what can I help you with today?" She climbed down, each wooden rung groaning under her heavyset frame. Pressing her fingers against her navy blue calico skirt to smooth it, she circled the counter.

"We've brought some supplies for you," I said as puddles from our clothes darkened the weathered oak floorboards.

Fair and sparse, Miss Smith's barely perceptible brows dipped. Her gaze shifted from the mess on her once polished floors to the window.

"We thought we could beat the storm," Whitney said with a slight hitch in her voice.

"I see." Her thin lips pressed together. "Ladies alone without protection isn't the wisest decision, what with rumors of the masked men roaming these parts again. They're holding up stagecoaches and carriages along the roads and robbing them blind. Folks are lucky to get away with the clothes on their backs, from what I hear. It'd be wise to bring a strong slave with you from now on."

"Yes, ma'am," I said.

"We'd best get those goods in here, and let's hope they're salvageable. Pull the wagon around back."

Later, with the supplies unloaded, I turned to bid Miss Smith a good day and found her studying me. Her set face held fast, but an unfamiliar softness filled her eyes. Pushing her spectacles up on her nose with an index finger, she said, "Your father was a good man. I miss his visits and doing business with a respectable and fair man like him. I don't deal with men of his caliber often. He treated me well, me being an outsider and all."

"Outsider?"

"Born and raised in the North. I came to Charleston after my family arranged a marriage between Amos and me. Before Amos and I could get married, he up and died on my journey here. Left this place to me."

I remembered the shopkeeper whose blond hair was more frizzy than curly. When I visited the general store with my father as a little girl, he'd let me pick out the biggest of the peppermint sticks from a glass jar he kept by his register. When I grew older, he lent me books from his personal library. His collection was the grandest I'd ever laid eyes on. While my father attended to business in town, I'd rummage through the books swallowing up Amos's cramped, dust-laden apartment above the store.

"My family is from Maine. Being a Northerner and all hasn't always been easy while living here in Charleston," Miss Smith said.

I recalled Lucille's harsh words from moments ago, portraying Whitney as the enemy. I'd known some folks viewed people from the North in this light, but with my father's businesses, we'd often dined and met with people from all over the world. The idea of treating them differently seemed absurd to me.

I'd always found Miss Smith unapproachable. Regarding her now, I wondered if there was more to Caroline Smith than what one would assume.

A knock on the back door interrupted my pondering. Miss

Smith's eyes brightened. "Here's my afternoon delivery. Will you please excuse me?" She turned, threw her shoulders back, and hurried to the rear of the store.

Delivery? In this weather? Whitney and I shared a look of puzzlement.

Miss Smith retrieved an umbrella propped against the doorframe and popped it up before opening the door and stepping outside.

While Whitney and I waited, we browsed through the store.

Minutes later, Whitney called out in a hushed voice, "Come here. You've got to see this."

"Give me a moment." I continued to flip through the pages of *David Copperfield* without looking up.

"Hurry," she said impatiently.

I replaced the book on the table. "All right. I'm coming."

Whitney hung in the shadows of the small window at the back of the shop, staring outside at whatever had piqued her interest.

"What is it?" I asked without lowering my voice.

"Shh! Don't let them see you." She grabbed me and pulled me into the darkened corner.

"Who?" I whispered. Being careful to stay out of sight, I took in the scene unfolding outside.

Miss Smith stood talking to a man of color. As we spied on the pair, I noticed Miss Smith's relaxed posture. The man grinned broadly without lowering his gaze in the submissive way slaves did. Was he a freeman?

The thumping in my chest intensified. Did she…? No. Were the pair romantically involved? Whites mingling with coloreds was not accepted around these parts. Miss Smith would be run out of town. And the colored man—heaven only knew what they'd do to him.

Miss Smith turned to head back inside, and we scurried to the front. Whitney's skirt brushed a stand displaying a set of china plates and set it teetering, and I jerked forward to catch them before they tumbled to the floor.

The door opened, followed by a gust of wind. Miss Smith shook off the umbrella and strode to the front of the store.

I stood by a shelf, engrossed in a forgettable vase that had suddenly become spectacular. The mallet vibrating in my ears jumbled the words she spoke to us. I kept my head down to avoid her seeing the guilt engulfing my face.

"I believe the sun is trying to break through the clouds, but the wind is picking up. You ladies should make for home now."

"I thought—" Whitney started to say, but I grabbed her arm.

I lifted my head, glancing from Whitney to her. "You're right. We'd best be going. I'm sorry for dripping water all over your floors."

Miss Smith's face was radiant, puzzling me. "Think nothing of it." She brushed it off with a wave of her hand. "It was lovely to see you both." She returned to the ladder, humming.

Lovely? What had happened to the gruff, unfriendly shop-keeper I'd known from before? I glanced at Whitney, and my puzzlement was reflected in her expression.

"And you, too," we responded in unison, and walked out the door.

CHAPTER
Five

NO WORDS PASSED BETWEEN WHITNEY AND ME UNTIL THE town faded behind us. As Miss Smith had predicted, the clouds parted, and the welcoming warmth of the sun beamed down on us.

"What are your thoughts on Miss Smith and her delivery man?" Whitney said.

"I'm not entirely sure."

"I've an inkling they may have feelings for each other. What else could explain the change in her puckered, tight face to the nauseating glow surrounding her?"

I laughed. "Are you referring to happiness?"

"Whatever you want to call it. She's an odd one. Something is going on between the two of them. I'm certain of it."

"You sound like Lucille, inserting yourself into other people's affairs."

"Are you looking to dine alone this evening?" She glowered. Tendrils of her auburn curls blew in the wind, cupping her face.

I chuckled and shook my head, then turned my attention back to the road. My mind drifted to the slave who'd lost his life but a short while ago. A heaviness fell over me. We'd failed him. Maybe we should've hidden him at the plantation until he recovered. Perhaps he'd still be alive. But to chance that meant putting our whole operation at risk.

The sun was settling onto the horizon as we rounded the

last bend before home. A rider on a chestnut bay approached us on the road. He rode right in the center of the narrow road, and like the men we'd met earlier in the day, he made no effort to move to the side.

"Are there no civil people left in this world?" I mumbled, slowing the horses to a stop.

The dark-haired man tipped the brim of his silk top hat. "Ladies."

Whitney picked up the rifle.

"Easy there; I mean no harm." His dark brown eyes roved over us, and an easy smile formed on his lips.

"One can never be too sure of the folks traveling these roads," I said.

"Yet you ladies are traveling them alone?"

"We can handle ourselves." Whitney cocked the rifle on her lap.

Unaffected by her attempt to warn him, he directed his words at me. "You must be Miss Hendricks?" He openly examined me from the top of my water-stained bonnet to the eyelets of my shoes peeking out from under my skirt.

I returned his bold inspection. He appeared to be in his early thirties, with the looks that would make any Southern belle bat her lashes and steal an extra peek or two. His clothes were of the finest quality. I arched a brow. "May I ask how you'd know this?"

"Your reputation as a woman of beauty and intelligence precedes you. Not to mention the boldness of your friend, Miss Barry."

"I see." I eased up on the reins.

"I purchased the plantation next to you."

"You mean the Widow Jenson's plantation?" Whitney said.

He rested a hand in a relaxed fist on his upper thigh. "It seems the widow couldn't handle the hardship of a woman running a plantation alone. She became downright frightened her slaves would rape her in bed after the uprising at the Barry Plantation a while back. Poor woman."

My father, who'd been known for being neighborly, had helped the Widow Jenson plenty of times. He'd send slaves over to help mend her fences and do other tasks around her homestead. Our blacksmith, Jimmy, had cared for her livestock on several occasions.

Father and I had often sat on her front porch, sharing punch and chatting about her brother and his family back East. I'd gathered that she got lonely from time to time, but to up and sell off without so much as a goodbye wasn't like her. She was tough and could put any man to shame behind a plow.

"I knew Mrs. Jenson well, and it seems odd that she'd up and sell overnight."

"It wasn't overnight. I was in town on business this summer and overheard her tell the shopkeeper, Miss Smith, how she was looking to move back East. After a few days of thinking about it, I inquired in town on her whereabouts. I rode to her homestead and approached her with an offer she seemed more than willing to accept. I moved in before you all returned at the end of summer."

"It appears you've inquired about our whereabouts." My breath quickened. Whitney stirred on the seat.

"We're neighbors, and it'd be my duty to ask about you. But no, you're wrong. Families often leave for their summer homes when the heat comes. Forgive me for assuming you'd done the same." He sat straighter in his saddle.

Oh! Heat crept over my cheeks. I'd jumped to conclusions, as I tended to do lately. The stranger's assumptions were right. Whitney, the twins, Ben, and I had gone to our estate in Rhode Island to avoid the fever that often plagued South Carolina in the summer months.

I mimicked the planter's perfect posture. "Mr.—"

"Silas. Silas Anderson." He half bowed.

"We need to get on home. If you'll kindly move out of the way, we'll be about our business."

"It's not wise to leave a plantation without its master. I don't know what your uncle was thinking, leaving it to be tended by slaves and mere womenfolk."

My hands tightened on the reins. The townsfolk had never been told about Ben being my real father, and I had no intention of making it known.

Whitney, who'd let me handle things so far, scoffed, "Listen here, you—"

I lifted a hand to silence her. "I assure you, Mr. Anderson, we're more than capable of attending to the matters at Livingston. As I'm the sole heir of the estate, my father thought it only fitting to teach me everything there was to know about running a plantation. You need not concern yourself with how us womenfolk run the place. In case you haven't been informed, I'm the master of Livingston, not my uncle, and I'm the one who says how things are run. It would serve you well to keep your nose on your own plantation."

"I see we're getting off on the wrong foot. Do accept a gentleman's apology if I insulted you. I'll do as you suggest and stay out of your affairs." He placed a noble hand to his chest and tipped his hat. "Good day, Miss Hendricks, Miss Barry."

Then he rode off.

With a click of my tongue and a smack of the reins, I urged the horses to head for home.

"That man makes me nervous. He's too close to Livingston for my liking." Whitney shuffled to cast a glance over her shoulder at the departed Mr. Anderson.

"Maybe he's only being neighborly, as he stated. We can't regard everyone as the enemy."

"Can't we? Until they prove otherwise, anyone who centers their eyes on us is Lucifer himself."

"That's been the approach we've taken so far, but it may not be the smartest choice for us to make."

"Not you too," she grumbled.

"What?"

"First, Miss Smith questioning if it's wise for us to be out alone. Then Mr. Fancy Pants with his question about our wisdom. Now you're suggesting the methods we've followed for the last year may not be 'smart'."

"We must be leery of people who are questionable. But I worry that if we go around looking down our noses at people while keeping everyone at bay, we may bring unwanted suspicion upon us. Mr. Anderson may be no threat at all. However, until proven otherwise, we'll follow protocol and be on high alert until we see what kind of man he is."

"And how do you suggest we do that?"

"One thing my father taught me is to embrace your enemy, find out everything you can, and use it to your advantage. And that's precisely what I intend to do. I expect Ben to be home before the Christmas season. Until then, we'll manage as we have so far."

Were we overthinking the situation? Or was there just cause to be concerned about Silas Anderson?

CHAPTER
Six

THE HORSES TURNED DOWN THE LANE TO LIVINGSTON Plantation. Above, the wind whispered through the foliage of the oak trees' canopy. The sun's rays yawned and stretched through the branches, guiding the eye to the main house bathed in sunlight at the end of the lane.

For the first time since we rode out in the early hours of the morn, I took a full breath. Home.

Jimmy entered the yard from the back and took the reins I handed him when I'd pulled the team to a stop. His speckled gray brows were drawn together, and his brown eyes roved over me as if making sure I'd returned undamaged. His expression revealed that he wanted to ask questions, but his eyes flitted away as he thought otherwise.

I wanted to fall into the warmth of his embrace and unload the grief that tormented me so. But it couldn't be. I'd tried to convince myself it was best this way. The childish girl of my youth had vanished. In her place stood a woman governed by secrets and crippling burdens. Burdens brought on by the acceptance of my lot in life. Meetings cloaked in secrecy, whispering in corners and behind closed doors, all the while looking over my shoulder for prying eyes. Had I become Charles Hendricks? The sheltered flame that burned in my belly for the rights of the Negro race held strong.

Whitney and I mounted the stairs to go inside the house as

Mary Grace's daughter's cries vibrated the windowpanes. "That squalling baby makes my ears bleed," Whitney said.

Baby Evie had come into the world screaming and hadn't been quiet for a moment since. I'd never been around babies until she was born.

Inside, we followed Evie's wails until we found Mary Grace, my childhood friend and handmaid, in the parlor with the baby strapped to her back. As she went around the room dusting the furniture, the child's small fists beat at her mother's back. Mary Grace's sweet voice sang:

O, go to sleepy, sleepy, li'l baby.
'Cause when you wake, you'll git some cake,
And ride a li'l white hossy.
O, de li'l butterfly, he stole some pie,
Go to sleepy, li'l baby.
And flew so high till he put out his eye,
O, go to sleepy, li'l baby.

She glanced up as we entered. Tears glistened in her eyes. "I'm sorry, Miss Willow. Usually I wouldn't have Evie at the main house when I'm working, but Sara can't get her to settle. I'm the only one that can, but today she's being impossible." Her shoulders sagged.

"Hand her to me," Whitney said.

"That's all right, Miss Whitney. I'll tend to my child."

"You look ready to collapse." Whitney moved forward and untied the child from her mother. The baby wailed louder.

"Squawk, squawk, all day long, driving us all insane," Whitney said to the baby as if she understood. She bounced the child in her arms while taking long strides across the parlor.

The baby's cries softened; she was most likely shocked out of her temper tantrum by the rough treatment she was suddenly receiving.

"Now, was there any need of all the fussing?" Whitney stroked her head of wooly curls. Evie cooed, and a gummy smile split across her face.

Mary Grace released a calming breath and mumbled a quiet prayer of gratitude.

"Miss Evie and I are going to catch some fresh air," Whitney said, heading for the door without a glance in our direction.

For some reason, the babe had taken to Whitney's boisterous ways. And as much as Whitney complained about her crying, she had taken to her too.

"The child will take my sanity." Mary Grace dabbed the corners of her eyes.

In the past, all infants of domestic slaves stayed with their families in the quarters, but I couldn't do that to Mary Grace. She'd been through enough. God had blessed her with a child created by her husband and not the men who still haunted her dreams.

I shivered involuntarily as I recalled the rape Mary Grace had endured at the hands of the overseer and his man from Whitney's father's plantation. It was a night we all tried to forget. Rufus and Yates had gotten what they deserved, along with Whitney's father. God had served justice to them, but death had been too kind for the likes of them.

I'd never forgotten the night of Evie's birth and how Mary Grace had relived the rape all over again with each labor pain that hit. Her blood-curling screams filled the cabin as I sat helplessly, mopping her sweat-drenched forehead.

After the birth, she'd refused to look at the child, afraid she'd see her rapists' faces staring back at her. She'd insisted we send the baby to a wet nurse down in the quarters, but Mammy was having none of it and demanded she take care of the child.

After the child had all but loosened the nails on the plank

boards of the cabin walls with her nagging wails, a sullen Mary Grace agreed to nurse the child. Mammy had brought the child to suckle, and much to our relief, the baby greedily drank her mother's milk. Mary Grace had sat with her head turned and her eyes squeezed closed. Only when Mammy told her, "Gal, you go ahead and luk at dat babe. She's as dark as a fine cup of strong coffee. Dat babe is Gray's chile for sho'," did she look upon her child for the first time.

Mary Grace had doted on Evie from that day on and was every bit the mama Mammy was to her.

"Mammy says Evie has colic and this stage will pass." I placed a hand of comfort on her shoulder. "But until then, we'll make bonnets lined with cotton to hug our ears and block out her wails."

Mary Grace laughed. "We may need to make them for the whole plantation. Sara says they can hear her screams in the quarters."

With the set of lungs Evie had, I was inclined to think Sara spoke the truth.

"For the moment, she's content. We'll all take pleasure in her contentment while it lasts. I'll be in the study if I'm needed."

She stared down at her hands. "Gone are the days of us lying up in your room, reading books and dreaming up fairy tales."

"Life has a way of forcing us into adulthood, whether we're ready or not." I, too, longed for days past. What I wouldn't do to go back to the days of being our younger selves, tucked away in my room, giggling and laughing and oblivious to the reality of the world we lived in.

"Nowadays, I feel as old as Mama looks."

"Don't let her hear you calling her old." I chuckled lightly as I walked down the corridor to the study.

CHAPTER
Seven

HOURS LATER, IN THE STUDY, I DIPPED MY QUILL IN THE INK AND stroked it neatly across the yellowed pages of the leather-bound journal that lay in front of me. The book held the names of the fugitive slaves my father had aided over the years, from the ones he'd helped while abroad to the ones that passed through Livingston. Beside their names were estimated ages and last known locations. Since then, the entries had changed from his scrawling penmanship to my neatly etched handwriting.

I ran my fingers over the names on the page. So many lives had passed through my family's hands. Lives of people looking to be free from the bondage in which my country held them.

After Father's death, I'd moved his manservant, Thaddeus, to Pennsylvania, where Father had tracked his family to their last known location. Currently, Thaddeus was employed as a butler for a white family.

Encouraged by my father's success in locating some families, I'd secretly started checking into Jimmy's daughter's whereabouts. It had proven to be impossible, as I had little to go on. I dreamed of reuniting him with her, but unlike the fairy tales Mary Grace and I had once read, their fairy tale was proving to have no happy ending.

I rubbed the aching muscles in my neck. Since my father's death, I'd muddled my way through the secrets surrounding my heritage and the man I'd thought was my father. I dove headfirst into his personal journals and ship ledgers, hoping to discover all his secrets. I'd come to understand that no matter how much I searched and read, I'd never truly understand the mystery surrounding Charles Hendricks.

The writing on the pages blurred as my tired eyes burned. Closing the journal, I wrapped the leather strings securely around it before I circled the desk to the movable panel on the mahogany wall. With a press of the bottom corner, the panel swung out, and I placed the book on the narrow shelf inside.

Back at the desk, I slumped into the chair, interlacing my fingers under my chin as I leaned back and stared at the image of my mother hanging over the fireplace. Her dark tresses were swept to the side in a mass of dark ringlets. The low-scooped neckline of her green velvet gown was trimmed in golden silk rope. Her green eyes shone like emeralds in a treasure chest, and her creamy-peach skin appeared soft and supple. Beauty adorning a queen, some might say. At first glance, one would think the woman with the alluring smile was happy, yet the artist had captured a great sadness in her eyes.

I'd found the painting, along with several others, wrapped in canvas in an outbuilding at our Rhode Island estate. I'd brought them back, and they now sat in their rightful place on the walls and mantels of Livingston. After all, my mother was the heart of Livingston and should be honored as such.

My mind turned back to the disturbing news I'd been told today pertaining to the masked men. "Copycats aiming to use the previous attacks of the masked men to their advantage, most likely," I said to the painting.

Rufus and his men's ashes had settled long ago. Whitney, Mary Grace, and I had burned all evidence of our involvement from the night we sought justice on the men.

But who were these impersonators, and what was their motive?

CHAPTER
Eight

I SHUT THE STUDY DOOR BEHIND ME AND AMBLED DOWN THE corridor toward the staircase. Behind me a commotion announced the entrance of the twins, Whitney's nine-year-old siblings, after an afternoon spent playing with the slave children. Whitney followed close behind.

Jack held his arms snug across his chest. "I don't want a bath. Can't we change our clothes and be done with it?"

"Why must you try me so, Jack Barry?" Whitney gave him a firm push toward the staircase. She'd met her match in her brother.

I smiled in amusement as she tried to lasso the wild child. She caught me smiling and gave me her I'll-speak-to-you-later look. I gathered the composure of a general reviewing his army before battle and stood aside to view the conflict going on in the foyer.

Jack stomped his mud-covered boots. "I'm about sick of all you womenfolk. I'm almost ten, and you treat me like a child. With Mr. Hendricks away, I'm the man of the house. I'm figuring that means I have a say when I get cleaned up."

Whitney's hands balled into fists on her slender hips. "Ten, twelve, or fifteen, you aren't too old for me to take you over my knee and give you a good spanking."

Over the last year, Jack had sprouted up and now stood about eye level with Whitney's chin. Yet I believed Whitney would still be capable of handing out a good tuning on his backside if need be.

Kimie, Jack's twin, differed from her brother and older sister. Never had I come across a child quite like her. From morning to night, she made her rounds on the plantation, nurturing and sprinkling a dusting of joy to all.

Mary Grace sauntered into the foyer, shadowed by my new handmaid, Tillie.

Kimie's eyes lit up, and she skipped over to them. The rays of the late afternoon sun streaming through the windows gleamed off her wispy blond curls. She slipped her dainty hand into one of Mary Grace's. "Can we use some of your pretty smells for our bath?"

Sunlight haloed Mary Grace's face. "You certainly can, Miss Kimie. I'll bring them up straight away."

"Women," Jack huffed with a narrowing of his eyes. "We need to have some menfolk around here. 'Bout time I moved on into town with Knox."

"You'll do no such thing," Whitney said with growing impatience. Almost weekly, Jack threatened Whitney with the same announcement.

"If you married him, then we could all live together."

Whitney let out a snort. "In an apartment in town? Stop talking such gibberish. There's no way you, of all boys, would be able to handle that." She took his arm and hurried him up the stairs.

Kimie followed but paused and poked her chin over the railing and said, "I like the one with the honey and lavender."

"Don't you worry your pretty little head, Miss Kimie; I'll bring all your favorites." Mary Grace smiled affectionately at the girl.

Pleased, Kimie turned and hopped up the stairs, her angelic

voice humming a tune. I stared after her, envying her innocence.

"Dat boy brings de whole yard of muck in wid him evvy time he goes out to play," Mammy said as she came charging out of the warming kitchen. The door swung fiercely after her. "Tillie, you go off and fetch a broom and git dese floors swept. I won't be having dis home luking lak no barn floor."

Tillie's lips moved, but her words were barely audible as she wiped her palms in the folds of her skirt.

"Heaven's sakes, speak up, gal."

"Yessum. I go straight away." Her voice squeaked as if an amateur violinist were playing it. She scurried off without so much as a creaking floorboard.

"Fool gal is scared of evvything. Walks around here wid her chin on de ground. 'Fraid to even luk a nigger in de face. Her skinny behind jumps at evvy creak and groan in de place."

I laughed in amusement at Mammy's sour disposition. "What's stewing under that head rag of yours this evening?"

"Nothin'," Mammy said dryly.

"You aren't joshing anyone with your lies. Now, out with it." I tapped my fingers on the banister post, awaiting her reply.

"You tell Miss Willow the truth." Mary Grace wrapped an arm around Mammy's plump shoulders.

"Gal, I done tole you not to be saying nothin'."

"Out with it!" I glanced from one dear face to another.

"I got...ya see—no, et be all right."

"Oh Mama, I can't put up with your crankiness any longer." Mary Grace turned to me. "She has a tooth that needs pulling, and she's too afraid to have it taken out."

"This is what this is all about?" I threw a hand in the air. "You can't go around with an aching tooth. It may get infected and cause you heaps more trouble."

"It's too late for that, I'm afraid," Mary Grace said

disapprovingly. "Infection set in days ago."

"You'll go down to see Henry in the quarters and get the tooth taken care of, or you'll be sleeping with the chickens tonight," I said.

Mammy's full bosom heaved, and she said with a snort, "I'd rather sleep wid dose critters dan let dat crazy-eyed nigger anywhere near me wid his belt of rusty tools. He's lakly to give me an infection far greater dan I already got."

I stifled a giggle at the wide-eyed, larger-than-life woman before me. Brief eye contact with Mary Grace informed me she wouldn't be far behind. Having them in my life was like a warm shawl on a bitter winter day in Pennsylvania.

"Henry will take good care of you. I've been to see him plenty of times." And I'd hated it every time. I referred to his chair as the chair of horrors. It was a known fact that he showed no mercy when pulling a tooth. He informed every patient that came to see him that he pulled his own teeth, and whipped his tongue out to loop up into the space that once held his two front teeth. Henry took his work seriously. He'd pin you down with a knee to your middle, one hand molding your head to the back of the chair, and he'd yank your tooth with the other.

"I ain't having none of et, I said." Mammy turned on her heels and strode out the front door with her arms swinging at her sides.

We waited for her to be out of earshot before we burst into unladylike cackling. Stitches ate at our insides, and tears glistened on our cheeks by the time we regained control of ourselves.

"Poor Mammy. She's scared to death, and I can't say I blame her much."

"I've got a plan that'll fix her up real good." A mischievous glimmer shone in Mary Grace's eyes.

"I know that look, and I'm half scared to find out what

you're thinking."

"You know that extra little something I put in Mama's tea the night we took care of those Barry men?"

I gasped. "You wouldn't! Mammy wouldn't fall for the same thing twice."

"You're right. But you see, I went to Henry one day and got some ointment to help with the pain—"

"And Mammy agreed to this?"

"I let Mama think I'd made it myself. I'm thinking tonight I add the same potion to the ointment and it will put Mama under so we can get Henry up here to yank out the tooth."

"You figure she'll be out for the whole thing?"

"Maybe not by the time the tooth comes out, but by then, it'll be over." She grinned, pleased with herself.

"You're a wicked, wicked girl." I laughed.

"Mary Grace, will you bring my bath tray?" a small voice called from above.

"Right away, Miss Kimie," Mary Grace called back.

CHAPTER Nine

AFTER THE EVENING MEAL, WHITNEY HEADED UPSTAIRS TO HELP prepare the twins for bed as I stepped outside onto the back veranda. Beau, our golden-red cocker spaniel, lay near the top of the steps. He lifted his head and looked at me, his tail waggling eagerly. I bent to scratch him behind the ears before straightening to look out over the plantation.

The moon hung lazily in the black velvet sky, bathing the plantation in a soft, shimmering glow. An outline of the horizon rippled its reflection along the Ashley River.

Everyone in the quarters had retired. The piercing reverberations of a hammer hitting metal cut through the peaceful quiet of the evening. Jimmy often could be found in the shop, fiddling on whatever task he could find to keep himself busy.

I descended the steps, holding a lantern high to guide my footsteps across the yard to the blacksmith shop. As I drew near, the fire from the forge bathed the outbuilding in a serene and rosy radiance. I watched Jimmy set aside his hammer, lift a set of tongs, and submerge the red-hot metal he'd been working into a bucket of water. It sizzled violently, and a gust of steam rose. Jimmy straightened and arched back his shoulders while rubbing his lower back.

Sensing my presence, he swung around, and a tender smile softened his weathered face. "Miss Willie!" He rounded the forge, and in a low voice asked, "How did ya fare wid de cargo?"

"It arrived damaged, and we had to dispose of it." I shrugged, and tears filled my eyes.

"Dere, dere, gal. Et ain't your fault. De goods were too spoiled from de start."

"It doesn't make the loss any less heartbreaking."

"Dat is true, but one person can only do so much."

"I wished I had—"

"Don't you do et, Miss Willie. No call to blame yourself for evvything dat goes wrong. You're doing your share of right in dis world, and dat's all you can do."

"But it's not enough."

He drew closer, coming to stand within arm's reach in front of me. "Et's 'nuf for one person. No one expects you to go 'bout taking on de whole world by yourself. You've done mighty fine on your own. You've done right good by dese folkses. Teaching dem to read and write, allowing dem to larn skills and crafts to better demselves, dat's more den any slave can ever hope for."

Jimmy had a way of instilling hope in me and relieving the debilitating anxiety that often consumed me. "How's the mood in the quarters lately?"

"Peaceful, for de most part. Some content wid de current situation, and others biting at de dust to head out on deir own."

I lifted my fingertips to my temples. "We can't afford to have unrest here if we're to continue my parents' work."

"Dat be so, but as long as dere be humans, dere will be unrest on dis earth. Et's jus' de way et be. Folkses talk of how you run dis place and what you do for dem. But some of dese people, all dey see is de invisible chains dat hold dem here." He peered around and leaned his head in, saying in a whisper, "Dere's talk amongst some of de folkses of making de journey to de promised land."

"I understand they want a chance at a life of their own. If I could, I'd set them all free." I sighed. "To think just a year ago, I thought I'd do exactly that. No person and no laws would keep me from doing what was right. At every turn, I challenged my father, making his struggles to run this place that much harder. I had so much to learn, and learn I have. That sort of childlike foolishness would only find me at the end of a hangman's noose. Then what good would I be to anyone?"

"Dat's what growing is all 'bout. But dat spirit and fire you have burning in you is what makes you de gal you are. Strength and courage dat sets you apart from all de other young fillies."

"Sometimes I don't want to be strong anymore. Some days, I want to run and keep running and leave all this behind. Maybe become a nun and forget all the pressures of this life."

His hearty chuckle stormed the walls and circled back. "You, a nun? I don't think dey would want de laks of Miss Willie dere. Meek and obedient ain't what you 'bout."

"At least there, no one would be questioning me on why I'm not married yet."

"Don't go letting de naysayers git in your head."

"I try not to, but sometimes I do think running this place would be easier with a husband at my side."

"I happen to know a young man who'd be happy to claim you for his wife."

My cheeks heated, and I averted my gaze. "I'm grateful for Bowden's faithfulness to me, but how long can that last?"

"Et takes a strong man wid an abundance of patience to put up wid a gal wid a mind of her own. I think Mr. Armstrong be dat kind of man. But don't hold him off too long, 'cause all men have deir breaking point."

"The thought of marriage frightens me. Even though I know my father was trying to do right by me, the worry of going back into a cage and being controlled keeps me from moving forward with Bowden."

"In time, maybe you'll see differently."

"Maybe…" I heaved a sigh. "I suppose I'd best be going. If you catch wind of any talk of running, you must let me know."

"I'll do jus' dat. We can't have dem putting de wrong attention on dis place, or gitting demselves caught."

"That's the last thing we need, and I can't protect them if they run off. By the way, have you seen anyone checking out the plantation?"

His eyes narrowed. "What do you mean?"

"The Widow Jenson has sold out to a Mr. Anderson."

"Sold out?"

"Yes; he mentioned that she was frightened for her life."

"Dat woman ain't afraid of nothin'. Tough as nails, dat one." He laughed and shook his head. "But maybe her place was becoming too hard to handle widout any menfolk around."

"This could be true, but you'd think she'd have at least stopped by on her way out and said goodbye. Whitney believes we've reason to be cautious of Mr. Anderson."

"And what do you think?"

"I don't know, but until we do, I think we need to be on the lookout for anyone watching the plantation."

Jimmy nodded. "Dat be wise."

"On another matter, have you heard mention of this person the Negroes are calling the Guardian?"

"Guardian?"

"The man mentioned he came here seeking the Guardian."

"I can't say I have." He stroked his beard, pondering the name that had played in my mind for the last few days.

"I may be able to help you there," a male voice said from behind me.

My hand went to my chest as if to still the sudden thud

of my heart. I spun around to find Jones, the overseer, leaning against a post a few feet behind me. I remembered the day he rode up to Livingston and asked my father for a job. It was the early spring before my tenth birthday. Although he was a trusted employee of Livingston, all these years later, I still didn't know much about the man, except he didn't mistreat the slaves, and there'd been no talk of him taking the slave women to his bed.

"You scared the life out of me. How long have you been standing there?"

"Not long. I saw you headed this way and needed to speak to you on a matter." He walked out of the shadows. The spurs on his boots jingled as he entered the light. "This 'Guardian' you speak of has been a rumor amongst the slaves around these parts for a while. They believe he lives in the swamps like a bushman and carries slaves away in the night."

"Carries them away?"

"Aids them in reaching the promised land, they say."

"Does the rumor hold any truth?"

"I think it may hold some truth, but I'm not certain this man lives in the swamps."

"No? Why?"

"It's the stirring of the townsfolk that's more of a concern to me than the whisperings of the blacks."

"The masked men?" I said.

His ink-colored eyes swept over my face. "The bigger thing you need to concern yourself with is why that injured slave came here, looking for the Guardian."

"That does concern me. The man seemed adamant he'd find the man here. Keep your ears open, the both of you, for any news on this Guardian and these masked men. I don't like this. Trouble could be brewing for us, and we need to be aware of it before it strikes."

Jimmy's keen eyes narrowed with concern. "Sho' thing, Miss Willie."

"Jones, you come with me. We'll walk a spell." I patted Jimmy's arm. "Try to find some time to relax."

"Don't you worry 'bout ol' Jimmy. I'll wander over to de cabin soon 'nuf." He turned and began to whistle the same sweet tune he always did. The familiarity of the tune stroked the knots in my shoulders.

"Come now, let us speak before I retire for the evening," I said to Jones.

We walked in the direction of the main house.

"I'll get right to it. You asked me to check the condition of your father's land to the south."

"I'm assuming you've something to report?"

"I reckon with some clearing of trees, we could build a house, and the ground, in time, would be workable and provide a good crop."

"That's great news! Please arrange a crew to clear the land."

"As you say. I'll have some men on it tomorrow."

"Very well. Is there anything else?"

"No, ma'am."

"Then I bid you a good evening."

He tipped the brim of his hat and backed away a few feet before turning and sauntering off toward his cabin. I stood for a moment, watching him. He stopped and fumbled around before placing something to his mouth. A flame sparked and flickered in the darkness, followed by white wisps that floated upward. He continued on, vanishing into the shadows from whence he'd come.

CHAPTER Ten

L ATER, IN MY BEDCHAMBER, I SAT AT MY DRESSING TABLE WHILE Tillie pulled the pewter horsehair brush in long, even strokes through my hair.

"He says he'll be in Charleston the first of February," I told her as I read over a letter from Kipling, the man father had tried to marry me off to. After my refusal of an arranged marriage, Kip had accepted my friendship, and we'd become steadfast friends. "Says he's bringing his assistant, Ruby, with him."

"Dat be nice," Tillie said.

"Ruby's a free black woman." I glanced at her in the mirror. "Her folks are white abolitionists. Along with her parents, Ruby has aided many fugitives to freedom."

"Is she dis Moses folkses talk 'bout?" She stopped brushing, but never lifted her gaze.

I'd met this "Moses" Tillie spoke of: a colored woman of the finest quality, a former slave who had taken her own freedom. No fear or worry could hold her back from creeping into plantations and stealing slaves away. Planters feared her, and there was a bounty on her head.

"No, but they uphold the same goal, to free all slaves."

"Lak you? Dey jus' be black folk?"

"I suppose so."

The brush began to glide through my hair again. I sat quietly for a minute, watching Tillie in the mirror.

After the birth of Evie, Mary Grace had moved to the quarters and shared a cabin with Tillie's mother, Sara. Tillie now shared the room by the back stairs with Mammy, never once complaining of Mammy's snores that rattled through the main floor like the rumbling of the train leaving Charleston station.

Tillie had never been much for talk, but she'd proven to be a good listener. Lord knows, she'd put up with my ramblings. The twins demanded all of Whitney's time. Mary Grace spent her free time in the quarters with her children: Noah, the boy from the swamp massacre, and her daughter.

Tillie was always there, hovering over me or standing back, waiting on orders. She was a skittish girl, and awkward in appearance, with arms almost as long as her legs. Whitney made it clear she thought I was out of my mind when I went to the quarters seeking Tillie. She said Tillie was absentminded. But there was something about the quiet, reserved girl that I liked. She'd proven herself to be loyal and trustworthy. I found myself talking to her the way I used to talk to Mary Grace.

Folks would frown and say the way I talked to my handmaid was improper. That I was a lover of a race thought to be nothing more than machinery, without emotions or smarts to think and fend for themselves. People were afraid that if the slaves claimed their independence, the South would crumble. For without their human machines, the planters would have to pay the wages demanded from the whites, or they'd have to invest in machinery and build factories like their Northern competitors.

"What do you want in life, Tillie?"

She froze.

I waited, urging her with my eyes in the looking glass.

She never looked up. Silence occupied the space between us. Down the corridor, the twins' laughter echoed.

Tillie said hesitantly, "I don't rightfully know."

"Do you want to be free?"

She wrinkled her forehead, puzzled by my ridiculous question. "Evvyone wants to be free, Missus."

"What would freedom mean to you?"

"I'm sorry, Missus, but I don't understand what you want from me."

"I'm not the enemy. Don't be frightened. If you were free, what would you do with your life?"

"I can't..." The brushing stopped, and I felt it tremble in her hand. "Mama says talking about such things can only mean death for a slave."

I turned to face her and removed the brush from her long fingers before clasping her hands in mine. "You can trust me. Have I proven otherwise?"

"No, Missus."

"Speak candidly." I gave her hands a gentle tug of encouragement.

"I'd... I'd lak to teach chillum to read and write."

"A teacher?"

She bobbed her head up and down.

"Why, that's a splendid and honorable purpose in life."

A smile curved the corners of her mouth. "I never cared much to larn to read and write. But wid de larning you bin doing wid me, I realize I want to give dat to others." She rushed to finish what she wanted to say, as if she'd lose the courage at any moment. "White folkses try to keep black folkses from larning 'cause dey scared ef we larn to read and write, we become jus' as smart as dem. Den dey can't keep us no slave no more," she said with a boldness I'd never witnessed in her before.

"You keep learning all you can, and when the day comes that all slaves are free, you use all the knowledge you've learned here on Livingston to make it on your own." I smiled, released her hands, and turned back to the mirror.

"Do you think dere will be such a day?" She began to braid my hair.

"It's the belief I hold to. Something we all must hold onto, because without hope, what do we have? I believe God has a plan, just as he did for the Hebrews in the days of Moses."

"Mama says I'm not to question de ways of de Lard. But I don't understand why he chose us colored folkses to place dis yoke upon."

I grew quiet. Her question had been one I'd asked God countless times. At night, in the sanctuary of my room, my screams of frustration were muffled in my pillow, my fist pounding at the linens as I wailed silently in my desperation to set things right. Why? Why? I begged for God to hear my cries and the cries of the slaves. Where was His mercy?

"Miss Willow?"

"Yes?"

"Why do you suppose de Lard let dis happen?"

I let out a weighted breath. "Why does he allow a lot of things? I don't understand it myself."

Finished with my hair, Tillie stepped back.

"I can manage from here," I said, pushing to my feet. "You run along and enjoy your evening with your mama. Tell her I send my greetings. You're dismissed."

"Yes, Missus." She curtsied, pivoted on her heels, and strode to the door.

"Tillie…"

"Yessum?" She swung back. Her eyes were directed at the cypress planking in front of her while her hands hung loosely by her sides.

"Maybe we can pick a day or two a week that you can help

in the quarters with the teaching of the children."

"I'd like dat." Her voice quivered.

"Very well, then. We'll discuss a schedule tomorrow."

"Mussiful be de Lard," she mumbled as she left the room and closed the door silently behind her.

CHAPTER
Eleven

Tillie

FROM THE WARMTH AND SAFETY OF THE BIG HOUSE, I CREPT OUT into the night. The oak trees and outbuildings painted the backyard with eerie silhouettes like deformed creatures. The far-off cry of a wild animal turned my head toward the dangerous cypress forest where they lay—waiting. Watching. Wanting to shred the meat from my bones.

The hoot of an owl threw me forward. My feet beat down the steps and I pelted toward the quarters like hell had been unleashed behind me, the lantern I held swinging wildly. My heart pounded in my ears as the unnerving noises closed in. Imaginary claws tore at my skirts, trying to pull me into the darkness beneath my feet. I pumped my legs harder.

Only when I reached the overseer's cabin did I slow my pace. Mr. Jones sat on the front porch, whittling away on a piece of wood. He stopped mid-stroke when he caught sight of me.

I tried to catch my breath while keeping my eyes glued to the bottom step of his stoop.

"What's your hurry, girl?" His voice sounded none too friendly.

"I jus' wanted to give my mama a squeeze." Men sent my knees a-knocking. Mama said never to trust no man. She said men were out to hurt girls like me. I still wasn't sure what girls like me were. But in my fifteen years, I'd seen a lot of ugly things before I came to this place. Things I'd never forgotten. Things that scar your mind forever.

Jones adjusted himself in his rocker and leaned forward.

I shuffled backward and became tangled in my feet, which landed me on the ground. Rattled my teeth clean up to my skull. Ignoring the pain stabbing through my cushionless backside, I scrambled to my feet. A grunt came from him, and the pulse throbbing in my head sped up.

"You bes' get at 'er, then," he said gruffly, and the slow glide of his knife on the wood resumed.

Dat be all? Dat man be an odd one, dat's for sho'. My brain had long ago given up trying to figure him out. For the most part, I steered clear of him.

Turning, I ran for the quarters.

At the end of the line of cabins, I pulled my racing feet to a casual walk. Menfolk sat socializing on the front stoops of their cabins. Chillum ran up the lane, diving in and out of cabins, playing a game of hide-and-seek. Cabin doors hung open, and on my way by, I snuck a peek or two inside.

Womenfolk sat in front of the fireplaces, attending to their family's mending. A mother stood over her son as he pointed at a paper on the table, reciting the alphabet. Unlike Masa Jack, the boy was eager to learn. Never would I figure out the whites. *Dey got evvything we've ever wanted, but dey still complain and cause a fuss.*

But not Miss Willow. I've never known a white person like her. She'd run herself ragged to make sure we got all we needed. A heap of trouble would be waiting for Miss Willow if the white folk were to find out about her doings here on the plantation. She had secrets as high as the tower of laundry on washing day.

Secrets, Mama said, would be the end of us all if information fell into the wrong hands. The white folk would send Miss Willow off to some prison overrun with rats and lice. A shiver rushed up my spine at the thought. She was too proper and kept for that sort of place.

Miss Willow's secrets were safe with me. I'd take them to my grave before I'd tell another soul. They could pluck out my eyes and pull out my fingernails before I'd give anything away. My fingers curled into fists, my nails biting into my palms.

Most days I worried about Miss Willow. Since before we left for the big house in the North, a great sadness had swallowed her up. She'd put the cross of all us black folk on her shoulders. I figured it was the reason she didn't smile no more.

In the days before she ran this place, her laughter could be heard around the grounds. Her steps were light. From the fields, I'd watched her float around the place in a vision of silks and beauty. On the heels of her pappy leaving on his long trips, she'd mount her horse and charge across the field, away from the plantation, dressed in his trousers. A sin, for sho'!

Her presence in the quarters was frequent and her visits breathed hope into the people. I'd come to idolize her in a way that wasn't Christian. Days when the sun blistered my skin and I was to the point of collapsing, I'd see Miss Willow's bonnet bouncing up and down as she drove a wagon toward us, bringing the field hands water. I gulped it back, letting the coolness trickle down my throat and cool my belly.

One day, I held out the empty ladle, and when she reached for it, her lingering hand folded over mine. Her fingers were soft, not calloused like my own. Shocked, I elevated my careless eyes to meet hers, and the warmness pouring from her face pinned my gaze a moment too long, before I turned my attention to the toes of her polished black shoes peeking out beneath her pale blue muslin dress.

Long after her wagon pulled away, I stared after her.

Soon, days came when her youthfulness was soured by a burden she carried. In those days, I'd heard talk in the fields and quarters of how she'd taken a liking to us black folk, a fondness that warn't normal for white people. No sirree! She and her pappy would fight rings around each other. I'd never known what for, but it was only when I became her handmaid that I got to truly see and understand the woman behind the fancy clothes.

Mama said it was a privilege Miss Willow chose me to be her handmaid, and I was mighty grateful her pretty eyes set on me. Many of us colored folks dreamed of being in the big house. Some people in the quarters had lots to squabble about when Miss Willow came asking for me. But there warn't room for us all up in the big house. Mama said I shouldn't be letting no jealous darkie make me feel wrong about what the good Lard saw fit to bestow on me.

It ain't as swell as they all were thinking. I missed my mama something fierce. But at least Miss Willow let me go visit her often. It was selfish of me to miss Mama so badly when Miss Willow ain't got none of her folks left except for her uncle. Though she'd recently rid herself of the dreary mourning clothes, it hadn't taken away the pain that hooked onto her heart over the loss of her pappy.

At my mama's cabin, Pete, a boy about my age and the perfect shade of dark, squatted on the front step. His body was angled away from me toward the woods. I sneaked up on him, and he didn't stir. For as far back as I can remember, people said to me, "Gal, dem feet of yours be lak wearing boats for feet," or "Poor gal can't steal up on a deaf man wid dose big feet." So I learned how to work my feet to touch the ground feather-light when it served me best.

"Evenin', Pete," I said.

He never flinched. Had he not heard me? "Evenin'," I tried again. Still, he didn't move.

"Pete!" I screeched.

He leaped off the step with his fist in the air, ready to pounce. Then he saw me. "What you be yelling 'bout? I ain't deaf, gal."

"I said evenin'."

"I ain't heard nothin' until you 'bout blow out my eardrum. What's wrong wid you? Slithering up on folkses. Got me eating on my own heart, et's thrashing so hard."

I smiled to myself. Whisper-quiet. My hips started to sway, and I dropped my eyes to the hem of my skirt as it swished side to side.

"How are things up in de big house?"

"Fine."

"What's dat?"

"I say dey be fine." I shifted my eyes to peer at his brown shoes. The stitching on the outer sole had given way, and the gap that showed his flesh had gotten bigger since last week. I'd studied a lot of shoes in my life.

"Gal, you got no need to be acting mouse-lak when you ain't in de big house."

I set my eyes on the curve of his glistening neck. "Dey don't make me act lak a mouse. Miss Hendricks and Miss Barry are real good to me."

"Is dat so? Den luk a man in de eyes when he speaks to you." His shoulders arched back, proud-like. Pete carried himself like he was a prized peacock. Dumb ox had forgotten he was a slave. Crowed all the time about being the son of an African prince. A medicine man.

At the swelling of his chest, fire zapped through me. "Who be saying you're a man? You're scarcely fourteen." I mounted the two steps leading inside.

He grabbed my hand on the way by.

My eyes flew up to his, and warmth swirled like a dust devil through me at the mess of feelings I saw there. I lowered my gaze. Like the mud of the bayou, his hand swallowed mine whole. Around Pete, I wasn't so oddly proportioned, but delicate and feminine like the other girls.

"Luk at me, Tillie."

I shook my head and focused on the sweat gleaming on his chest at the opening of his shirt.

"You'll be my gal someday."

"Says who?"

"I knowed et. Your eyes tell me dat your heart swells for me, de same as mine does for you."

"Oh, rubbish!" I shook my hand free, stomped inside, and closed the door behind me. I leaned my head back against it and closed my eyes. The sun had gotten to Pete's head today. His gal! Imagine dat.

"Dat you, gal?" a husky female voice called out.

I opened my eyes and found my mama sitting in a rocker in the corner, her pipe clenched between her teeth. She squinted in my direction. "Yes, Mama."

"Come closer so I can feast my eyes on you."

I placed the lantern on the table and moved toward her. "Where is evvybody?" With Mama's failing eyesight limiting what she could do, Miss Willow had given her the new position of minding the chillum. I leaned in to give her a hug. The smell of tobacco in her hair and clothes tickled my nose.

"Dey be off visiting other folkses. Mary Grace took Noah and de babe to play wid Esther's young'uns."

I moved a rocker closer and sat down.

"You eat?" she said between puffs of her pipe.

I coughed and swiped a hand through the air to clear away

the clouds of gray. "Yes."

She was silent except for the creaking and swishing of her rocker. Mama was tall and willowy, like me. Some said she was a handsome woman, but I guess I'd taken more after my pappy. Whoever he may be. Mama didn't speak of him.

Her rocker squeaked as she leaned forward. "Let me git a good luk at you." Her milky eyes ran over me. She smiled, revealing yellowed, tobacco-stained teeth. "You luk healthy. Miss Willow's taking good care of my gal, I see."

"Dat she is. Maybe takes more care of me den me her."

"Dat's good. Tell me all 'bout your travels to dis Rhode Island place."

"But Mama, we talk 'bout dis evvy time I come."

"You please an old woman and tell me again. I laks to tell de chillum 'bout your travels." She removed the pipe from her lips and waved a hand in the air like she was painting a vision for all to see. "My Tillie, off traveling de world lak she's a white girl."

"Miss Willow, Miss Whitney, and Masa Ben are fine people. Masa Ben takes my arm and helps me up lak a Southern gentleman. Same as he does for Miss Willow. He acts lak we are equal."

"Hush now. Dat's hangin' talk. In de white folkses eyes, you'll never be equal to no white woman. As long as your skin be dat beautiful coffee color, you be a slave."

"Now, Mama, you stop all dat negative talk. You're as free as we can be here on dis plantation. Et jus' de papers dat says differently, and a white man's court."

"De only way we are free is when we leave dis country behind, or our hearts stop ticking," she said.

"In de North, dere be free blacks wid free papers. Why, Miss Willow said not but a few years back, a slave by de name Henry Brown mailed himself in a crate, all de way from Richmond to Philadelphia, right to de doorstep of de Anti-Slavery Society—"

"Et don't matter ef you're in de North or de South. I've heard of nigras gitting all de way to freedom in de North and den gitting nabbed by de cursed slave traders and sold back into slavery. A person's got to git demselves to Canada."

Her words dumped a wagon of lead in my stomach. *Surely et warn't so? Free is free, warn't et?*

Mama's eyes shone with devotion. "Free doesn't matter to me dat much anymore anyhow. Dis plantation is de closest I'm ever going to git to freedom. I sho' don't know why et tuk de good Lard so long to send us here. But et doesn't matter dat much anyhow, 'cause de missus's cause is de best thing I've done in all my life. Et makes me feel alive, helping other folks along de road to freedom. Besides, I'm too old to run anymore."

The door opened, and a hush fell between Mama and me. Mary Grace and the children, along with the weaver woman, crowded into the cabin for the night.

After visiting Mama and the others, I returned to the big house. Mama's words hung over me like Preacher John's sermon on Sunday after I'd been sampling sweet potato pie from the kitchen house.

CHAPTER
Twelve

Willow

DRESSED FOR BED, I FOLDED BACK THE COVERS AND CLIMBED IN, releasing a long, drawn-out breath as I pulled the covers over me. I stared up at skillfully etched patterns in the plastered ceiling.

Things will be better tomorrow.

My eyelids drooped as the nightly singing of the slaves around the fire down in the quarters drifted into my room, lulling me. The exhaustion of the day carried me away into a fitful sleep.

I dreamed of running blindly through the swamp under a blanket of darkness. The bayou mud pulled and gripped at the hem of my skirt. The howls of the bloodhounds grew louder as they closed in. Globes of light glimmered around the slave traders' torches, visible through the trees.

A man stepped from the trees with a torch in hand. Terror froze my steps. The face of Mr. Thames lodged a scream in my throat. Then screams, not my own, echoed around me. Screams that jolted me upright in bed. My heart pounded wildly.

The silvery-white moonlight spilled into my room, illuminating a long, narrow windowpane pattern across my floor.

It was just a dream.

A scream came from the main floor, and I jumped from my

bed. The clang of something hitting the floor sent me running for the door.

We were being attacked! The masked men? Had they come to rob us?

I grabbed my dressing robe from a chair in a dark corner of the room. Opening the door, I slipped out into the dimly lit corridor, pushing my arms into the sleeves. Then, each step light and soundless, I crept down the stairs.

"Stay away!" Mammy cried.

Shadows moved in the corridor, cast from the room to the right of the staircase. My stomach lurched. I remembered the revolver in the top drawer of the desk in the study. How would I get across the corridor undetected? Panic surged in me, but I forced myself to concentrate on stealth. The stairs were cold and hard under my feet.

As my foot touched the last step, Mammy cried out again. "I knowed you were up to somepin'. Did Miss Willow put you up to dis?"

"No, Mama, she had nothing to do with it."

"I bet she didn't." Sarcasm oozed from Mammy's voice. "De two of you are always up to no good. I heard you cackling earlier. Think you can fool me after de last time?"

I tiptoed down the corridor to the back room where Mammy and Tillie slept. The door hung open. On the floor lay a tray, shattered glass, and a puddle of liquid mixed with what appeared to be one of Mary Grace's herbal concoctions.

Tillie sat on the edge of her straw bed, wearing only her shift and a nightcap. The whites of her eyes were prominent as her head swung back and forth between mother and daughter.

Mammy stood in the middle of the room, her eyes spitting embers at Mary Grace, who blocked the doorway with her body.

"You've got to get it pulled. There's no way around it," Mary

Grace pleaded, sounding frustrated.

"I said no. No, no, no! Dat be et, gal. Now, you wander on down to de quarters and take care of your chillum. Your mama be jus' fine."

Mary Grace didn't move.

"Go on, now, git." Mammy shooed her with a hand.

"But, Mama." Mary Grace broke into sobs. "Why must you be so stubborn?"

"Hush now. No 'mount of tears is going to make me change my mind. Dat crazy nigger won't be yanking out my tooth tonight or any other night."

"Enough of this wailing and screaming," I said.

They all jumped, and all eyes in the room turned to me.

"Mammy, you scared me half to death. With you carrying on so, I thought we were under attack. That tooth is coming out tonight, and I won't hear another word about it." I warned, giving Mammy a hard, authoritative glare. "Tillie, go to my uncle's room and fetch some opium. Mary Grace, you administer a small dose. I'll go get Henry." I hurried from the room before Mammy could get a word in.

Lantern in hand, I moved hastily down the back steps, across the yard, past the riverbank, and behind Jones's cabin to the quarters. Henry's cabin was the first one on the right when entering the quarters. I rapped on the door.

Inside, whispers gave way to the shuffling of feet.

"Et's de missus," a woman's voice said, followed by, "What she be wanting dis time of de night?" in a lowered voice.

The door creaked open, and a woman I knew to be the wife of Owen, the carpenter, poked her head out. "Dere be a problem, Missus?" Her brow wrinkled.

"No problem. I've come seeking Henry."

Her strained face eased. "Henry, et be for you," she called

out, and her head disappeared back inside.

Minutes later, Henry stepped out onto the stoop. His wild gray hair stood on end. He looked at me, or to the side of me—I wasn't sure. His lazy eye made it hard to tell.

"Mammy's tooth is still bothering her."

"I'll git my things." He disappeared back inside and soon returned with the dreaded rolled-up leather pouch.

We retraced my tracks to the house, but by the dock, a movement paused my steps. I held the lantern high and squinted to see.

"What is et, Missus?" Henry asked at my sudden stop.

"I'm not entirely sure." I leaned forward to get a better view.

The moonlight poured over Jones, standing on the far end of the dock. He leaned forward with an elbow resting on his knee, speaking to what appeared to be another man in a skiff. I couldn't be sure, because a dark hat and the tall reeds concealed the figure's identity. Who was Jones speaking to? And furthermore, what were they doing here at this time of night?

The light breeze carried the masculine tones of their voices, and I became sure Jones's visitor was indeed another man. I strained to make out what they were saying, but their words were unclear. "You head on up to the house. I'll be right behind you," I said to Henry.

After he was gone, I followed the beaten path the short distance to the dock.

Jones heard my approach and straightened, whispering something to the man. Without hesitation, the skiff started moving away from the riverbank.

Jones stalked toward me, his boots echoing on the planks. "Miss Hendricks, what are you doing out here at this time of night?" Was there a hitch in his voice? Or was I imagining things?

"I've come to get Henry. Mammy has a tooth that needs

attention." I glanced at the skiff floating farther down the river. "Who's that you were speaking to?"

"A friend," he said, walking past me in the direction of his cabin.

"What did he want?" I called after him.

Jones came to a stop. Half turning, he said, "I asked him to keep an ear open for news on those masked men."

"Already?" I'd only just mentioned my concerns to him. He certainly hadn't wasted any time.

"Had you preferred I wait?" he said gruffly.

"I suppose not. Thank you for seeing to matters straightaway."

I left him and returned to the house, Jones and the stranger in the boat forgotten as Mammy's yelling hurried my steps to the back room.

"Stay away, you savage! You come near me, and I'll take your head off your shoulders." Mammy swung a broom in the air, holding Henry at bay.

"Aw, Rita, et be over in no time," he said. A grin of amusement parted his lips, and the black hole between his teeth was a reminder to us all of how Mammy had every right to be scared stiff.

Tillie hovered in the corridor, and the unsuccessful Mary Grace stood in the room with a brown glass bottle in her hand.

"Mama, please," she begged.

This wasn't going to go down as planned.

"Tillie, get a couple of men from the quarters."

"Yessum." She disappeared down the corridor.

There was only one way that tooth was coming out, and it was with force.

CHAPTER
Thirteen

WEEKS HAD PASSED SINCE THE SLAVE HAD SHOWN UP ON THE doorstep. So far, Mr. Thames hadn't traced him back to Livingston, and the more days that passed, I believed he never would.

On the riverbank, I waited as Jones and a gang of slaves pushed off the dock in a riverboat loaded with supplies headed for town. "Don't forget to pass along my message to Miss Smith," I called out.

Jones nodded and half waved.

After they disappeared around the bend in the river, I strolled back to the house. I'd reached its corner when I heard the clip-clopping of a horse coming up the lane. I shielded my eyes to see who the rider might be.

"It's Silas Anderson." Her face pinched, Whitney stood on the front veranda, observing the approaching rider. I followed her gaze.

He rode with the air of a grand duke, his broad shoulders thrown back, his chin jutting up. He was dressed in tan breeches, a matching coat, and a silk cravat. Beneath his brown, soft-crowned hat, dark wisps of hair touched the tips of his ears. His knee-length black leather boots glimmered in the morning sun as if recently polished. Most would consider him a handsome man with an awareness of modern trends.

He tipped the brim of his hat as he pulled his mount to a halt.

"What can I help you with?" I said after pleasantries had passed between us.

"I'm finding myself short of help. The homestead came with a handful of slaves. They ran off shortly after I purchased the place."

"Ruth and William too?"

"The widow took them with her. Said they weren't included in the sale," he said nonchalantly.

The widow had a fondness for the husband and wife. They'd been with her for as long as I could recall, and I could see her not wanting to part with them.

"And the others? You didn't track them down?"

"If a man wants to run, he'll run. I don't have the manpower to be tramping through the swamps and trails I'm unfamiliar with to search for them."

"But they're an investment." My curiosity perked at his non-chalant dismissal of the slaves. He'd said he'd been in town on business when he'd heard the widow mention wanting to move back East. Perhaps he was not from these parts?

"I prefer to hire white folk willing to work without their eyes on the lookout for an opportunity to run. My man Caesar has been with me since his mama ran off with a salesman passing through. He was barely six years old. I don't consider him a slave. More like my right-hand man. I depend on him more than I should. If he were to get it into his head to run off, I don't know how I'd manage. He does the work of three men."

"Your views on the importance of slavery are odd for these parts. If you don't mind me asking, where did you drift in from?"

"Jamestown. Jamestown, Kentucky. My pa was a miner."

He didn't come from a planter family. If his father was a miner that meant Mr. Anderson didn't come from elite society. And the likelihood of his family owning slaves would be low.

Maybe there was truth in his words. The ache of the tension gripping me eased.

As if sensing this, he broke into a winsome grin. "Will the defendant go free?" His eyes twinkled with a mixture of boyish glee and amusement.

My cheeks burned. "Yes." I hid my face with a dip of my head.

"I was beginning to think I should climb down off this horse and ask if I might sit awhile until you've finished your investigation of me."

"I apologize," I said, peering up at him. "With all the rumors, I'm a bit on edge lately, as you can understand." It wasn't a complete lie.

"Certainly; think nothing of it. But perhaps from here on out, we can forgo the interrogation and have a conversation that's more pleasant for the both of us."

"I'd like that."

"Very well, then." He leaned his elbows across the neck of his horse, the reins hanging casually in his hand. "I intend to hire a woman from town to do the cooking and cleaning at my place. But I've yet to have a moment to inquire about someone. I wondered if you'd be so kind and hire out a slave until I find the time. Man or woman, it doesn't matter none. As long as they can cook. I do enjoy a proper meal."

"I don't make it a habit of hiring out my slaves. Maybe you can inquire with the other neighboring plantations."

"I've inquired at the Armstrong Plantation. Mr. Armstrong was none too welcoming."

His statement stilled our conversation. His eyes remained fixed on mine.

A niggle of doubt rose in my mind. Bowden hired out his slaves. Why hadn't he offered the service to Mr. Anderson? "Mr.

Armstrong is a busy man," I said in his defense. The air seemed to thicken at the mention of Bowden's name. All summer I'd tried to block out any thoughts of him.

"One should never be too busy to offer proper hospitality to a neighbor," Anderson said, breaking through my thoughts.

The approach of heavy footfalls turned my head. Whitney's stiff face and compressed lips reminded me of my teacher, Miss Davis, at the uppity boarding school I'd attended. Cold and inquisitive, Whitney squinted up at Mr. Anderson. I wanted to jab her in the ribs and knock her from the judge's seat she sat upon.

"Miss Barry," he greeted her, his expression sober.

"Anderson," she replied with a nod of her head. "I couldn't help but overhear you were looking to hire a slave." Her tone softened.

"That was my intent."

"We'd consider hiring out for a good price."

My mouth dropped open. I was dumbfounded at her willingness to send someone into unknown territory.

"Is that so?" He looked at me in confusion.

"Miss Barry has forgotten her place," I said sharply. "As I stated, I do not hire out slaves."

Whitney whirled to face me. "I do not mean to overstep my boundaries after you've been so kind, but the gentleman is right. It's our duty to be good neighbors and help in whatever reasonable way possible." She set her eyes on him, slid a hand to her throat, and lowered her thick auburn lashes. "Forgive me if I came off harshly," she said. "Willow's always telling me I judge people unfairly. I hope you won't allow my poor behavior to reflect badly on her." Her lashes swept up as she regarded him.

She couldn't be serious! She was acting like all the girls she detested. Did she think she could use flirtation to make him retreat from the cliff she'd cornered him on with her hostility?

What was she up to? Furthermore, was he accepting the white flag she waved? I swung my eyes back to him, my throat clamped with worry.

Whitney held his attention. His look of confusion had slipped into one of disapproval and unnerving dislike. He hadn't fed into her change from a baying hound on the hunt for blood to the lamblike demeanor she'd so poorly executed.

Never could Whitney pull off the blushing Southern belle. It would take years under the watchful eye of Miss Davis to mold Whitney into a proper lady. Yet, even that seemed impossible. Woman or man, it didn't matter to Whitney. She stated her mind and stood firm in her beliefs. Society didn't take to women conducting themselves as boldly and outspokenly as Whitney did. From the beginning, it was the trait I'd admired most about her. However, in this moment, I wished she was anything but that woman.

"What do you say, Miss Hendricks? You made it quite clear the other day that *you* were the rightful owner of this plantation." A hard glint settled in his eyes as he looked to me. I couldn't blame him. When Whitney's quills were up, she didn't provide the most welcoming company.

"Will you excuse us for a moment." I smiled through clenched teeth. Not waiting for his reply, I grabbed Whitney by the arm and dragged her out of earshot.

"Willow—"

"Are you trying to get us found out?"

"No!" she whispered, a flash of remorse crossing her face.

"What are you thinking? Hiring someone out could endanger us all. Not to mention the way you marched up, looking to go into battle. You must control yourself for the sake of us all." I felt tightly strung, pinging with building anxiety. Sweat formed at the nape of my neck.

"You're right." Her sweaty palm touched my wrist. Her eyes darted past me to eye Mr. Anderson. "Hear me out, and then you can make the final decision."

"Out with it."

"Sending the right person could provide us with information we can't possibly obtain ourselves. If he's who he says he is, then there is no real loss. If he's pretending to get into your good graces for some reason, then we'd have the upper hand."

"I don't know—"

"Please don't be pigheaded, and trust that I may be right."

I folded my arms across my chest. I wasn't the only pigheaded one. I opened my mouth to speak and then thought better of it. Maybe Whitney was right. He seemed harmless enough, but if Anderson was a danger to Livingston, we had to know.

I swung to look at him where he sat observing us. He sent me a charming smile that sent heat washing through me.

Whitney gave my elbow a rough shake. "Don't let his good looks throw away all your common sense."

"I'm not," I said in exasperation. "We'll do it your way for now. But it needs to be someone he'd underestimate."

"Who do you have in mind?"

"Tillie."

"Tillie?" she screeched before catching herself. "You can't be serious," she whispered. "She's the last person you should send."

"You need to trust me on this one," I said firmly.

"As you say." She sank into an exaggerated curtsey.

I resisted the urge to roll my eyes. "In the meantime, find some manners, and let's send Mr. Anderson on his way," I said.

She rose to her full height and arched back her shoulders. "I'll send him on his way all right, with a swim in the pond." I stifled a laugh. She looped arms with me, and we strolled back to Anderson.

CHAPTER
Fourteen

"TILLIE, WHERE ARE YOU?" I CALLED OUT, MY VOICE SOUNDING strained to my own ears as I swept from room to room in search of her.

"Here, Missus," Tillie said from behind me.

"Come out from behind my skirts so I may speak to you," I said, more firmly than I'd intended. I gently took her arm and pulled her from my shadow. "Follow me."

"What is et, Missus? I ain't done nothin' wrong, have I?" Her arm trembled under my fingers.

"No, you need not worry. There's an important matter I must speak to you about."

In the study, I released her arm and gestured for her to take a seat as I closed the door. Strolling across the room, I came to stand in front of the mahogany desk my father had imported from the Caribbean. Tillie mauled her apron with her hands, mimicking what I felt was happening inside my chest. *I can't do this to her.* Nausea swirled in my stomach. *A week. Only a week, and then she'll be back.* I suppressed the panic coursing through me and pushed forward.

"We've been together for a while now." My voice quavered. "You've proven your trustworthiness and your desire to be part of the movement here at Livingston. With this knowledge and understanding, I've got a favor to ask of you."

Tillie's head hung reverently.

Devoted to a fault.

"What is dis favor you speak on?"

"Mr. Anderson, our new neighbor, has come here asking to hire someone to do some housework and cooking at his farm. Whitney doesn't care for the man and thinks he's up to no good. We need someone we trust to be our ears and eyes and see if he poses a threat. I believe that person should be you."

Tillie's body hunched inward, and through quivering lips she said, "Who'd care for you?"

"Don't you be worrying about me. If you're too frightened and don't wish to go, I'll try to find someone else."

"What ef he's a bad man? What ef he hurts slaves?"

I swallowed hard. She spoke the words I'd feared most. What if I was sending her into danger? Was I risking her life? I crumbled. "Your concerns are valid. I've no right to ask this of you. We'll come up with another plan."

I moved around the desk and collapsed into the chair. What was I thinking? This was all wrong. Come what may, I couldn't send her or any other slave without knowing precisely what I was sending them into.

"I'll go," she said.

"It's all right. We'll figure something else out. It was wrong of me to suggest such an idea. I can't seem to think clearly lately."

"Missus, please." Her voice cracked. "Et be true I'm scared. More scared den I've ever bin, but dis is my chance. My chance to do somepin' good for folkses. I'm tired of being scared. Ef you think dis man is a danger to us, I'll go."

"That's just it. I don't know this. But one can never be too careful, you know?" I looked at her for understanding.

"You're awful good, Missus. Better dan any white woman or man I've ever known. You take many risks for colored folkses. I want to be lak you, the Moses woman, and Miss Ruby from de

North. Dis here be my turn." She pulled her shoulders back and thrust out her chin.

I went to her and knelt before her, lowering my head so I could look her in the eye. She had pretty eyes. Kind and trusting. Eyes that weren't meant to stare at the floorboards or some cob-webbed corner. "You must know I can't promise safety. I can't stop by to check on you. When you leave here, you're on your own. Do you understand that?"

Her fear-filled eyes searched my face for courage.

I cupped her chin and smiled. "You're a courageous girl. If anyone can do this, you can. I've seen how you creep around un-noticed. You probably frighten the ghost."

Her eyes grew large. "You thinking dere are ghosts at Livingston?"

I laughed and stood up, pulling her up with me. "No. It was a figure of speech."

"What do you mean?"

I wrapped my arm around her and led her to the door. "Nothing. There's no ghost. I told Mr. Anderson I'd deliver a slave myself tomorrow morning. If you're certain you can do this, we'll move forward with the plan."

"Yessum, I am. But…I was wondering…can you keep dis from my mama? She'd worry, and her heart ain't strong as et used to be."

"But your visits to the quarters… She'll suspect something is amiss."

"Not ef you tell her I'm caught up at de big house."

"Very well. I'll conjure up something to tell her. We'll leave for the Anderson farm in the morning, right after breakfast. If I get a feeling something is amiss when we arrive, the plan is off."

"I trust you to do right by me."

"Your courage won't be forgotten," I said.

Closing the door after her, I turned and leaned against it, sliding down until I sat on the floor in a cloud of petticoats and fabric. Drawing my knees up, I rested my cheek on my arms.

Tears did not come. Nor did the sadness. Emptiness and numbness enveloped me, controlling me like a disease as it ravaged through every fiber and crevice of my body.

And with that, I placed the well-being of Tillie into the hands of Silas Anderson.

~ CHAPTER ~
Fifteen

MIDMORNING, PREPARING TO TAKE TILLIE TO THE ANDERSON farm, I tacked up my horse, grimacing at the drumming of a red-bellied woodpecker high in a sweetbay magnolia tree. It elevated the pounding in my head left by a sleepless night. The muffled sound of a horse's hooves lifted my head, and I peered over the back of my mount. Through the veil of my riding hat I made out Mr. Sterling, a neighboring farmer and the constable for this area, trotting up the lane.

A friendly smile pushed aside his jowls as he pulled his mount alongside me. Bending, he held out a bundle of mail. "Morning, Miss Hendricks." On trips to town, Mr. Sterling and my father often picked up the mail for the folks in the surrounding area who could afford the cost of sending and receiving mail.

I returned his smile as I accepted the bundle. "How go things with you and the missus?"

"Waiting on the grandbaby to arrive. My Alice says it should be any day." He removed the tattered brown hat he always wore cockeyed and scratched his balding head while glancing around the property. "Always loved this place. It's like a little piece of heaven hidden away by these oak trees."

I smiled, looking over my shoulder at the view around me. "It has a certain charm, doesn't it?"

"I was a little boy when your grandpa built the place. My pappy and your grandpa were good friends. Pa would bring me along sometimes when he came to visit. I remember the slaves lifting those columns into place on that front veranda there." He waved his hat at the main house. "I remember your mama, too. Pretty little thing with eyes that ate through a man's soul." His voice conveyed deep appreciation.

I stiffened and turned back to examine his face. "You knew my mother?"

"What man didn't?" He clapped his leg in mirth.

I frowned at his remark, and his eyes widened in horror. "Wife's always saying my words don't come out right. What I was fixing to say is it was her beauty, I suppose, that made folks' tongues waggle. Women beat their men with their parasols if they so much as craned their necks your mama's way. Beauty was her curse. She never gave folks no cause to say the things they did. Your mama was made of a pure heart. Folks will always be folks. Nothing better to do than construct stories."

We'd never spoken about my mother. Why was he saying all this now? Prickles zapped under my skin.

Oblivious to the raw emotions his words ignited in me, he continued. "Many afternoons when I'd stop by, your mama would greet me with a cold glass of punch." The deep creases in the corners of his eyes softened. "Couple of times, I seen her out riding with your uncle. One day, I rode up on them sitting on a blanket in the grass all cozy-like. I spied on them for a moment or two." A pinkish tinge seeped through the gray scruff on his cheeks. "They were laughing and chatting, causing nobody no harm. I couldn't help but wonder if she might love him. But then she married your father, and soon after, her belly grew with you. Around that time, your mama changed."

"How so?"

"Her eyes became vacant. The sweet, carefree gal she once was was gone. After you were born, a spark of that gal returned.

For a while, she'd bring you out to greet me. Other times I'd see her over there by the pond, reading to you."

Through his memories, I envisioned the phantom of my mother with a small child.

"Olivia loved you more than anything, as sure as I'm sitting here on this horse. Never could figure out why she ran off. After all these years, it still doesn't sit right in my gut. She wouldn't just up and leave you." His wind-chapped lips formed a firm line. It was apparent that the mystery around my mother's disappearance that had tormented me still troubled the man.

It felt as if hands squeezed the breath from me as he continued. "Some say she bewitched the Hendricks brothers." His shoulders slumped, and a haunting sadness darkened his gray eyes. "After she took off, your pa wasn't ever the same. He became consumed with his businesses, and the other brother vanished altogether. People took to saying Olivia had run off with the younger brother and you. I wondered myself when the three of you disappeared. Then there were the rumors of the younger brother drifting in and out of town over the years.

"It was some years later that Charles started being seen around town with a wee one. Folks contrived a story that helped them come to peace with the situation in their minds."

"I don't see why they should concern themselves with other people's lives." I folded my arms across my chest, biting down hard on the corner of my lip.

"Folks always going to pry into others' affairs. With your pa gone, I know that's got to be hard on a young lady. Sure glad your uncle stuck around to help you run the place. Charles refused to speak about Olivia and him being gone, but I wanted you to know, no matter what folks say, your mama loved you. If it weren't for the height you inherited from your pa, I'd say you were Olivia in the living flesh."

Tears scratched at the back of my throat. Mr. Sterling wasn't one for an idle tongue. He wanted me to know this. The genuine kindness on his face cracked the defensive shell I'd formed around myself. "I appreciate you telling me about my mother. For many years, I've wanted to know more about her, aside from the tiresome gossip of her running off with another man. I suppose I'll never know for certain if the rumors hold any truth."

I'd allow the town to savor the theory they'd concocted about my mother. Ben had told me everything he could about the passionate and fearless woman I aspired more and more every day to emulate.

"Your parents would be proud of the young lady you've become."

"Thank you, Mr. Sterling." I willed a cheerful smile.

"I'd best be on my way." He pulled his reins and circled his horse back down the lane. With a wave over his shoulder, he took off at a gallop.

I flipped through the stack of mail. My heart caught when I noticed one from a William Still. Did he have news? What if...? I tore the letter open with trembling fingers.

Philadelphia, October 2nd, 1852

To Miss Hendricks,

It saddens me to inform you that I have no update on the girl Mag, whom you seek. With little information to go on, it does seem impossible to locate her. But I will keep searching.

W. Still

I dropped my hand to my side and blinked away tears. Mr. Still's letters continued to snatch all hope from me with their endless dead ends. I tucked the mail into my saddlebag and leaned my forehead against my mare, clenching my eyes shut to cut off tears. I had to find her! But how?

Jimmy led a horse into the front yard. Tillie sat on the horse, gripping her carpet bag and the saddle.

"Lard, keep me on dis horse. Don't let him git no funny ideas," she whispered.

"Oh, Tillie, you'll be just fine. The horse is the least of your worries," I said, stepping on the carriage stone to mount my horse. Then we were off.

ᘒᕣ CHAPTER ᕣᘒ
Sixteen

OUR HORSES HAD BARELY BROKEN A SWEAT BY THE TIME TILLIE and I arrived at the Anderson farm.

As with Livingston, the Ashley River was the farm's backdrop, but this property lay wide open, without the cozy appeal of lush gardens and trees. A smaller two-storey house sat in the center of the property. Over the years the white paint had cracked and chipped, revealing the weathered gray boards underneath. An enclosed porch extended from end to end at the front of the house. Knee-high grass swallowed up the two outbuildings and barn that sat to the right of the main house. A couple of slave shacks overlooked the river.

A few peacocks scurried around when I rode into the front yard, but aside from them and the hogs in the pasture, the property appeared lifeless. Where was Anderson? I'd expected him to come out to greet us. I rose up in my saddle and looked around. "Hello?" I called out.

Nothing.

"Mr. Anderson, it's Willow Hendricks."

No answer came.

I climbed down and tied the horse to the hitching post before removing my riding gloves.

A light cough came from Tillie, and I glanced up at her. Though her eyes were engrossed in the mane of her horse, a fleeting shift in her facial expression warned me of Anderson's approach before he called out.

"Miss Hendricks, what a pleasure." His gait was wide and fast as he entered the yard from the back.

Most women would swoon at the heart-pattering smile he offered me but, focused on the task at hand, I delivered Silas Anderson a flawless fixed smile while forcing myself to take full, even breaths. "Tillie here is one of my kitchen slaves. She's a fine cook and can get your house in order. As we discussed, she'll be in your service for one week and one week only."

"You have my gratitude, Miss Hendricks." He bowed gracefully.

I turned my back on him to face Tillie. "You go on now and get off that horse."

Tillie hesitated.

"Come, girl, move along," I said sternly.

"Yes, Missus." She slipped from her horse.

Tillie held out the reins with a surprisingly steady hand. The tips of her fingers touched mine as I took the reins. Gathering her skirt, she spun to face the house, her shoulder blades angled back and her chin thrust out. With the courage of the African warrior prince Mammy had often told me stories about as a child, Tillie mounted the steps and disappeared inside, the door shutting silently behind her.

Worry and despair expanded in my chest as I stared after her. Pleading in my head that she transmit her courage into me, I fought against the sting of telltale tears. *Stay strong. Keep the faith,* I told myself.

Without warning, a massive, moving shadow engulfed me. My heart snagged in my throat and I stepped back, dropping my gloves. My hands came up, ready to fend off my attacker.

A man. A huge man, vast and wide. As he shuffled toward us, I imagined the shaking of trees and the crumbling of the earth beneath his feet. I inched back as he stopped beside Silas. "This is Caesar. He's harmless," Silas said, motioning for me to relax with his hand.

Head bowed, the man clasped his paw-like hands tight in front of him. He stood like a beast in an opium-induced trance.

"He was born a mute," Silas said. Did he think that made the man less intimidating?

"Yes, well now, on to the reason I'm here," I said, disregarding the slave. "I am hiring the girl out to you in good faith. I pride myself on being a businesswoman. Slaves are an investment, and a slave marked will decrease their value. I can't have that. I choose to have my stock of slaves in good health. I'd expect you to treat my slave no differently. If she's returned to me marked or damaged in any way, I'll come looking for the price I paid for her and the price for the inconvenience of finding another. Are we clear?" Sweat trickled down my inner thighs. I imagined it pooling in my boots.

"You have my word," Silas said, his visage of a well-mannered gentleman never faltering.

I released a breath, nodded once, and turned to my horse.

Leaving the farm, I whispered a prayer of protection for Tillie.

❧ CHAPTER ❧
Seventeen

Tillie

F ROM THE WINDOW IN THE PARLOR, I WATCHED MISS WILLOW ride away. I could barely hear my own thoughts from the drumming of my heart.

Please don't leave me.

Be brave, Tillie, I imagined Miss Willow whispering back. Yesterday I'd found my courage in her, but now, without her, I could feel it slipping away. Down...down it went, fading with each breath I took.

You got to be strong. Ef folkses can run from deir masas and follow de North Star to freedom, you can do dis small ting de missus ask of you. One week, Miss Willow said, and den I'll go home. I swiped the moisture from my eyes with the back of my hand.

From behind the musty-smelling blue gingham curtains, I spied on Mr. Anderson and the slave man. Never had I seen a black man like him. His shoulders seemed as wide as the Ashley River, and his head could touch the top of a mountain. *I ain't ever seen a mountain 'fore, but I'd say he'd be 'bout dat big.*

Mr. Anderson and the slave exchanged a few words before Mr. Anderson strode toward the house. The slave turned to leave but then stopped and looked at the house. His eyes moved to the window where I stood, and he waved right at me like he knew I was spying. Then he dashed around back to the working yard.

The squeak of the front door opening sent me scurrying to the other side of the room. Grabbing the dusting cloth I'd found earlier, I glided my hand along the mantle. An imprint of my long fingers left a trail in the dust.

Mr. Anderson's boots clicked across the floor. *Click...shuffle... click...shuffle* they went. Each step strummed the fear thrumming through me all morning. The third floorboard in the hallway right next to the double sliding doors outside the parlor creaked.

Then his footfalls stopped. His eyes were on me. I could feel them piercing through my back. *Sweet Jesus, protect me.*

"They call you Tillie?" he said, his voice flat.

I dug the heel of my left shoe into the floor plank and slowly turned around. Sticking my eyes to the clawed wooden foot of the settee, I said, "Dat's right, Masa."

"I see you've searched the place out." In the yellow pattern on the floor coming from the window, I saw his finger poke at me, or at the cloth I held balled in a fist at my side.

Was he displeased? The thumping inside of me felt like it exploded. For a second that's all I could hear. "I thought you'd want me to git right to work, Masa."

From the low growl that rose from his chest to the way he shifted his weight to one foot, I listened and noted it all. A gray spider scurried from the oak baseboard over the flower-patterned hooked rug and across the toe of Mr. Anderson's boot. The boot that was worn more than the other.

"You head on out to the kitchen house. You can start there. Supper is to be served at 5:00 p.m. sharp every night. Understood?"

"Yes, Masa."

"Good. I'm not to be disturbed. Now, off with you."

Out the back door I went, without another word. I scurried across the yard to the first outbuilding, where my feet caught at the doorway. My heart sank at the sight I saw.

"Oh, Lard have mussy!"

I'd found the kitchen house, all right, but it didn't look like no kitchen house I'd ever seen before. It seemed like the critters from the woods had turned the place upside down and inside out. I took a deep breath and climbed the two steps into the house. A wooden table sat in the middle of the small room, heaped right full with dirty pots, plates, cups, and utensils. Muddy footprints trailed from the fireplace to the table to the cupboards.

Miss Rita would be piping mad if she could see this place. She'd go up one side of Mr. Anderson and his slave man and down the other, sending them running away with their faces hanging low and red with shame. I snickered at the thought. Besides, there was nothing to do but laugh. It was either laugh or squat in the corner and bawl over the task ahead.

So I did what needed doing.

⚜ CHAPTER ⚜
Eighteen

Willow

S EVERAL DAYS HAD PASSED SINCE I'D LEFT TILLIE AT THE ANDERSON farm. And with each passing day, my stomach twisted into knots. I couldn't eat or sleep. I paced the corridor all hours of the night. I'd considered spying on the farm, hoping to spot Tillie and ease my mind over her well-being.

Today I sat on an afghan by the edge of the pond, under the shadows of the moss-covered limbs of the grandest live oak on the plantation. On a lily pad in the center of the pond, a bullfrog croaked. White swans circled, dipping their beaks in the water and snapping up vegetation. A lone swan swam near the shoreline, extending and flapping its massive wings and showering me with droplets of water.

Gazing at my reflection in the pond, I traced my fingertips along the thick pink scar trailing up my neck, left by the lash of the whip and the night I tried to forget. The guilt I felt over Mary Grace's rape had become increasingly harder to bear. Mary Grace had been free all along. Mammy should've taken her and left long ago. But because of me, Mammy had stayed, and because of me, her daughter had suffered a fate no woman wants for another. *If only* had played over and over in my head since I'd learned the truth that they were, in fact, free.

The workload of running Hendricks Enterprises and

Livingston numbed the madness inside my head. Had my father felt the same? Had guilt cut away a little piece of him each day, changing him as it was changing me?

My parents had fought against slavery for decades, yet we owned slaves. Ownership of slaves on Livingston dated back to my grandparents. From those slaves came families, and as time progressed, families continued to grow. With that, more lives became enslaved at Livingston. As with all slave owners, we were bound by the legislative law that restricted the freeing of slaves. Laws might prevent me from setting them all free, but I wouldn't allow it to keep me from doing what was right for the slaves.

Livingston was envied for its beauty and its prosperity. Unbeknownst to me, Father had used this advantage to transfer slaves in and out of Livingston. Risking being arrested, he'd hidden fugitives on his ships and moved them around the world. Many passed through Livingston before being moved along the channels to the next station, and many had enlisted right here to aid Father in the cause.

I'd spent so many years being a self-absorbed child, believing he wanted to keep my mother from me, that I hadn't noticed the operation going on right under my nose. Though at times the past threatened to consume me, I forced myself to move forward. In secret, I encouraged slaves wanting to learn to read and write. We taught them trades to better themselves in hopes that one day the brighter future we all believed in would come. More and more folks all over the country were taking a stand against slavery.

As it was for the slaves here, some days were darker than others for me, and then my faith would dwindle. But we had to keep the faith, or all we'd striven for would be lost.

Lost on the battlefield inside my mind, I hadn't heard anyone approach until a husky voice rescued me from my thoughts.

"I was told I could find you here."

"Bowden!" My voice hitched, and for a moment my breathing stopped.

"The one and only." He bowed extravagantly before straightening to his full height.

A soft, genuine smile curved the corners of his lips, a smile that cut at my heart. Guilt flared over the way I'd left things last spring before leaving for Rhode Island—an emotion I hated above all others. I'd been avoiding him since my return. And from the look on his face, I guessed he knew it.

He lowered himself to the ground beside me, one knee bent, the other outstretched. He removed his hat and placed it on his bent knee. His dark waves shone in the sunlight, and his blue-green eyes captivated me with their intensity. In them I read longing and a burning passion.

I averted my eyes. The pain in his gaze was too great. "I've been meaning to let you know we were back, but I've had my hands full with things here. When did you get back?"

"A month ago," he said.

He gazed out over the pond, his jaw-length hair partially hiding his expression from me. A desire to reach out and tuck his hair back so I could see him struck me, but I lowered my eyes and instead traced the outline of the tiny pink rosebuds on my ivory gown.

I'd missed him greatly, but my life was so busy, and time for matters of the heart wasn't a priority in my life. I'd meant to write and tell him I needed more time to give him the answer he sought, but time had a way of slipping away. And with me trying to sort out my family's affairs, I'd spent the summer meeting Father's acquaintances, locating the station depots, and meeting my father's station masters in the Northern states.

He deserved better.

"I knew falling for a girl like you would bring its challenges," Bowden said.

"A girl like me?"

"A wild bronco," he said with a dry chuckle.

"A horse? You're categorizing me as a horse?" I laughed.

"I tend to enjoy horses. They're magnificent creatures."

"And me?" I needed to know he still loved me. No sooner had the desire to hear the words filled me than I quickly admonished myself for such a selfish thought.

He turned to look at me, and the pain in his eyes tore at me. "Irresistible."

I swallowed hard and tried to slow the feverish beat of my heart. He lifted his hand and traced my jaw with his fingertips in a slow, enticing rhythm. The pounding of my heart resounded in my ears. He was everything and more that a woman could want in a man. I wanted—needed—to feel his warm, inviting lips on mine. But I couldn't push away what my heart was telling me.

"Things are complicated. With all the discoveries I've made about my father's affairs, it's overwhelming. I don't know where to start."

His hand hesitated in its movement, and the muscles in his jaw grew taut. "Marriage would allow a man to take away some of the burdens—"

"You men think we women are weak, and that irritates me. I—"

"Now, don't go letting the bees stir under your bonnet. I only meant that a plantation is a great responsibility for anyone."

I blew out a calming breath. "Forgive me for my assumptions."

"I've grown used to your hostility," he said with a shrug.

"If you didn't get under my skin, then maybe I wouldn't get so hot around the ears."

"Maybe if you heard people out before jumping to conclusions, you wouldn't get so riled up."

"You made your point," I warned. "I did miss you, and I'm pleased you stopped by."

"Are you?" His eyes settled on my lips. Cupping my chin, he stroked my lips with his thumb as his head lowered.

This is wrong. I can't do this! But...as his lips touched mine, my body filled with warmth and a welcome familiarity. Involuntarily, my arms circled his neck, and I clung to him. My fingers looped through his hair as I soaked in his scent.

He groaned, fighting the desire our kiss awoke and pulled back, releasing me. He turned to gaze once again out over the pond. "I've had the summer and most of the fall to think. I've come to understand that snaring you into being a married woman is more trouble than I anticipated."

We'd courted longer than most, and a piece of me wanted to continue to court because the thought of losing him was a pain I couldn't bear. "Why do we have to follow the ways of the world around us?" I laid a hand over his on the grass.

He withdrew his hand. "Why do I feel that you go out of your way to defy the ways of the South?"

"I refuse to be molded into what any man says I must be. I've been restricted too long, and now that I have my freedom, I'll not allow any man to dictate to me what I should do or feel. This is who I am, Bowden. You were aware of this from the beginning. I've never pretended to be anything else."

"I was aware of it. But I thought—"

"You thought you could change me?" I laughed, and the scorn in my voice shocked me as much as it did him. He stiffened, and I wished immediately that I could recant the bitterness in my tone. I hurried to explain myself. "I can't promise you that I'll ever be the marrying type. I know it's unfair of me to say, but

I do love you."

"There will never be another woman for me." His voice thickened with emotion.

"I'm sorry I can't offer more." A weight settled in my chest. He deserved to be treasured and loved by a good woman. A woman that would bear him children and care for him and put him first. But I wasn't sure I'd ever be that kind of woman.

"Then that's your answer?"

"I wish I could say yes, that I'd marry you, but I can't. God help me, I wish I could!" Tears sprang into my eyes.

"They've consumed you," he said, releasing a long, drawn-out sigh.

"Who?"

"The slaves, that's who! Along with your obsession with changing our way of life."

A lump formed in my throat at his words. The differences in our belief systems would always keep us apart. "I'll not stop trying to set right the wrongs we've done to them. It's who I've become. Maybe it's who I've always been."

"*We* are slave owners. Our businesses rely on their labor."

His emphasis on *we* stung. "Times are changing. People grow restless. What if slavery was no longer our source of labor? What if we employed the blacks and gave them the freedom to choose what they do with their lives? Is this idea so insane?" If only he could see the wrong in our ways, all this pain and emptiness between us could be resolved.

"Of course it's insane. Our prosperity depends on the slaves, and without their labor, it would be our demise. Why can't *you* understand that!"

"I do understand it, clearly. But what is wrong is wrong, and no amount of profit can wash away the sins of our nation. Enslaving a race out of the belief that their skin color makes them inferior is evil and beyond my understanding. You may consider my thoughts and ideas childish or foolish, but this will always divide us. How can I marry a man who holds to a belief that questions all the values I hold dear?"

"Willow—"

I put up a hand. "No! We must be honest with ourselves. How can you and I unite as one when we are two extremely different people? You're a good man, but your belief system is one I can't abide, and I can't, in good conscience, be your wife, knowing where you stand on slavery. We'd be miserable together, and I'd grow to resent you."

My voice fractured. I needed him and couldn't imagine my life without him, but how could I change him? I couldn't. No amount of love could change our core beliefs.

I wept.

He gently stroked my shoulder, then stood. "There will never be another," he said softly.

The whisper of his boots on the grass grew and then faded altogether.

⟋ CHAPTER ⟍
Nineteen

Bowden

T HE COUNTRYSIDE FLASHED BY ME IN A BLUR. THE SILVER MANE of my dapple-gray thoroughbred billowed in the wind as we charged toward home. His need for speed and my eagerness to put distance between Willow and myself propelled us onward. Dust kicked up around us, gritting up my teeth and lips and scratching at my eyes. The thunderous hoofbeats resounded in my chest as Willow's words milled around in my head.

Had I thought I could change her? I suppose I had, but hadn't she felt the same?

"Damn fool!" I blurted, my voice caught and carried by the wind.

Willow drove me to the point of madness. Made me want to stomp my foot like a scorned woman.

Charles Hendricks had spoiled her by lavishing her with trinkets, books, and the finest silks and fashions money could buy. Maybe he'd felt guilt over her not having a mother, or any female relatives, to teach her all the things only a woman could. Or that his businesses had taken him away for long periods of time, leaving Willow to be raised by her mammy and house slaves. He'd played a hand in the unhealthy bond she'd formed with the Negroes. I couldn't fault her for loving them; they'd practically raised her.

Her passionate belief that all slaves should be free and that she could change the world to one of her making not only went against everything I'd ever known, it was dangerous. I didn't condone the cruelty I'd seen unleashed on the Negroes any more than she, but people didn't take kindly to Negro lovers. Willow finding out about her mother's murder had only driven her deeper into her obsession to be a voice for the Negroes. An obsession that terrified me.

Any man with common sense would've washed his hands of Willow long ago. Some would say she wasn't the sort of woman a gentleman should take as a wife because she lacked obedience. Her love for all humanity was admirable and spoke volumes for the heart that pounded behind her beautiful full breast. In ways, she reminded me of my mother and how she'd offered her love without restrictions. Could a man find happiness with a woman like Willow?

Last spring, before Willow had gone off to Rhode Island, we'd taken a ride in the countryside. As we'd sat in the grass, I rested my chin on the top of her head while holding her in my arms. That afternoon, I'd asked her to marry me, and she'd left me without an answer.

The next morning, she was gone. Soon after, I'd left to spend the hotter months in California with my brother, Stone. Not a rustle of skirts had passed me during my time away without sending my heart into spasms and hope surging through me that the face I'd look upon would be Willow's.

Over the months away, I received a couple of letters from Willow, but she never mentioned my proposal. In her last letter, she'd spoken of Kipling's visit and the wonderful things he was doing in the North. I'd cursed the man and shredded the letter. Had he stolen her affections? My heart ached at the thought.

Armstrong Plantation soon stretched out before me, and I slowed my horse to a trot as we passed under the wooden sign that hung from wrought-iron arms on the double-wide stone archway. The lane led from there up to the two-storey brownstone house with its many windows framed by freshly painted ivory shutters. A grand staircase rose to the front doors, today open to catch the afternoon breeze.

At my arrival, my manservant, Isaac, stepped out onto the piazza and stood waiting on my instructions. Gray jogged toward me as I reined my horse to a stop. The sunlight caught his slave tag through the opening in his shirt. Swinging my leg over my mount, I dropped to the ground.

Gray dipped his head in a bow and took the reins I held out to him. "Did you see my Mary Grace and chillum, Masa?"

Embittered by Willow's rejection, I wasn't in the mood for idle chatter. "It wasn't a social call. I merely stopped by Livingston to clear up a personal matter between Miss Hendricks and myself."

He nodded. His hands fell limp at his sides, as though he'd waited all morning for me to return, holding onto a glimmer of hope that I'd have something to report about his family, and with my blunt words, I'd snatched it away.

I sighed with regret. "I did, however, see Mary Grace sweeping the front piazza. She looked to be in fine health."

Relief washed across Gray's face, followed by a bigger-than-life grin. "Dat's good, Masa."

"Sunday will be here soon, and you can see for yourself how your family fares." The tightness in my jaw eased, and I clapped his shoulder.

"Sunday is a blessed day," Gray said before leading my horse out back.

I tarried a while, considering the slave who stood out against the rest. Physically, Gray was strong and outperformed any slave on the plantation. He was ambitious, a trait that would threaten other masters, but it was his ambition that made him valuable and dependable. He finished his tasks long before the others. If hired out or sent on errands, he always returned home. His work ethic was strong and purposeful.

One thing drove Gray, and that was freedom. He'd saved every coin he'd earned with the idea of buying his freedom. Yet even if he saved enough to buy his freedom, the courts would have the final say. Documents signed by a slave's master freeing him had become more restricted and held little value. I couldn't find it within myself to dim that light in Gray's eyes by telling him the dream he desperately clung to was next to impossible. I was afraid to witness the defeat in his face. The truth was, Gray was a man more honorable than most of the white gentlemen in my social circle.

"Horses are property, Mr. Armstrong. Humans aren't!" Willow's words from long ago echoed through my head.

I removed my hat, swiped a hand through my hair, and forced her from my mind. Climbing the stairs, I passed my hat to Isaac, then paused to drain the glass of water he held out to me.

"Mr. Tucker is waiting in the parlor, sir."

Ahh, Knox. Now, he was someone to brighten the day.

Inside, I found Knox in my favorite armchair. He sat with one booted ankle crossed over his knee. Abigail, the cook, hunched over him, filling his glass with wine.

"I can't leave for a moment without you taking the liberty to help yourself to my home, my best wine, and my chair," I said, entering the room with widespread arms. Knox grinned broadly, starting to rise, but I motioned for him to remain seated.

"I quite enjoy coming out here and dabbling in the finer things in life. My apartment is drab and stuffy. I felt the need for a little country air."

"Town life isn't suiting you?" I seated myself on the sofa opposite him as Abigail offered me wine. I shook my head. "Cognac." I'd need something stronger to make it through this day. I ducked my head around her to look at Knox.

He seemed absorbed in the burgundy sea at the bottom of his glass. His visage was serious, an expression almost foreign on the jokester I considered my best friend. Knox leaned forward, resting his elbows on his knees, and the globe of his wine glass disappeared between his large hands.

Abigail returned with a bottle of 1827 Albert Jarraud. Removing the red seal, she poured an inch of the rich amber-brown liquid into a glass. I tilted the snifter to my lips and took a sip. The spice and oak flavors circled over my tongue.

"I've been thinking," Knox said, "of asking Whitney to marry me."

As he blurted this, I gasped, sending the fire of the cognac trickling down my windpipe. "You've thought this through?" I wheezed. Behind a closed fist, I released a hard cough to clear the fiery liquid.

"I have. I love her, and being alone doesn't hold the same appeal it once did." He focused his brown eyes on me.

"Are you sure you can handle a woman like her?"

"Time will tell with that." His muscular chest expanded and fell as he sighed. His worries rekindled the despair over my own fading love affair. "But I love her...and the twins. The children need a father, and young Jack is a handful for Whitney. If we got married, maybe I could ease some of her burden."

I wasn't sure if he was trying to convince himself or me. "So...you're doing her a favor?"

"I guess so."

"If I were you, I wouldn't be voicing that knuckle-brained

thought to her," I said. I envisioned Whitney coming undone and landing Knox on his backside. Amused by the mental image, I wished I could be a bird perched on a limb nearby if he was fool enough to verbalize such a thought.

"You have a certain charm with the ladies. What would your approach be in asking a lady to marry you?"

Disgruntled and anguished over how Willow had run off last spring without so much as an "I'll think about it," I'd avoided mentioning the proposal to Knox, or anyone else, for that matter. "I don't know if I'd be much help. Willow flat-out refuses to marry me."

He arched a brow. "You've asked her?"

"Last spring, and she gave me her answer today."

Pulling himself from his own dilemma, he really looked at me for the first time since I'd sat down. I didn't try to hide the despair I felt.

"She turned you down!" he said. "But why? Willow has been in love with you since she was a child."

"Sometimes love isn't enough," I said, and gulped back the cognac. Lifting the bottle, I refilled the snifter.

Knox sat back in his chair. "We're a sorry pair, aren't we?"

I laughed bitterly.

"Maybe I put too much trust in your gentlemanly swagger. What's happening to us? You're losing your touch with the ladies of Charleston, and I'm considering giving up my bachelor life for a family."

I chugged back another mouthful. The warmth of the cognac numbed the agony I felt and blotted out the soft chestnut locks and alluring green eyes that hounded my every waking thought. "What's your plan? Move them all into town? Your place is too small for the four of you."

"I have some money saved up—"

"Since when? I've never known you to be capable of saving."

"I told you, things are different now."

Women had a way of doing that. They crept into the fibers of your very soul and spun their webs. Once they had you entangled, they pounced, and you became their victim, helplessly wrapped in the silk of their web.

"I'm thinking of purchasing some land and building a home on it. It'd be small and nothing like what she's become accustomed to at Livingston."

"Something tells me Whitney isn't a shallow woman."

"But most of her gowns are imported from Paris and England." The toe of his boot tapped repetitively on the floor.

"I wouldn't concern yourself with that. Her father left her almost penniless, and she isn't capable of purchasing the things she once did. Speaking of building a home, what about the Barry Plantation? Whitney owns the land, and you two could build a homestead there."

"The men down at the docks say the place is haunted. They say the ghost of Mr. Barry roams the land, seeking his revenge on the slaves for killing him."

I chuckled. "The townies like to hear themselves chatter. The ghost of ol' Mr. Barry, the masked men, and this swamp man called the Guardian—what next?"

"But the masked men are no laughing matter. I was at the pier when their first victims tore into town. The coach was peppered with bullet holes, and the driver was dead. I saw it all. It's no made-up story."

"Maybe there's truth in these men. But tell me: what have you heard about this Guardian fellow?"

"I went for a drink at the saloon a while back, and Thames was there with some locals. He was drunk, but he was adamant that this fellow had a hand in his slave's disappearance. There's talk of the constable getting a patrol together to sniff him out. Folks are getting riled up. They won't sit by and allow slaves to go around killing. First the Barry slaves, and now the Thameses' slave killing their overseer. Folks are on edge. If one slave so much as looks at a white man the wrong way, there'll be trouble, and what happened in those swamps out there will be like sipping afternoon tea."

My heart hammered in my chest. A patrol going from plantation to plantation looking for lawbreakers couldn't happen. What would this mean for Willow? God only knew what she was up to over there.

"I've heard mention of how Mr. Thames treats his slaves, and I'm sure his overseer was no different," I said.

"You're saying the overseer got what he deserved? It's against the law for a slave to strike a white man, and to kill one is suicide."

"Taking a life isn't right, no matter how you look at it. How some slave owners treat their slaves isn't right either."

"What about owning slaves as a whole?" Knox said.

"Some days I question it, but it's the way things are done. The way they've always been done."

"I will not own a slave. If Whitney honors me by becoming my wife, we'll make our own way in life."

"How do you intend to work the land?"

He waved his hands in the air. "With the two hands God gave me."

My stomach dropped as I studied him with unmasked envy. He had a chance at happiness. What I wouldn't do to be rid of this plantation and start over…

After Knox's departure, I left the parlor and strolled down the corridor to the library. Portraits of my grandfather, my parents, Stone, and me lined the dark paneled walls. I paused in front of the portrait of my parents. Time had dulled the pain over their death, but on days like today, I yearned to sit in their presence one last time. To seek their advice, not as the selfish boy I'd been the last time I'd seen them alive, but as a man willing to hear.

Maybe it was time for a change. South Carolina held nothing for me anymore. Perhaps I'd go back to Texas and take up ranching. Something had to change. Life without Willow seemed impossible, but her living a stone toss away was suffocating.

I'd prospered over the years while running this plantation, but it had never been my calling in life. When grandfather fell ill and needed help, I'd just finished medical school and came home to care for him. Helping people had been all I'd wanted to do in life, but somehow life had led me here.

Loneliness consumed me as I turned to glance out the French doors. To the left of the formal gardens, the new overseer sat on his mount, speaking to Gray. The head overseer had needed the extra help and hired the young man while I was in California. Gray, never one to cause trouble, stood submissively before the man with his head bowed. The man raised the butt of his whip and landed it on Gray's temple.

I tore toward the French doors. The glass rattled in the frames as I shoved the doors open and charged through like a bull released from its corral. "Collins! You come down off the horse immediately," I said, the inferno sleeping in me ignited. My feet bounced in my boots as I glared up at him.

Collins sat unmoving, either out of shock or intimidation, I wasn't sure. I'd come unhitched, and I knew it, but I didn't care.

"You have two seconds to dismount, or I'll remove you myself."

He quickly dismounted.

"Were you informed by Milton of the rules here?"

"Yes, boss."

"Then you're aware of my strict policy about the abuse of slaves. And that under no circumstance is it permitted."

"Yes, boss."

"Then clear out your cabin and be gone within the hour."

"But...boss, I need this job."

"You should've thought of that before you struck Gray."

"He's just a nigger, and he was questioning me on my—"

"Masa...I jus' tole Mr. Collins dat Lilly May ain't well 'nuf to be working in de field. De tumor is eating away at her. She can hardly stand most days."

"Is this true, Collins?"

"Ain't nothing but a lazy nigger looking for an excuse not to pull her weight." His face contorted with hatred, and he intentionally landed a spray of tobacco juice on Gray's shoes.

Red darkened my vision. My fist clenched at my side as the desire to lay him flat surged through me. "Gather your belongings and ride on out of here," I grated. "I'll see to it that Milton brings you payment for your service, but you won't be employed by me a moment longer."

Sweat dotted his forehead. "But...my folks are counting on me for the money."

"It's a little late to consider that. Now, get out of here before I drag you out by the collar."

Collins led his horse to his cabin.

Minutes later, I stood speaking to Gray when the pounding of hooves made us look up. Collins was charging toward us, whipping his reins wildly from one side of his horse to the other, his eyes bright with fury.

I grabbed at Gray and leaped aside.

Collins spewed a mouthful of tobacco juice at us on the way by and screamed, "Nigger-lover! I'll be sure folks hear of this."

I removed a handkerchief from my pocket and wiped the disgusting liquid from my face. "Here." I handed the cloth to Gray.

He wiped his face and handed it back. "I'm sorry, Masa."

"It isn't your fault." I clapped him on his shoulder. "You get back to work, and I'll check on Lilly May's condition."

CHAPTER
Twenty

Willow

THE COMFORT OF MY BEDCHAMBER CALLED TO ME, ALONG WITH my desire to escape from watching eyes and wallow in self-pity. But the demands of the plantation didn't allow me to go into hiding after Bowden's departure took the last of my spirit with it.

Our love for each other couldn't change the differences between us. In time, maybe we'd learn how to move on. If we'd been fool enough to marry, it would've been tainted from the start. A marriage built on lies and deceit would never last.

I was the one to blame. I was the one with all the secrets. I'd told Bowden of my mother's involvement in helping a slave that ended with her murder. But I couldn't tell him what really went on at Livingston or that I was involved in aiding more fugitives than the one time he knew of. I suspected that he knew to some extent but turned a blind eye, and for that, I loved him even more.

"Miss Willow?"

"Yes, Parker?" I shook my head free of daydreams and returned to the glowing circle of light from the candle in the center of the table, and the chatter of the others in the small cabin.

"I don't care to larn dese white folkses' books." His voice squeaked with the changing of a boy into a man. "I want to be a sailor."

"A sailor?"

"Yessum. I want to feel de sea water on my face and see de world. I ain't been nowhere but South Carolina. Last time Captain Gillies was here, he tole me I'd make a fine sailor." He played with the pages of the book that lay open in front of him.

"Is this so." I smiled.

"Parker always has his head in de clouds, dreaming of things impossible," his pa, Owen, said from his chair in front of the crackling fire.

"Dreams give us something to look forward to." I glanced from Parker to Owen as an idea popped into my head. "What would you think of Parker accompanying Captain Gillies on his next voyage?" I saw Parker squeeze his mouth shut as he held his breath, eyes on his father.

Owen sat forward in his chair. "I don't want de boy's head filled wid ideas dat can never happen for a slave."

"This is an idea that's quite obtainable. If Parker proves to be a good sailor, we could find him a position on our ships. He could earn some coin."

Parker pushed back his chair and, using his walking cane, pushed himself to his feet. "I'm going."

"Now, wait a minute, boy." Panic widened Owen's eyes.

"Pa, I got to go. De missus is offering me a chance slaves don't git. I ain't meant to be tied down. Please, Pa, I need to go."

"De boy is right. Ef de missus is saying he can go, den you need to let him go," Owen's wife said from beside him, her eyes intent on the rug she was weaving out of corn husk.

"Pa, I know et's only bin you and me, but now you got Rosy here, and she'll take good care of you."

Tears welled in Owen's eyes, and sadness far greater than any of us could understand swept over his face. He settled back in his chair and stared long and hard into the flames of the fire.

"Time comes when chillum move on. Better I know you're out enjoying life den sold off to another plantation. Et could be far worse, I suppose."

His walking cane knocking across the planked floor, Parker shuffled over to hug his father. Owen embraced his son in loving arms, his face streaming with tears. I felt a twinge of guilt. Parker would get his wish, but his father would remain behind, missing and yearning for his son.

Leaving the cabin, I wandered back to the house, but instead of going inside, I sat on the back steps and peered out over the river. Beau's nails clicked across the veranda, and I felt his head nudge my side. I lifted my arm and scooped the dog closer. "Always faithful, aren't ya, old boy?"

He whined and rested his head on my lap. I patted him as I let my thoughts carry me away to a world I had formed in my head long ago. A world where any boy could sail the seas of his own accord. A world where the slave quarters didn't distinguish Livingston as a slave-owning plantation. Where the slaves singing their freedom songs was a thing of the past.

What would that world be like?

And where would I belong in that world?

CHAPTER
Twenty-One

Tillie

MISS WILLOW SAID TO KEEP A LOOKOUT FOR ANY FUNNY business happenin' at the Anderson farm. So far, Mr. Anderson had kept his distance, and nothing was amiss, but I had my eye on him. Miss Willow trusted me with an important task, and I'd let no trickery slip by me.

At night I slept in the quarters, same as most slaves do, but there warn't any slaves there except the man Mr. Anderson called Caesar. The slave was as dark as a widow's gown. His head hung low and didn't shift up nor left or right.

The past few days, I'd been thinking maybe Mr. Anderson wasn't as wealthy as he was letting on. Or perhaps Mr. Anderson believed, like Miss Willow, that people aren't meant to be owned. Because besides Mr. Anderson, Caesar, and me, there wasn't a soul around the place. No overseer, no hired men. No visitors besides the man that paid Mr. Anderson a visit a day or two back.

I blew out the candles in the kitchen house and stepped into the night, closing the door behind me. Turning, I glanced up at the big house. The light from the candles in the parlor that doubled as a study let me know Mr. Anderson was still up. Mr. Anderson never left me alone in the house, and he hadn't left the farm to do any errands, so I'd had no chance to snoop around in there.

Mr. Anderson's silhouette leaked out onto the ground from the window. It moved back and forth as Mr. Anderson paced the floors. Through the window, I saw him waving his hands in the air, and his mouth moved like he was talking to someone. His hands shifted to grip the sides of his head, and then he disappeared and reappeared. He jabbed a finger in the air, and his mouth was still moving. Poor Caesar was getting it good.

Beelining it for the quarters, I threw a look over my shoulder to make sure they hadn't spotted me and ran straight into something solid. The impact sent me reeling backward. Paws reached out, snatching me in their powerful grip. "Lard Jesus, help me!" I said as my bladder let loose. Squeezing my eyes shut, I lifted my arms to shield myself as I waited for the first strike of its claws or snap of its powerful jaw.

When I didn't feel any pain, not even a scratch, I eased open an eyelid. My squint made it blurry, but I recognized Caesar. My eyes snapped wide open, and I swear my jaw landed on my chest. "You git your hands off of me. I don't take no laking to men's demands." I wiggled and thrashed under the pressure of his fingers. My supper of cornbread and salted pork scurried up the back of my throat.

He grunted, and his eyes turned toward the house.

I eased my struggle for a moment. If he was standing here, who was Mr. Anderson talking to? To my recollection, no one had paid Mr. Anderson a visit.

Caesar's dark eyes moved back to me, and my pulse pumped wildly behind my windpipe. He hauled me toward the quarters.

"Sweet Jesus, show mussy!" I cried, digging my heels into the ground. "Please, I ain't ever bin wid no man 'fore. Let me go. Don't do dis!"

The beast ignored my pleas and dragged me to the shack I'd been staying in. The crushing grip on my arm relaxed. Again he grunted and gave me a shove toward the door before stepping back.

My brows lowered. He wasn't going to have his way with me? I wasn't sticking around to ask questions. I bounded up the rickety steps and threw open the door. Inside, I closed the door behind me and wedged myself against it. I waited for him to hammer on the door and push his way in.

Minutes passed, and no movement came. Opening the door, I stole a peek outside. He'd vanished. It was as if the night had swallowed him up.

The eerie sounds of the low country animals fell on my ears, and I slammed the door shut.

Later, as I lay in bed, the tree limbs scratched and groaned across the side of the cabin. The moonlight whitewashed a line down the center of my dead-still form on the corn husk pallet on the floor. A whispering of voices sounded in my head, and I curled up on my side like a new babe. I pulled the cover over my head, and the moldy smell plus the scratchy burlap plucked tears from my eyes. *Please, Lard, help me through dis night. Don't let dem murder Tillie in her sleep.*

CHAPTER
Twenty-Two

Willow

T ILLIE RETURNED AND BROUGHT WITH HER NO INFORMATION TO give us cause to be leery of Mr. Anderson.

Whitney, of course, wasn't letting go of her gut feeling. "He's good. Not one to be underestimated."

"Oh, poppycock." I glowered at her as we sat on the swing on the front veranda. "I don't want to hear any more about him. We've far more important things to worry about."

"Mark my words, there's more to him than what meets the eye." Her jaw set with determination.

"I hope you're wrong." I gave her a second glance, my uncertainty rising.

"Here she comes." Whitney stood.

I gazed out over the fallow field to the road and the flatbed wagon headed our way. Caroline Smith, the shopkeeper, had sent word with Jones that she'd accepted my offer to share tea with Whitney and me.

When she arrived, we stood to wait for her at the end of the pathway. She'd come alone, forgoing her own advice to bring a man for protection. Instead, there was a rifle propped against the seat next to her.

"Miss Smith, we're delighted you could join us," Whitney said.

Caroline gathered her skirts and stepped over the gun onto the carriage stone, then descended to the ground.

"I was surprised to receive your message from Mr. Jones," she said, stroking the neck of the horse while glancing around the plantation. "I've never been out here. I often dreamed of what it would look like. Words don't do the place justice." She stood as if in a trance. Miss Smith's cheerfulness during our last encounter was a faded memory, and the sternness I'd associated with the woman stood front and center. Yet, today there was an aura of despondency around her.

"We'll be having tea in the garden house today," I said.

Startled, Caroline blinked repeatedly, then stepped away from the horse. One finger at a time, she painstakingly removed her black leather gloves.

When we were seated in the garden house, I poured tea into Caroline's cup.

"Thank you." Her eyes settled on me. I smiled uneasily. "I must know what's so important that you'd request I come all the way out here," she said.

I quickly reiterated our concerns over Mr. Anderson buying out the Widow Jenson's farm and her sudden departure.

"He said he was in your store when he overheard the widow mention wanting to head back East," Whitney said.

"I recall the day. The widow had come into town with her slave William to purchase some supplies. She did mention something about going back East. I can't recall exactly what she said."

I gave Whitney a *See, I told you* look and smugly took a bite of my groundnut cake.

Whitney set her teacup down with a clank.

Caroline observed the silent battle between us and asked, "Why the concern?"

"With my father gone and my uncle away, we're a bit on

edge without any menfolk around." I fed her the story we'd concocted.

"I see," she said, and I glimpsed the dolefulness I thought I'd witnessed earlier. "The town lost a great man when your father passed." Her shoulders slumped, and she peered at her hand lying on her lap. "There will never be another Charles Hendricks." Her face twisted, as though she was wrestling with unresolved emotions.

Confused, I asked, "You knew him well?"

"After I arrived in town and found Amos had been struck down with yellow fever, I figured there was no need for me to stay and planned to go back home. Then I was informed by Amos's disgruntled brother that he'd willed his store to me. Charles came upon the man when he had me cornered and was threatening me, telling me that if I didn't hightail it out of town pronto, he'd make sure I was run out. Charles took me to see his lawyer, Mr. Bennick, and they saw to it that Amos's will was honored. Some days, I wonder why I stayed, especially now..." Caroline's voice drifted.

"Why did you?" Whitney said.

She heaved a sigh and turned her eyes on me. Softly, she said, "I'd hoped...I hoped Charles would one day see me as more than a friend and a business relationship."

Taken by surprise, I gasped. She'd been in love with him! The sadness enveloping her was the emptiness she felt over my father. The same sorrow buried deep inside me. "You loved him..." I whispered.

"Yes, but his heart would always belong to another. Even if time had permitted us to form more than a friendship, Charles could never completely give himself to another." Tears pooled in her eyes.

Raw and vulnerable, she sat before me. Like a rose, the

delicate petals that protected the heart of Caroline Smith fell away, revealing the tremendous ache she suffered for the loss of a man we both loved. My heart broke for her. In her vulnerability, she shared with me a longing for a man never destined to be ours.

"Your father spoke of you with the greatest affection. Though he did worry about the affection you showed toward the slaves." Her questioning eyes held mine.

Every nerve in me pinged to attention. Had she used her feelings for my father as a ploy to break down the defensive walls of my fortress?

"I too care what happens to the Negroes." Caroline's voice cut through the panic seizing my breath.

"I'm not sure we follow you," Whitney said, shifting in her seat. I'd almost forgotten her presence.

My mind skipped back to the delivery man at the store. Recovering my voice, I advanced with caution. "Why don't you enlighten us on what exactly you're alluding to, Miss Smith?"

"Ripping families apart and selling them as if they were mere hogs," she said bluntly.

"At one time in my life, I'd pass a colored person on the street without so much as a nod of acknowledgment. My family employed a colored woman, but at night she went home to her family. I'd heard how it was in the South, but it wasn't part of my life, so I didn't give it any thought.

"Since my arrival, more times than I can count, I've been disrespected and mistreated for merely being an outsider." She glanced down at her hands, but not before I saw the shame on her face. "I hate to admit it, but being an outcast myself finally opened my eyes to the evil befalling the Negroes. I found myself relating to them more than the fine folk of Charleston. I've made it my mission to help them in whatever way I can."

"What does this all have to do with me?"

She glanced around for eavesdroppers and said, "I know your father was an agent and used his ships to move cargo."

On the surface, I maintained my composure. Inside, I struggled to control my rising anxiety. "What else do you suppose you know?"

"The day you came by the general store, you made a delivery to the docks first. How am I doing so far?"

I gulped. "How do you know this?"

"I have my sources. But as you know, leaking information about conductors and stations could be the derailment of the railroad. Do you follow now, Miss Whitney?"

Whitney looked wide-eyed from her to me.

"My father would never tell you about the network unless—" I gasped as the realization hit me.

"Unless I was his source." She smiled knowingly. "You see, Miss Willow, I'm not as spooky as you've always believed. I don't cook children and eat them at luncheons."

My mouth gaped open, and the burn of my embarrassment reached the tips of my ears. I'd spoken those exact words to Mary Grace when we were little girls, waiting in the carriage while Miss Smith and Father had stood engaged in conversation.

❧ CHAPTER ❧
Twenty-Three

Ben

T HE CREW STRUGGLED TO CONTROL THE VESSEL AS THE STORM battered the *Olivia II*. Waves thrashed against the ship, threatening to rip it apart with each violent blow. Wooden crates and barrels squeaked and groaned below as they strained against their lashes.

The candle burned low in the cabin as I scanned the entries in Charles's journal. Sam Bennick, my brother's lawyer and our childhood friend, had found the journal and a slave ledger hidden in Charles's townhome in London.

I paused on a page where the ink smeared and dripped down the page. Reading the excerpt, I swallowed hard as I envisioned Charles sitting where I sat now, writing the entry.

July 25, 1845

My dearest Olivia,

Months have faded into years. Yet time doesn't ease the ache I've felt since they took you from me. Guilt fills me each day with the knowledge that I didn't seek justice for you; neither have I found the ones responsible for ending your life.

Willow is growing into a remarkable woman. Raising her has proven to be challenging. I feel I may be failing her as a father. She is settled in the boarding school you attended and is none too happy about it. It grieved me to leave her, but it's for the best. I don't know the first thing about raising a child. The girl is spirited and a replica of you.

In her veins runs a great love and admiration for Livingston, as it did in yours. Willow's love for the blacks outweighs all reasoning with her. She is headstrong and determined that she'll be the one to set all blacks free. She aims to defy me at every turn. She will send me to an early grave.

I miss her greatly, but I can't have her drawing attention to Livingston and the work we are doing with her outspoken ways. The secrets I carry and the truth I must keep hidden from her are a wedge that divides us. I fear most days she despises me, as her father does…

From time to time, I hear from Ben. The closeness we once shared as brothers is gone. His haunted eyes are something I understand all too well. I fear he hates me for laying claim to all that should have been his. God punishes me for the envy I hold in my heart toward my brother. I begrudge him your love and the child you bore with him.

I wonder, if circumstances had been different and you'd met me first, would I have been the one who won your heart?

Months at sea give me nothing but time to reflect on my life and the wrongs I've done. Nights when I'm troubled, my mind tricks me into seeing you skimming across the water with outstretched arms, only to fade as you draw near. Even from the grave, you haunt me.

A knock at the door startled me.

"Come in." I closed the journal and looked up as the door opened.

Sam poked his head around the door, and his eyes fell to the journal. "Did you find any resolution in there?"

"If you mean understanding my brother, the answer is no."

Sam shook the rain from his coat in the corridor before entering. He strolled to the narrow bed under the single small window and sat down. Age had left traces of silver threading through his dark hair.

"Charles and I were practically strangers. I thought, with all these months of living his life, that I'd begin to understand who he'd become. Maybe I'd find closure for the rivalry of our past. But I've come to feel like I'm chasing a ghost."

Most of my life, I'd carried guilt over the hurt Charles felt because Olivia had loved me. Then there were times I'd wished I'd not given in to my brother's demands and claimed Olivia as my own. But Charles and Olivia had quickly married after her father suffered a heart attack. She blamed herself. She believed she'd brought on the attack after she refused to marry Charles.

The scandal of me stealing my brother's wife and folks finding out about Willow's illegitimacy was something none of us could risk. Olivia would've been shunned and Charles humiliated. Where would that have left Willow? I loved them all too much to put them through that.

Charles's death had changed everything. I'd emerged from the shadows and became part of my daughter's life. However, Willow yearned for the only father she'd ever known, leaving me to roam in the shadows of my brother in her heart.

"When are you going to tell Willow about the girl?" Sam's voice cut through my pondering.

"Soon."

"It's been a year."

"She's been through so much. I worry about her well-being. I don't want to push her over the edge."

"She's a strong girl."

"But one can only be strong so long."

"Don't make the same mistake Charles did. Secrets have a way of coming out, and with them comes disaster."

"I will tell her when the time is right."

"I urge you not to wait too long."

"Damn Charles for leaving me to clean up his mess! What have I become, my brother's keeper?" I stood and swiped my hands through my hair, then gripped and tugged on it.

The ship rocked under the force of another wave, and I clutched the desk to steady myself.

"You can't get back the years that were stolen from you, but if you continue to live in the past, you'll only rob yourself of a future with your daughter."

"That's the last thing I want to do. I won't see her suffer anymore. I can't see the pain in her eyes..." My voice clogged with emotion.

"You can't control what life bestows on us. Nor can you protect her from the truth."

I sighed. I knew Sam was right, but how did I begin to tell her...

CHAPTER
Twenty-Four

Willow

S OME WEEKS HAD PASSED, AND LUCILLE SENT A SLAVE TO INFORM me of Julia's arrival. As expected, I returned an invitation for the ladies to join Whitney and me for a luncheon.

The morning the ladies were to come, I sat at the breakfast table, reviewing the preparations, assuring myself that everything was in order for the arrival of the scathing Lucille Carter.

Whitney slid into her seat and stubbed her foot on the leg of the table. Her face crumpled in pain, and she muttered a curse under her breath. "Must we endure this day," she said sourly.

"I feel the same as you, but if we want word to spread, Lucille is the one to do it."

"The thought of enduring her company makes me ill. Perhaps I should come down with something." She covered her mouth and feigned a cough.

"Perhaps you should be a good friend and help me. We'll conduct ourselves as gracious hostesses. I'll stroke Lucille's ego and coo and giggle, even if it nauseates me to think of behaving in such a shameful and false way."

Mammy entered the room from the warming kitchen.

"I, for one, will not lower myself to kissing Lucille's feet. Besides, I'm sure they're grotesque. Hairy and hideous," Whitney said with a smirk.

"What?"

"Her feet." She laughed and in a haunting, low voice intoned, "Nightly, she patrols the corridors, while below her, slaves huddle together and peer at the ceiling, paralyzed with fear by the sound of the curled toenail on her big toe scoring the planks as she hunts for the goblet of her handmaiden's blood." Her eyes twinkling with amusement, she took a big gulp of her water.

"Whitney Barry!" I burst into laughter.

Mammy sputtered, and the platter of eggs she carried clanged as she nearly dropped it on the table. A low cackle came from her.

My stomach ached from laughter, and I patted my index fingers under my eyes to wipe away the tears. Whitney had a way of breaking the tension, and I loved her for it. "We'll get through this engagement. I hope I can count on you to take it seriously."

"I promise to mind my manners and be dressed in my Sunday best." She rolled back her shoulders and folded her hands in her lap.

I laughed. Whitney never let anyone's opinion of her deter her from being herself, and I envied her. To be comfortable in one's skin was an admirable trait.

"I look forward to catching up with Julia and hearing how she's faring in married life up in the province of Canada," Whitney said.

The twins dashed into the room with Mary Grace scurrying to catch up.

"Stop telling me I can't marry him," said a teary-eyed Kimie.

"Girls are dim-witted!" Jack plopped into his chair.

"What is all the fuss?" Whitney asked.

"Kimie thinks she's going to marry that boy from the quarters. And I told her a white girl never mixes with the darkies."

"He isn't a darky. He's my friend." Her pink lips pouted.

"Jones says all slaves are darkies," he shot back.

"Enough!" Whitney's palm hit the table, rattling the glass-ware and utensils. "Jack, why do you insist on starting every morning like this?"

"I'm not. Kimie needs to start talking sense."

"You need to worry about yourself and stop trying to father your sister."

"Maybe if she had a father, then she wouldn't be so brain-less!" He looked away, his bottom lip quivering.

Whitney, caught off guard by his response, sat still.

"Ben will be home any day now, and I'll ask him to take you to see the ocean. What do you think of that?" I said.

He turned to me, and his dejected face brightened. "When?"

"I'm not sure exactly, but soon."

His narrow shoulders relaxed, and the trace of a smile formed on his lips.

"All right, apologize to your sister for being rude and hurt-ful," Whitney said.

Jack muttered an apology, and all was forgotten between the siblings. But Whitney remained oddly quiet for the duration of the meal.

CHAPTER
Twenty-Five

THE ENCLOSED BLACK CARRIAGE ENTERED LIVINGSTON IN THE early afternoon. All morning I'd paced my bedchamber, glancing in the looking glass and adjusting my hair. Much to Tillie's dismay, I switched from one gown to another to the one I presently wore.

As of yesterday, all literature, paper, pencils, inkwells, and slates in the slave quarters had been removed and placed in trunks in one of the barns. The folks in the quarters were used to the protocol. Everyone fell into step to assure nothing was out of place and took their positions.

A breathless Mary Grace entered my chamber. "They're coming, Miss Willow."

I squeezed her hand on my way out of the room. "Make sure the children stay out of the house while they're here."

"Yes, Mistress," Mary Grace said with the utmost obedience, sweeping low in a grand curtsy. One outer corner of her mouth inched up as her smiling eyes touched mine.

"And to think people consider you innocent and sweet. Wicked to the bone is more like it." I shook my head and strode from the room.

Nausea roiled in my stomach as I descended the staircase.

Mammy stood at the bottom of the stairs, waiting for me.

Taking a deep breath, I patted my ringlets and smoothed my hands over the waist and skirt of my pleated blue taffeta gown.

Sweat dampened the whalebone corset cutting into my prickling flesh.

"Et'll be all right, gal," Mammy said, warmth and encouragement radiating from her face. "Don't let dem fillies scare ya none. You're de Lady of Livingston. Now, git on out dere and show dem your regal self."

"Regal?"

"Tillie said dat means lak a queen?" She grinned proudly.

"I'm hardly a queen, Mammy. But thank you." I leaned in and quickly kissed her cheek.

Head held high, shoulders rolled back, I straightened my spine and headed for the front doors. "This is for you, Father," I whispered.

Acting like the Mistress of Livingston and daughter of the respectable, departed Charles Hendricks, I grasped the bronze doorknobs and pulled open the doors. I swept onto the veranda with a fixed smile on my lips.

The carriage came to a stop beside the carriage stone. A footman circled the carriage and opened the door, the brass buttons on his brown velvet coat glinting in the sunlight. He held out a white-gloved hand, and a small gloved hand emerged from inside the carriage and lightly gripped it.

Ostrich feathers and the ivory and pink flowers on a high-brimmed, periwinkle-blue hat poked out. "It appears the plantation hasn't gone into disrepair with the passing of your father," Lucille said, performing a quick inspection of the property.

The fixed smile on my face vanished. I clenched my teeth and winced as I tasted blood from biting my inner cheek. Whitney's warning rang clear in my head: *She's a meddlesome chinwag with no intention but to find out what is happening here.*

I hadn't forgotten anything. I'd made sure everything and everyone had their place. Had I forgotten anything? Panic and fear squirmed in my gut.

A swishing of material and the crunch of footfalls on the crushed stone drive turned my head. Whitney strolled toward me. Relief ran through me, and we exchanged tight smiles. Together we swung back to our guest.

"Hello, ladies," I said, ignoring Lucille's cool reference to my father's passing.

Lucille had exited the carriage, and Josephine and Julia followed.

Josephine preferred to sit amidst the clouds rather than dwell amongst the living. Today, however, a radiant smile reached her cornflower-blue eyes—an oddly whole smile.

"Willow, my darling." Julia pushed her way between the hoops and fabric of Josephine's and Lucille's skirts. She threw her arms around me, and I teetered backward, trying to catch my balance. "I'm so happy to see you."

She stepped back and adjusted her lopsided silk and velvet hat. "Whitney, always a pleasure." A sheen covered her freckle-dusted face. Her eyes watered with happiness.

"It appears married life suits you," Whitney said, considering her a moment longer than usual.

"You think so?" Julia giggled, twirling about in a wave of scintillating burgundy taffeta and ribbons.

Whitney and I nodded in agreement.

"And to think not long ago she was beside herself with melancholy because she had to marry Jeffery," Josephine reminded us.

The apples of Julia's cheeks glowed rosy. "That's true, but I've grown since then."

"Haven't we all," I said. "Mammy has set out—"

Lucille snorted with disgust. "Honestly, Willow, you're a grown woman. You'd think you'd have stopped calling your slave

Mammy by now."

I blew out a calming breath. *Play the gracious hostess and send her on her way.* I talked my hands into relaxing at my sides when all they wanted to do was feel the smoothness of her delicate neck under my clenched fingers. "Does it really matter to you?"

"I suppose not, but how do you expect to be taken seriously if you still act like a child?"

"Lucille, shut up!" Josephine snapped.

Lucille's jaw hung. "Josephine...I...well...never in my life...I was simply stating—"

"Every impolite thought that comes into that rambling brain of yours need not be spoken." Josephine stepped forward and looped her arm in mine. "I'm starving."

My mouth unhinged in the most unladylike manner. "I—I... yes."

"Refreshments will be served in the parlor. If you ladies would like to move inside..." Whitney almost sang as she bestowed a doting smile on Josephine, relishing the embarrassment mottling Lucille's face. Josephine had just earned herself a spot in Whitney's good books, a difficult task to accomplish.

Off to a great start! I grumbled inwardly, and allowed Josephine to lead me inside.

CHAPTER
Twenty-Six

THE AFTERNOON PROCEEDED AT AN EXHAUSTING PACE, WITH Lucille jabbering nonstop, relaying the newest gossip she'd heard, Josephine's scolding forgotten entirely. Lucille's lack of intelligent conversation dulled my senses.

Mammy and Mary Grace had outdone themselves with the spread of food displayed on the white-clothed table. Hot tea biscuits, stewed fruit, tart preserves, fancy cakes, grated coconut... the dishes went on.

Behind Lucille, Mary Grace stood against the wall in the far corner. Her keen eyes focused on the back of Lucille's head, and I could only guess what she was thinking.

My attention turned to Josephine. Something was different about her. Her face appeared fuller, and the usual restraint in her thin face was gone.

"These tea cakes are divine. You must let your cook know," Josephine said, lifting her napkin to remove the crumbs from her lips.

"I'd say so. You've eaten almost the entire tray. You must stop overeating. You're nearly the size of a whale. Your father will have to charter one of Willow's ships to take you out to sea," Lucille said haughtily.

The tightness returned to Josephine's face, and her shoulders curled forward.

I wanted to chastise Lucille and put her in her place once and for all. Darting a glance at Whitney's hands gripping the sides of her gown and the pain etched on her face, I knew she was about at her breaking point. "Mammy will be delighted to hear how much you enjoyed the cakes. No matter what Lucille's opinion may be, I've never seen you lovelier than you are today," I said.

Josephine's eyes softened.

Lucille's hackles rose. "Delighted? Do those creatures even have feelings? My father says they're black demons without souls. At least when we reach heaven, we'll be rid of them once and for all!"

Dumbfounded and appalled by Lucille's comments, Julia had gasped several times over the course of the afternoon. But she'd remained quiet, hiding behind a lace hand fan. Her discomfort was evident in the tornado winds the fan now threw off.

The poison of Lucille's company was becoming too much for us all.

Heat surged through me, and before I could catch myself, I blurted, "Do you suppose the good Lord will let the likes of you through the pearly gates? Heaven is said to be a place of love and peace. I can't imagine having to endure your hateful and condescending attitude for an eternity."

Silence. Neither whisper nor movement followed. No one breathed.

I set my cup on my saucer, and the porcelain clang echoed in the deadly quiet room. My eyes sizzled through Lucille. Under my gown, my crossed ankles vibrated as I willed myself to stay seated.

Lucille's mouth gaped open, and tears glistened in her eyes.

"Cry all you want. You're an evil, hateful woman!"

Whitney's breath caught. Mary Grace's eyes widened in horror.

Lucille leaped to her feet. "I've never been treated so poorly in all my life. You, Willow Hendricks, are the rudest person I've ever met."

"Hardly!" Droplets of my spit flickered in the air. "First you invite yourself to my home. Then you openly disrespect the memory of my father. Then you go on to insult my guest. How dare you! You selfish, impudent child!"

I glanced to Mary Grace, who shook her head in warning. I closed my eyes and exhaled deeply. God help me! I wanted to squeeze the life from Lucille.

The shocked whisperings of the slaves in the corridor reminded me of the reason why I'd allowed the ladies to visit. I'd failed miserably, and I had to set things right for the sake of everything I held dear.

"I would have expected this from Whitney, but not from you." Lucille's tears had turned into a full-out pout.

"I'm…I'm sorry. I don't know what's come over me. I was a shameful hostess. Please accept my humble apology." Trying to quell the shaking of my hands, I clasped them tightly in my lap.

Lucille turned her body away with the intent of shunning me. A sour taste filled my mouth. I'd have to work her harder, no matter how much it sickened me to do so. "You're *right*, Lucille." I paused to let the emphasis sink in.

She gave me a sideways glance and a slight nod, as though she was giving me permission to continue.

"I do find it hard to run this plantation alone. Maybe it's time to find a gentleman to take care of me. With us being the weaker of humankind, it may be best. What would you suggest I do?"

Her sourness disappeared. "I'm glad to see you still have some common sense in that head of yours." She settled back in her chair, looking smug.

The walls, lurking slaves, and guests breathed in relief as

tensions melted.

"While we're speaking on the subject of marriage, I wanted to inform you ladies that I expect to be married by the end of the summer," Lucille said over the top of her teacup.

An image of her choking on the hot liquid rushed into my mind. Shame at how it would bring me pleasure curdled in my stomach, and I rebuked myself and shook the horrendous thought away. Who was I becoming? The pressure of everything was getting to me. Lucille had a way of bringing out the worst in everyone around her. Why God created horrible, ill-mannered people like her, I'd never understood. "Who's the lucky gentleman?" I said in a sickly sweet voice, nauseating myself. But I'd redeem myself with Lucille, even if I had to eat a picnic table full of humble pie.

Courting? Lucille? I couldn't imagine the poor soul who would find her personality compatible. Beautiful or not, her negativity erased all appeal.

The ladies appeared to be as shocked as me at her news. "Yes, do tell us. We're dying to know," Julia said.

Lucille sat straighter, and she tossed a ringlet over her shoulder. "Silas Anderson."

"Our neighbor?" Whitney squeaked in bewilderment.

No! Absolutely not. This was the worst possible news ever. Silas hadn't mentioned Lucille before. How could this be? "That's delightful news! Your parents must be thrilled. When is the wedding?" I said. My stomach churned at the sugary sweetness in my voice. It was becoming too rich for my liking.

Lucille delighted in the attention. "Oh," she threw back her shoulders and lifted her nose elevated, "we haven't set a date yet. We aren't even courting. But we will be."

"Oh…" several voices said.

When Lucille set her mind to something, she usually

achieved it. I found myself feeling sorry for the unsuspecting Mr. Anderson.

"With you being neighbors, I wanted you both to know that I lay claim to the newcomer." She leveled a stern *you'd better not forget* look on Whitney and me.

Whitney inhaled the crumbs off her tea biscuit, and it sent her into a coughing spell. Tears ran down her cheeks as I poured her a glass of water and held it out to her. Then I held my hands up to Lucille. "You've no cause for concern on my part."

"And hardly on my part," Whitney scoffed. One glance at Whitney told me she had a sermon of things to say, but she held her tongue.

Lucille directed her next statement at me. "Well, it's a known fact you've been courting Bowden and stringing him along. People assumed by now you'd be a proper Southern belle and settle down. If you've no intention of marrying Bowden, the ladies of Charleston would be more than grateful for you to release him from the spell you've placed on him. Plenty of ladies would line up to win favor in his eyes."

"Lucille!" Julia gasped.

Finally, she speaks! Heat surged through me. But…I would not fall a second time into the trap of the Charleston Trumpeter. I remained as cool as the iced water in the glass I lifted to my lips. I took a long, thoughtful sip.

"Mr. Armstrong is free to do as he chooses. I do not hold claim to him, nor do I hold him prisoner," I said.

Lucille fluffed the layers of her gown. "That's what you claim, but we all know he has only had eyes for you."

"How's that her fault?" Whitney piped in.

Lucille's eyes regarded me with contempt. "You play with his heart."

I swallowed hard. Her words scored on my conscience.

But I set him free, I wanted to shout. "I'm unsure how to reply to your—"

"Nor do you need to," Josephine said, rising to her feet. "I grow weary of your relentless muttering, Lucille."

"But, Josephine?" Lucille's hand fluttered to her chest. "You—"

"If you croak out another word, I will slap you myself," Josephine said, shutting Lucille's whines down with a flick of her hand.

Speechless, Lucille sat gawking at her. No "But—but—" spilled from Lucille's lips. Only sweet silence draped the room. Glory be praised! I wanted to jump from my chair, throw my hands in the air, and parade around the room shouting Josephine's praises. Josephine finally had stepped from the shadows of Lucille's hoops.

"I'm feeling tired. I want to thank you for your wonderful hospitality," Josephine said, clasping Whitney's and then my hand in hers.

Lucille grumbled under her breath as she stood.

"Let me show you to your carriage," I said, more than happy that the painfully draining afternoon had come to an end.

"Willow, would you mind if I stayed for a while?" Julia said, a serious expression on her face. "Jeffery is visiting nearby and will come for me later."

My hopes of putting the afternoon behind me dimmed. The façade I'd struggled to uphold for their visit had already fractured, and I wasn't sure how much longer I could keep it up. "That will be fine," I said, touching her elbow. I turned to the others. "Ladies, let me show you out."

CHAPTER
Twenty-Seven

J ULIA AND I STROLLED ALONG THE RIVERBANK, DUCKING UNDER THE low-hanging limb of an oak tree that stretched out over the river, casting a mural on the brownish-green ripples. Redfish and speckled trout scurried upstream. A blue heron stood tall and proud on a slick black boulder rising out of the water.

Julia's face was tightly drawn. We walked in silence, until finally she said, "I wanted—" Her hands twisted in front of her. "Willow..."

I slowed and turned to take her hands in mine. "Speak freely."

Her gaze flitted around, as if the woods held listening ears. She caught her bottom lip between her teeth.

"For the sake of all that's sacred and pure, out with it!" I said.

"All right." She took a deep breath. "I know you're a woman of integrity, but I'm concerned that what I have to say may not be viewed favorably by you. You could very well have me thrown off your property."

"It would have to be something awful," I said with a laugh. But the worry in her blue eyes stifled my laughter. "What is it that troubles you so?"

"Things have changed for me since moving to Canada...I've changed."

"How so?"

We began to walk again.

"My husband has changed me."

I arched a brow. The dull husband she was dismayed to be marrying not two years ago? *One cannot change another.*

"I don't view things as I once did. Sometimes, I feel like a traitor in my own skin, and to the South. I love this place. It's my home. But I can't deny what's burning in my soul."

Silence came yet again. Dread accompanied the prolonged silence as I waited. The call of the chickadee in a nearby tree resounded over and over.

"Are you waiting for me to perish?" I laughed nervously, coming to a stop. What was troubling her so? I turned to her and waited.

Her lips parted, but she hesitated a moment longer before she said, "I am part of a network."

Network? As in the Underground Railroad? My heart lurched. "What kind of network?" *Go on...please, go on,* every part of me begged. Could it be possible she spoke of the same network?

"Jeffery and I are abolitionists."

Never would I have dreamed that dear, sweet Julia would be an abolitionist. I'd never viewed her as one to take chances. She was more of a person who settled for whatever life handed her. Like an arranged marriage. "I see..." I said.

"And your thoughts?"

"I don't...I'm not. You have to follow what your heart tells you, and if befriending the Negroes is where it's leading you, then you must follow it." I wanted to scream, *Me too.* Yet something held me back.

"I know I've never been one to speak on politics and have been quite content being a decent Southern girl most of my life. But that isn't the case anymore." A determination filled her eyes. "I, for one, can't sit quietly by any longer. Where does the South get off thinking we're superior to another race? After all, didn't God create us all in his own image?"

My heart hammered against my breastbone. Her words sang to the yearning in my soul to right the injustice in a world that was devouring every piece of me. "Why do you tell me all of this?" I said carefully.

"I want to enlist your help."

"My help? How could I possibly—"

"I don't know you to be an unreasonable person. You may be an owner of slaves, but I believe you're made of a finer quality than girls like Lucille and Josephine. You have an empire at your fingertips. With businesses and homes all around the world, you could aid in helping free thousands of slaves."

"The Fugitive Law forbids such thoughts. Besides, why would I want to do that? The South needs the Negroes. They're our source of income," I said, testing her.

She threw her hands up in the air. "Your income! Taking another human being and claiming him as property is wrong. Can you people even hear the absurdity in your words? People can't be owned. People claim to be Christian folk, but they turn a blind eye to what the good book clearly states." Her pale skin reddened with the passion running through her. The passion she carried for all to view.

In her…I saw me. A vision of my former self, a girl that voiced her thoughts without caring who might be watching or the danger that came with it—bold opinions that needed to be harnessed. "Shh! You must calm down," I whispered, scanning our surroundings.

She pulled a handkerchief from inside her sleeve and dabbed the tears streaking her cheeks.

"You must control your emotions. You'll do no one any good behind prison bars," I said in a low voice for her ears only.

A line appeared between her eyes, and she whispered, "I've come to Charleston seeking your help. I sent you a letter after your father passed, but you never responded. I figured you were too stricken with grief."

I'd received the letter some months after the funeral and intended to respond, but I was too caught up in trying to sort out the truth that had been dumped in my lap. Which proved to be overwhelming, to say the least.

"I know your father ruled this plantation with an iron fist, but only a fool would fail to realize what a good and decent man he was."

Like me... The familiar heaviness settled in my stomach. "More decent than his own daughter could see."

"Don't be so hard on yourself. We often don't see what is right in front of us. Look at my husband, for instance. I thought I'd live a loveless life filled with boredom. But that isn't the case at all. He's a man of honor, filled with passions beyond my wildest imagination. He's exciting and treats me as if I'm the most precious thing to him."

The love and admiration in her expression filled me with longing. "It pleases me to hear that."

"Thank you. Back to the reason I wanted to speak to you. A man has gone missing. A free black man who has gone to great lengths to help free slaves. We've reason to believe he's been sold into slavery, and our sources tell us he was placed on a ship headed for Charleston. I know you must have access to information and people that can help you find out where he may be."

"What? Why would—"

"Because you have ears everywhere. Like your father, you're an important and powerful person with contacts around the country."

"But I've barely scratched the surface of my father's affairs. With my uncle away, I have all I can handle with managing this place."

"Please, Willow, will you at least try?"

I paused a moment. "I can try."

She leaned forward and crushed me in her arms. "I knew I could count on you."

I gasped, trying to catch my breath. "I can't promise anything, but I'll try."

She pulled back and said firmly with a tug on my arm, "You must do more than try. His name is Toby, and he's around thirty years of age and on the fair side in skin tone. He bears no marks that set him apart, which will only make it that much harder to find him."

"And you figured I'd be the one who could achieve such an impossible mission?"

"Jeffery and I have been searching ourselves, but so far, nothing has surfaced. Maybe your crew at the docks has heard something."

Later, Whitney and I stood in the yard until the noise from Julia and Jeffery's carriage dwindled.

"Why did you decide to keep quiet about your involvement in the cause?" Whitney asked.

"Worry, I suppose." My shoulders rose and fell.

"Of what?"

"Her making a slip-up and turning the focus of folks' simmering paranoia on us. She's only recently broken away from the only mindset she has ever known and lacks the composure to keep our secrets. I couldn't chance it. I'll see if I can find this Toby she speaks of, but I fear it may be like searching for a coin at the bottom of the ocean."

Whitney draped an arm over my shoulders as we turned toward the house. "I fear you may grow old before your time, my friend, and me right along with you."

CHAPTER
Twenty-Eight

BEFORE THE EVENING MEAL, I WANDERED DOWN TO THE FORGE TO find Jimmy. Not seeing him there, I moved on to the stables. I found him alone and grumbling to the horse whose hoof he held between his knees. His head was planted in the horse's side.

"Stay still, you ornery creature. I'll fix you up ef you mind me for a minute or two."

My skirts brushed a path through the straw-covered floor. "What's the matter with ol' Betsy?"

Jimmy craned his head to look at me, all the while keeping it positioned against the horse's side. "Appears to have an abscess. Must have stepped on somepin'. Trying to git de dang critter to soak ets hoof in dis bucket of salts and warm water to draw out de infection."

The horse took advantage of Jimmy's distraction and jerked its leg free, knocking over the wooden pail of salt solution. "You blasted creature!" Jimmy stepped back and wiped his brow.

"Let me fetch a new pail of water, and I'll give you a hand." I hurried off, not waiting for his protest that followed after me. Soon I returned, hauling a slopping pail of warm water.

Jimmy added the salts, and together we got the horse to cooperate. After it was cleaned, Jimmy applied some ointment, then bandaged the leg. He straightened and arched his back to stretch out the kinks.

"I needed to ask you a favor."

He looked at me. "What dat be?"

"I need you to ask around about a man named Toby."

"Toby?" His brow furrowed.

"He's a free black man that was nabbed a while back. Sources say his last known location was a ship headed for Charleston. He may have been sold to a plantation around here. That's if he hasn't been sold off and moved elsewhere."

"Ef anyone is going to git de information, et be de black folk."

"They're our best hope of finding him." People underestimated how widespread the grapevine of the slaves was, and how resourceful they were.

I couldn't get the freeman off my mind. Had he been born free, or was he a slave that earned his freedom? Did it really matter? As long as his skin was dark, he was never free of the threat of being sold back into slavery. My thoughts ran to Ruby and someone nabbing her. A shiver crawled down my arms.

"What's dat hanging face 'bout?"

"I was thinking of my friend Ruby, the Northern girl I told you about, and how she's at risk daily of being plucked off the streets and sold. She believes she was once a slave. Escaped on a ship to the North when she was a little girl. But she doesn't remember her past before ending up in New York. Doesn't even know her own age."

"Our chillum are taken from deir mamas and papas and sold off to new masas. Forgit where dey're from." His Adam's apple bobbed up and down, and a quiet gasp of anguish escaped. "No 'mount of praying will bring dem back. Et's lak de Lard turned off his ears to us long ago." His shoulders slumped. "Ain't no use crying over et anymore. Et's de way et's always been, and I'm guessing et ain't ever gonna change. 'Less white folkses see de wrong in deir ways."

"We must believe it'll change." *We have to. It's the only way I can face each day. The only way I can endure the longing reflected in their eyes for their missing children, husbands, wives, mothers, fathers...grandparents. The only way I can step outside and look out over all I own and convince myself I'm not like the other slave owners.* Silent tears escaped me and rolled down my cheeks. His pain carved out my heart.

If only I could set this one thing right. If I could find Mag, maybe I'd erase some of the scars from his soul. "You ever wonder where she ended up?" I asked, my voice hushed.

He lifted his eyes to meet mine, allowing me to fully see the pain he carried. "You mean my Mag?"

I nodded, afraid to breathe.

"I used to. Den I let myself believe my gal was daid. Et's too hard to think of her suffering." His breath became ragged.

"But...what if, like Ruby, she's searching for you?" I could barely hear my own voice.

His face twisted, and an unusual hardness transformed his features. "Dat's crazy talk! When we git sold off, we never see our loved ones again. I tole you dat's de way et is wid us. For years I hoped and asked any new slave I came across about my gal. But de Lard, he has forsaken me. I'm an ol' man...I'll never see my gal again, and I've larnt to live wid dat."

I had to tell him the secret I'd been keeping. He needed to know I was searching for Mag. But what if the news angered him? What if he resented me for it?

I gripped the fabric of my skirt, and my voice came out hoarse. "There's something I've meant to tell you. Something I've wanted to tell you but didn't know how." I hesitated, tipping my head to peek at him.

"What is et, Miss Willie?" He frowned.

"I've been searching for her."

"Fool gal! Why you doing a thing lak dat? No need to go wasting your time when you got too much on your young shoulders as et is." His voice cracked, and tears glistened in his eyes.

I couldn't hold back my tears, and they flowed freely. "Because I wanted to bring her back to you. Your heart is stuck back with your wife and Mag. You've never moved on to marry again or have other children." My legs trembled, but I pushed on. "As foolish as it may sound, I want you to be happy. And I know you can never be happy staying here. I need to let you go, but I can't…God forgive me, I can't!"

When I spoke the treachery in my heart, it was as though the floor parted beneath me, and I fell to my knees, sobbing. "I love you. I need you. Without you, I'd just die!" The last year of heartache and anguish tore through me, and I didn't care who heard. I squeezed my eyes shut and folded my arms tightly over my chest as grief rocked my body.

I heard him kneel before me, and gentle hands pressed against my shoulders. His voice strummed softly, like the fingers of a harpist. "You be de light in my life, Miss Willie. I've watched you grow, and wid each year, I saw my Mag in you. When you ran and played, I'd stand back and imagine you were her. When you stormed down here, all full of fire and opinions 'cause your pappy didn't let you have your way, I gave you de same advice I'd give her. You see, Miss Willie, to me, my gal lives in you. Widout you, I'da done away wid myself a long time ago."

I threw my arms around his neck. He stiffened and then relaxed, and his arms circled me. I allowed the warmth of his arms to soothe me. Tucked away in the stables, hidden from wandering eyes, a broken woman found comfort in the embrace of a broken man. Color did not define us, and for a few precious moments, the world stood still, and we were equal.

All too soon, we stood and placed the appropriate distance between us. I brushed off my skirt and wiped my tears with the back of my hand. After saying goodnight, I left him to return to the house, my heart weighted with desperation to find Mag. To restore her to her rightful place alongside her father. But how?

I lifted my skirts and ascended the back steps to the veranda. Pausing, I pressed my hands against the wrought-iron railing while I glanced over the grounds.

Smoke wafted from the chimneys in the quarters to vanish beneath the Big Dipper as it blinked in the sky. In the distance, a lone wolf howled. A breeze ruffled my skirt and swept tendrils of hair across my face. I thought about the slaves that might be chasing their freedom this very night.

"I will find you," I whispered.

From the quarters, the nightly hum of the black spirituals rose.

Go down Moses
Way down in Egypt land
Tell all pharaohs to
Let my people go!
When Israel was in Egypt land
Let my people go!
Oppressed so hard they could not stand
Let my people go!

Each word echoed with their desire to be free. And with each word, my chest tightened.

I turned to go inside, but a movement to my right caught my attention. Jones had opened the side door of the stables. I watched him cast a look around before exiting.

I hadn't noticed him in the stables. I'd become so distressed that maybe I'd missed him. What had he been doing in the stables? And why hadn't he made himself known?

CHAPTER
Twenty-Nine

A FEW WEEKS LATER, WHITNEY AND I MADE A TRIP TO TOWN IN search of new gowns for the upcoming Christmas ball at the Abbotts Plantation. A day away from the plantation would be good for the soul, Whitney had said.

Late morning, our carriage rolled down the cobblestoned streets of Charleston, with Whitney and I bouncing and swaying on the red velvet cushioned seats. I leaned forward and pulled back the dark curtain to look out into the bustling streets.

Ladies strolled down the boardwalk, carrying silk parasols, with their gloved hands tucked in the crook of their gentlemen's arms. Jewish peddlers hustled to sell their goods to passersby. I held a handkerchief over my nose; the stench of horse dung was stronger in town than I was used to, out on Livingston.

Across the street from Market Hall, our carriage came to a stop. The coachman opened the door and offered a white-gloved hand. Alighting from the carriage, we opened our parasols and strolled along the boardwalk, stopping to peer through the windows of various shops on our way to the dressmaker. A bulletin board clustered with notices, everything from runaway slave and *Wanted* posters for bank robbers to scheduled meetings hung on the wall of one building.

One poster in the top right corner of the board caught my attention. "Look at this," I said, halting. It read:

WANTED

The Guardian

Believed to be male. Race still undetermined. Any information on his whereabouts is to be given to the sheriff. Any person or persons aiding fugitives will be subject to Section Seven of the Fugitive Slave Act.

"Everyone's talking of him," a voice said behind us.

I braced myself and swung around to face Bowden. The mere sight of him sent butterflies fluttering in my stomach. "And what are your thoughts?" I said.

"Well," he studied the poster, "folks say he's a colored, as no reputable, intellectual Southern gentleman would go risking his life and all he owns for a slave."

I stood pretending to be intrigued by the poster. "Is that so? You think the same?"

"I think it may be a woman," he said in a low voice for our ears only.

Puzzled, I lifted a brow. "What makes you think that?"

He leaned close in a manner not appropriate for a gentleman, and certainly not in public. The warmth of his breath chased goose bumps up and down my skin, but it was the words he whispered that snatched my breath. "Because you required my friend's help, if you recall."

He stepped back, his face drawn with concern. "Folks say they're going to search every inch of the swamps until they burn out any hiding coloreds and the one they deem the Guardian."

My grip tightened on my parasol, and I tried to quell the trembling of my hand. The thought of another massacre made me feel queasy. Suddenly, I felt faint.

Whitney clasped my elbow to steady me as I began to sway. "Are you all right?"

"A bit parched is all. If you'll excuse me, I think I'll find something to quench my thirst." *I've got to get out of here.* I squeezed between Bowden and Whitney and fled down the boardwalk.

People whispered their disapproval as I wove between them, mumbling my apologies. A woman's words to her husband didn't fall on deaf ears as I passed: "With her father gone, I'm afraid the girl has lost all sense of proper etiquette. Running through the streets like common trash. Such a shame." The woman followed that with a *tsk-tsk.*

Tears blurred my vision, and I ducked between two buildings to get out of sight. Leaning against the brownstone wall, I closed my eyes to blink off my tears. *Please don't let it happen again. Don't let them slaughter the innocent. Protect the one they're calling the Guardian.*

Taking a moment to gather myself, I wiped my cheeks and blew out an angry breath before slipping out onto the boardwalk. I collided with Whitney and grabbed her arm to keep her from landing on her backside.

She steadied herself. "Do you intend to bring reproach on yourself by running down a public street?" she said in a low voice before sending a leery gaze over her shoulder. Her smile looked more like a grimace as she nodded at people pausing to send us questioning stares. She cupped my elbow and turned me in the direction of the dressmaker's shop. "What did he say to get under your skin?"

"He made reference to me being the Guardian," I whispered through the side of my mouth.

"What?"

"He mentioned the time we asked Knox to help us."

"Out in the open like that? The nerve of him."

"I'm afraid his pride has been wounded and he may be angry with me."

"What in heaven's name for?"

"I told him I can't marry him. That our views about political matters are too different."

"Oh, Willow…" Whitney stopped and pulled me to the side. "But you love him. I know you do."

"No amount of love can change the differences between us." I lowered my eyes and tried to still my trembling lip.

"Why didn't you tell me? Is this the reason for the emptiness in your eyes?"

"It's that obvious?"

"I thought it was your grief over your father, along with everything else, taking a toll on you. I should've known. I've been so preoccupied with the twins and trying to figure out what to do with Jack that I've been a horrible friend. I'm sorry."

"Don't be. No one can fix what is broken between Bowden and me. Sometimes I fear fate has my life planned out to be one of loneliness and misery like my mother's."

"Nonsense! We have a hand in our own fate. Bowden will come around. The man loves you. His eyes tell it all."

"I don't know—"

"Ladies." A male voice interrupted our whisperings.

I glanced in the direction of the voice, and Whitney and I immediately pulled our heads apart.

"Mr. Anderson. A pleasure," I said.

"Miss Barry, Miss Hendricks."

I offered him a hand, and he bent low and lightly clasped it in his, touching his lips to the top of my hand. Over his head, I saw Bowden strolling toward us. When he caught sight of Silas he stopped, and his expression became hooded.

For a second, the thought of stroking Silas's attention to make Bowden jealous entered my mind before I shoved it away. I felt my neck and face heat.

Whitney noticed Bowden and began to wave wildly. "Bowden, please join us."

No! I wanted to throttle her.

Silas pivoted on his heels to look at Bowden as he moved toward us with his eyes pinned on me.

"Mr. Armstrong; we meet again." Silas held out a hand.

Bowden shook it. "Anderson; how's the homestead?" He sized up the man before him.

"Everything's moving along smoothly. A special thanks to the lovely Miss Hendricks for allowing me to hire one of her slaves." Silas smiled.

Bowden's eyebrow rose as he peered at me.

"However, I may need to hire her again," Silas said.

"You're in town, Mr. Anderson. What stops you from seeking the hired help you so clearly indicated you intended to hire?" Whitney asked, her lips twitching.

I elbowed her in the ribs, making her gasp.

Neither looking in her direction nor hesitating at all, Silas said, "I assure you, Miss Barry, it's my intent. I've inquired around town but have come up empty-handed so far. I'm sure, in time, someone will answer my ad."

"I'm sure they will," I said.

"I've meant to ask you, Miss Hendricks, if you'd consider teaching a fellow who's new to the planter way of life a thing or two about how you manage your plantation. A man could learn from a woman such as you. After all, an empire such as Hendricks Enterprises and Livingston would need a woman with a remarkable eye for business and exceptional skills to function."

Bowden's stance widened, and he sent an inquisitive look at Silas. His jaw set, but he remained silent.

Silas's flattery wasn't lost on Whitney. She sputtered with brash, contemptuous laughter, at which Silas's jaw clenched. I sent her a disapproving look, and she collected herself and stood quietly.

To Silas, I said, "I must ask, how do you know—"

"Of your family's business ventures?" he finished for me. His broad smile lit up his dark eyes. "Everyone knows of the Hendrickses. Why, your father's savviness as a businessman is known for states around."

"I see. You'll forgive me if I decline for the time being. Social season is upon us, and as is the case with most ladies, I do find my time occupied."

"Perhaps when your time is in less demand, you'll allow me to call on you?"

A grunt came from Bowden, and I flashed him a look. The cords stood out in his neck, and his glare burrowed into Silas.

"Perhaps," I said, inclining my head.

"Very well. You ladies enjoy the rest of your day." He boldly eyed Whitney as if he were letting her know she didn't intimidate him. Then he touched the brim of his hat.

I watched him leave, and for the first time, I noticed a shuffle in his walk. Bowden cleared his throat, and I snapped my head away from Silas's retreating back.

"I've come back to apologize. I was wrong earlier, and I'm sorry," he said, regret shadowing his face.

"Are you trying to cause me harm?"

"Never." He dropped his eyes, swiping back his hair with a hand. "I behaved less than decorously. I was angry, and I know that's no cause to behave so poorly."

"I wish things could be different between you and me. I really do."

"And Kipling?" His jaw tensed as he leveled his eyes on me. "What about him? Are you in love with him?"

Whitney cleared her throat and shuffled in discomfort, an unwilling bystander to Bowden's and my troubles.

"Of course not! How can you think...do you think that's what this is all about? I'm in love with Kip?"

"Are you?"

"No! I love *you*, you daft man! I've never loved another."

His shoulders dropped, and he expelled a deep breath. "All right."

That's it? All right? I wanted to reach out and beat at his chest with my fist. I wanted him to be what I needed him to be. To forsake all his ways and rescue me from the misery that confined me. "I'm sorry. Truly, I am," I whispered. I swerved past him.

"She loves *you*, you toad." Whitney said behind me.

Catching up, she tucked a hand in the crook of my elbow and gave my arm a gentle squeeze. No words needed to be said. Whitney knew my most profound thoughts, and I hers. Her friendship had been my foundation over the last year. I placed a hand over hers as we continued down the street.

❧ CHAPTER ❧
Thirty

"**H**E's BACK! MASA HENDRICKS JUST RODE IN." A breathless Mary Grace blurted as she entered the library.

I dropped the book I'd been reading and leaped to my feet. "Truly?"

She bobbed her head, her eyes alight with happiness.

I ran down the corridor and past the staircase to the open front door. My heart soared at the sight of Ben speaking to Mammy in the dim light on the veranda. Tillie and our butler stood on either side of the double doors, waiting for instructions.

"Welcome home, Masa Hendricks." Mammy beamed.

I'd heard recently from Mary Grace that Mammy thought Ben was a catch of a fellow. I smiled to myself.

"Thank you, Miss Rita. I trust all is well?" He touched her shoulder with his hand.

"Yes, Masa. De best et can be."

He turned, and his handsome face brightened at the sight of me. He moved toward me with widespread arms. "Willow, my darling."

I walked into his embrace. "You're home. You're finally home! How I've missed you," I muffled into his chest.

He chuckled. "A man should leave home every day, if he's to come home to a welcoming such as this." He squeezed me tighter before leaning back. Holding me at arm's length, he inspected me. "As beautiful as ever, I see."

I blushed under his praise. "You're too kind, Uncle."

He winced at the term "uncle."

I tucked my hand into the curve of his arm, hoping to relieve the hurt caused by the name I'd given him. "I couldn't be more pleased that you've arrived. We've important matters to discuss, and with Christmas just around the corner, I'd hoped we'd all be together."

He removed a gold pocket watch—a gift from my mother—from his vest pocket and flipped it open with his thumb. "Let us move inside and get cleaned up before the evening meal."

Whitney stepped onto the veranda as we turned to go inside. "Mr. Hendricks, you're home at last." Her smile was reflected in her eyes.

He grinned in return. "It's been too long."

"Mr. Hendricks!" Jack and Kimie bounced down the stairs.

Ben knelt and held out his arms, and the twins sailed into them. He kissed the top of Kimie's blond curls and tousled Jack's hair before planting a kiss on each of their cheeks. My heart swelled at the exchange of affection.

Jack stepped back and straightened to his full height. Trying for a deep voice, he said, "I was about done with all these women. It's a mighty good thing you showed up when you did."

Ben's chuckle made the room feel weightless and life not so burdensome. "Too many womenfolk for too long of a spell can't be good for any man's sanity." He tossed his hat on Jack's head. The hat dropped below the boy's ears.

Only the impish grin that spread across Jack's face was visible until he pushed back the hat and peeked up at Ben. "You got that right."

"All right, children, run along and let Mr. Hendricks settle in," Whitney said.

"But we—" Jack started to protest, but Whitney took him by the shoulder and spun him toward the door. "Fine." He scowled, then said over his shoulder to Ben, "I'll see you later, sir."

"I look forward to it, young Jack."

Kimie gave a small wave and trailed after them and up the stairs.

I turned to Ben. "After you've freshened up, would you care to join me in the library?"

"I expect a full rundown of the plantation and the warehouses." He leaned in and kissed my forehead, then mounted the stairs.

CHAPTER
Thirty-One

THAT NIGHT, I DESCRIBED TO BEN ALL THAT HAD HAPPENED while he was away. The next morning we rose early to go over finances and business prospects before breakfast.

At the end of breakfast, Ben wiped his mouth, pushed back his chair, and stood. Strolling to the window with hands clasped loosely behind his back, he ducked his head to take a gander at the skies. "A day such as this shouldn't be wasted." He turned to us. "I don't suppose you young folk would enjoy a ride to the ocean?" His eyes gleamed as he shot me a wink. I smiled knowingly. He looked to the shining faces of the twins.

"You bet we would!" Jack scraped back his chair and threw his napkin on the table.

Whitney's hand slipped up to cover her heart.

"What do you say, Whitney? Do you think Jack and Kimie have behaved well enough for a day by the ocean?" Ben said.

She nodded vigorously and tilted her head to peer at the lackluster ceiling, trying to tip back the tears threatening to spill.

An hour later, loaded with blankets and a picnic basket, the enclosed carriage bumped down the road. Whitney and the twins sat across from Ben and me. Jack and Kimie chatted and giggled with excitement over the day ahead.

Jack held his sister's hand while pointing out the window with the other. "Lookie there, Kimie," he said, referring to something of interest he'd spotted. She ducked her head close to him to take a peek.

I shared a grin with Whitney and then looked to Ben. I found him watching me as if he was studying me. I smiled, and he returned one of his own. He reached out a hand and covered mine where it lay on the seat.

"Is everything all right, Uncle?"

His smile widened for my benefit, but in his eyes simmered a darkness that confused me. "Absolutely. Couldn't be better," he said, giving my hand a gentle squeeze.

"Good." I pushed the uneasiness from my mind. For one day, I wanted to relish the moment and forget about the rest of the world.

Without warning, the carriage jerked, and our driver Thomas's voice called out, "Whoa!"

Whitney and I exchanged a look before we turned troubled eyes on Ben. His brow wrinkled, he pushed back the curtain and popped his head outside. "What appears to be the problem?"

"A tree has fallen, blocking de road, Masa," Thomas called back as we came to a stop.

Ben opened the door and stepped out. "Let me help you, Mr. Hendricks," Jack said, hopping out behind him.

"Very well. The more manpower we have, the sooner we'll be on our way." Ben squeezed his thin shoulder, and they disappeared around the front of the carriage.

"Having Mr. Hendricks home will be good for Jack," Whitney said.

"It'll be good—"

A gunshot split the peacefulness of the morning.

Cold panic rushed down my body.

Whitney's face drained of color, and she grabbed for Kimie.

Another shot cracked.

"Get down!" I cried.

They dove to the floor in a heap of petticoats and fabric. Whitney shielded Kimie with her body. Fear like I'd never heard before sounded in Whitney's voice. "Jack is out there."

My tongue thick and dry, I nodded in acknowledgment.

Jack. Ben. Thomas.

Her fear was my own.

Was it the masked men?

I crouched low in the seat and slid a hand up to draw back the curtain and peeked outside. The thundering of horses' hooves tightened my chest. Another shot rang out, followed by a scream. I dropped my hand and squeezed my eyes shut. *No. Please...no.*

"A fine morning for a carriage ride," a coarse voice rang out.

"So the rumors are true," Ben said with disdain.

"In fact, they are," came a reply.

"What do you want from us?"

"I'll ask the questions."

I heard a meaty thud and then the unmistakable sound of bone snapping under a blow. A grunt and a string of curses chilled my blood.

"I wouldn't if I were you," the stranger said. "You—remove his holster."

"All right, you in the carriage, out, now!"

Kimie started to scream.

I pushed open the door with my foot, and Whitney stepped out and turned to reach for her sister. Kimie pushed back against me, shaking her head no as her screams turned to whimpers. My hand shook as I brushed back Kimie's sweat-drenched hair. "Go to your sister. We can't stay here," I whispered.

Her eyes large with panic, she inched toward the waiting arms of Whitney.

"Come on, hurry it up," the man barked.

On shaking legs, I exited the carriage and looked around.

Thomas's eyes begged the ground to open up and swallow him. Ben stood with an arm around Jack, who had his face buried in Ben's side. His soft mewling gripped at my heart. Blood from a gash on Ben's left cheek trickled down and curved under his jaw. Ben's shoulders were arched back, and he boldly stared at our attackers.

Perched on horses sat three masked men. The speaker was on the taller side, the middle man was of average height, and the one behind them had a huskier build. Their horses weren't branded. Fully cloaked in coats, hats, gloves, and the masks, the men's identity proved impossible to guess.

The speaker cocked his head in our direction. "Well, what do I have here?" He nudged his horse with his heels, and the beast moved toward us. The man stopped inches from my face. A sweet, faint odor emanated from him. His mount snorted its protest, and its saliva splattered my face.

I didn't move. The saliva ran down my face, over my lips, and darkened the neck of my high-collared cream blouse.

Save for the dark eyeholes, the man's mask concealed all facial features. He sat upright in his saddle and swerved his mount back toward the other two. His closeness pinned me against the carriage. "You collect their valuables." He motioned to the huskier man and then circled his attention back on us. "One movement from any of you, and you'll wish you'd never awakened this day."

The huskier man jumped down from his mount, his feet hitting the ground with a heavy thump. He strode over to Whitney. Without speaking, he pulled her locket from her neck and dropped it into a small potato sack before continuing on to me. I removed my garnet earrings and the cameo broach pinned on the collar of my blouse and shoved them into his hand.

Moving to stand in front of Ben, he reached for his pocket

watch, and Ben's hand flew up.

A gunshot echoed.

Ben jerked back, and I screamed and leaped forward.

"Not another movement, or it will be the last thing you see." The leader's voice froze me; his gun was now aimed at my forehead.

Jack's screams elevated the terror inside me. His hands mauled at his ears. Kimie's wails added to the nightmare unraveling around us.

Without turning my head, I glanced sideways at Ben, who stood clutching his shoulder. Tears poured from me. He was alive.

That thought was plucked from me at the sound of a thud. All eyes swerved to Thomas, who lay crumpled on the ground. Still. Lifeless. The shot fired had grazed Ben's shoulder and found a new mark in Thomas's neck. A burgundy puddle stained the ground. My throat constricted.

"No…" Whitney cried softly. "No…no." Thomas, the driver from the Barry Plantation, had found refuge at Livingston after the slaves set the fire that took Whitney's father's life, along with his overseer and his men.

"Thomas!" Kimie started to run to him, but Whitney grabbed the back of her dress, pulling her back, as the leader fired a warning shot at the child's feet.

"Get control of the child, or I'll spill her guts where she stands." His cold, emotionless tone sliced through me. "You, get the boy to shut up, or he gets the next one." He cocked the gun and gestured for Ben to silence Jack.

"All right," Ben said. "No more bloodshed." He scooped Whitney's lanky brother into his arms. Jack buried his face in Ben's neck, and quiet sobs shook his body.

A deep, sinister laugh came from the third man who'd remained quiet until now.

"Silence!" the leader ordered. To the collector of our valuables, he said, "Get that pocket watch."

A stony grimace formed on Ben's face as the man stepped forward to remove the watch. There was a hard glint in his eyes that I'd never seen before.

"Hand it to me." The leader extended the fingers of his brown riding gloves.

The collector yanked the watch from Ben's vest pocket, then moved, his footfalls heavy, to stand in front of the leader. The collector dipped his head to peer at the ground as if in reverence and held up the watch to his boss.

The man snatched the watch and rolled it over in his hand. A scornful snort came from him, and he read aloud the engraving on the back. "'To the keeper of my heart, Olivia.' Well, ain't that nice." Loathing echoed in his voice. His grip tightened on the watch, and he mumbled something I couldn't pick up before slipping it inside his saddlebag.

He signaled with two fingers in the air, and he and the other man spurred their horses. The horses took off, sending Whitney, Kimie, and me diving to get out of their way. I hit the ground with a hard jolt.

The collector mounted and nudged his horse forward. He pulled on his reins as he hovered over me. He craned his neck, and a grunt sounded in his throat. A shot whizzed by the head of the collector and ripped through the side of the carriage.

I shut my eyes, and the dirt scraped at my palms as tremors coursed through me.

"Come on, you damn fool!" the boss man hollered.

I sputtered, spitting out the earth kicked up by the collector's horse as the rider wheeled it and touched its ribs with his boots.

"Willow." Ben's voice quaked with emotion. The scuffing of his boots was followed by the blinding sunlight in my eyes as he pulled me back to inspect me for injuries. "Are you shot?" His painted gaze roved over me.

"No, I'm all right," I said through a flood of tears.

I felt his wince as he crushed me to his chest. "Your arm, is it bad?" I wiggled out of his protective arms. His blood had blackened the shoulder of his coat.

"Nothing I can't patch up when we get home." He stood and pulled me up with him. Concern shadowed his face as he peered at Whitney and Kimie. "Are you all right?"

"Shaken, but fine." Whitney sat on the ground with a teary Kimie.

Jack stood next to Ben and me. His lip quivered. I reached for him, and without a second thought, he wrapped his arms around my waist. Gone was the boy wanting to be a man before his time. In his place was a child looking for someone to soothe away the terror coursing through him. "Everything will be all right," I whispered, pulling him back and cupping the sides of his face. "Ben's here now. He'll take care of us." I looked past him to Ben.

Ben's face was set firm, a look that reminded me of my father. Sadness and determination filled his eyes; anger and worry. "Get the children in the carriage," he ordered before hurrying to Thomas's side.

Maybe it was the doctor in him, but regardless of a status we already knew, Ben checked for a pulse on the dead man. He heaved a sigh and hoisted the man over his shoulder and laid him on the driver's seat, then climbed up himself as Whitney shuffled the children inside. Ben's once-white cotton shirt shone crimson with the man's blood. "Please, Willow, get in the carriage," he said, his voice abrasive.

At a speed that sent his passengers grasping at the ceiling and door frames to keep from being thrown side to side, Ben raced the carriage toward Livingston.

～ CHAPTER ～
Thirty-Two

MAMMY BOUNDED DOWN THE STEPS WITH MARY GRACE AND Tillie on her heels as our carriage raced up the lane. Ben jerked the carriage to an abrupt stop.

"What happened?" Mammy's expression was sharp and assessing as she pulled open the carriage door.

Kimie stepped out, and Mammy pulled her into an embrace at her side. Her hand stroked the girl's back. "Oh, Mammy, it was awful. These men, they—they—" Her voice broke.

"Hush now, chile. You don't have to speak on et," Mammy said.

Mary Grace reached for Jack as he stumbled out of the carriage in a daze. No tears came from the boy, only hiccups from previous tears. He stared, emotionless.

Jimmy and Jones ran into the yard. "Help me with him," Ben instructed, lowering Thomas's body to them.

The men laid the body on the ground.

"Come, chillum." Mammy placed an arm around each twin's shoulders and guided them toward the steps.

Whitney's eyes never lifted to meet mine as she patted my arm. Her face was pale and blank as she trailed behind Mammy and the twins, as if she'd removed herself from the present moment.

"Miss Willow, are you all right?" Mary Grace's brow puckered with concern.

"I'll be fine. You and Tillie go assist Whitney and the children. I need to talk to my uncle." I smoothed my hair with my hand.

They nodded and hurried off.

Jimmy and a field hand carried off the body. Ben stood speaking to Jones.

"Get two horses saddled. You and I'll be paying the constable a visit," Ben said.

"Right away, Mr. Hendricks," Jones said. His eyes fell on me as I came to stand by Ben. "You get a look at them, Miss?"

"One spoke, but his voice wasn't familiar. They were covered from head to toe. Nothing stood out that would reveal their identity," I said.

Jones expelled a heavy breath, and his eyes dropped to the ground.

"All right, get the horses and make sure you're armed."

Jones flipped back his coat to reveal his gun in its holster.

Ben dipped his head in acknowledgment. "Very well."

Dismissed, Jones left to fetch the horses, and I followed Ben inside.

He disappeared down the corridor to his room and returned with his medical bag. I helped him out of his coat and shirt. "Please get my uncle a fresh shirt and coat," I said to Tillie, who waited just inside the threshold.

"Yessum."

Ben tended to the wound, which appeared to be nothing more than a flesh wound, for which I breathed a prayer of thanks. Dressed in a clean shirt and coat, he moved to the gun cabinet and took out Father's Colt revolver. He cracked back the hammer and peered down the barrel.

Unnerved by the morning catastrophe, I said, "I'm coming with you."

"No." His tone was harsh. He lifted his head to look at me, the revolver still arched in midair.

Angry tears welled in my eyes. "I'm not sitting around here, waiting for your return. I'll be sick with worry."

"Jones and I won't be back until evening. I need you here managing things."

"But I—"

"Willow, I said no!" he snapped. His eyes narrowed, and the man before me melted. In his place stood Charles Hendricks.

I swallowed hard and stepped back. Silent tears spilled from me.

Ben's eyes widened, and his expression grew distressed. He held up a hand. "I didn't mean to come off so harsh. We don't know who these men are, and if they choose to come after Jones and me, I can't risk you being in the way. If something were to happen to you..." The gun dropped to his side.

His words did nothing to soothe my worry. I whisked the tears off my face. "As you say, Uncle," I said, my own voice hard. I glowered at him.

"Willow...I..." His words withered on his tongue. A grimace contorted his face, and his gaze shifted downward.

I felt a pang of remorse. He didn't deserve to be shunned because he reminded me of my father. Nor because fear of losing another person I loved was a constant in my life. I placed a hand on his arm. "Please forgive me. I'll take care of things here until you return."

His eyes captured mine. The pain I read in his eyes thickened my throat. Building a relationship with a daughter he didn't know couldn't be any easier on him than it was on me.

He lifted a hand and cupped the back of my head, bringing my forehead to meet his lips. Stepping back, he rested his hands on my arms. "I love you, daughter. We'll sort this out together."

"Be careful."

"I promise." He tucked the revolver into his waistband and strode toward the doorway, where he paused and turned back to me. A haunting softness shone in his eyes. "I'm not my brother."

"I know," I whispered.

He nodded and left.

I placed a hand against the wall to steady myself.

Please watch over him.

CHAPTER
Thirty-Three

AFTER BEN PAID THE CONSTABLE A VISIT, PATROLS ON THE ROADS sent the masked men into hiding, and for the time being, the folks of Charleston and surrounding areas breathed easier.

Christmas arrived, and for the first time in years, Livingston wouldn't be hosting its annual ball. Though I'd removed the mourning attire from my wardrobe, I continued to use my father's death as a way to get out of social engagements. When Josephine's family sent an invitation inviting us to the Christmas banquet at their plantation, I wanted to decline, and Whitney concurred, but at Ben's insistence, we accepted.

Tonight I sat in our best carriage on the way to the party. Next to me, Ben's legs were lost in a sea of silver silk making up my gown. Whitney, the model fashion plate, sat across from us. Her ivory gown was accented with matching rosebuds that pulled up a layer from the hem, revealing an underlayer of beautiful lace. She'd donned a green cape over the dress.

The glow of lights on Josephine's family's plantation came into view, and the driver turned up the lane leading to the front of the home. Soon we came to a stop, and the carriage door opened.

As we stepped outside, the music from the band drifted from inside. I'd visited a time or two when I was younger, but now the white house with its black shutters was luminous in the abundance of lanterns that lined the path to the front steps. Holly and greenery wrapped the railings of the front veranda.

Mr. and Mrs. Abbotts, Josephine's parents, stood just inside the front doors, greeting their guests as they arrived. After an exchange of pleasantries, Mr. Abbotts guided Ben off to introduce him to some other gentlemen. To folks, the mystery around the appearance of the other Hendricks brother was a topic of conversation, and like my father, he'd caught the eye of the unwed ladies of Charleston. People were eager to peel back the layers of the newcomer.

Josephine swept toward us as a finely dressed manservant took Whitney's and my wraps. Her rose-colored gown reflected a pinkness in her plump and gleaming cheeks. Long, elbow-length gloves covered her hands, which she rubbed as if to relieve an ache. She bestowed a grand smile on her mother. "Mother, I'll see to our guests."

"Do enjoy yourselves," Mrs. Abbotts said. She gripped her daughter's arm and leaned in and whispered in her ear.

Josephine's face paled.

"I mean it, Josephine Abbotts. On your best behavior," Mrs. Abbotts said with a hard bite of her jaw before wandering off to mingle with her guests.

After she was gone, Josephine turned back to us. "I'm delighted to see you two." But sullenness had replaced the warm girl from the last time we'd met.

"Your home is beautiful." I glanced around in appreciation before resting my gaze back on her. "As are you." I touched her hand.

A wan smile brightened her face. "I don't deserve your and Whitney's kindness. Lucille and I haven't exactly been cordial over the years." The sadness returned.

"Sometimes the company we keep has everything to do

with it." Whitney regarded me with an admiring smile.

I waved a hand in dismissal. "A real friend should lift you up."

"Lately, Lucille finds any reason to belittle and humiliate me. With my recent weight gain, she's been rather cruel. She has a way of demoralizing me."

"We've all become a target of hers at one time or another. But you choose to be her friend, whereas we do not." Whitney shrugged.

I placed a hand on Whitney's arm to stop her forwardness before she offended our hostess in her own home.

Unaffected by Whitney's blunt opinion, Josephine said, "It's quite all right, Willow. I wish I had Whitney's courage to speak my mind." Her eyes drifted past us, and I swerved to see what held her attention.

The slave who'd taken our wraps stood against the wall with his head lowered, waiting for further instructions.

"Her nagging is as bad as my mother's," she said dryly, returning her eyes to us. "Lucille will come undone with Father's announcement this evening."

"Announcement?" I asked.

She dropped her voice. "Father will be announcing my betrothal to Theodore Carlton."

A gasp came from the slave behind us, and I cast a glance in his direction. He quickly composed himself and moved to take the top hat and coat of an elderly man.

Josephine led us down a corridor for privacy.

"This Mr. Carlton, are you in love with him?"

"No, of course not! He's old enough to be my grandfather, and his lustful eyes unnerve me. But he comes with a fortune, and that's all my parents see." Tears welled in her eyes.

I stroked her arm.

"My only hope is that he's one step from the grave. I had such grand ideas for my future, and it seems I'm meant to live a life of misery. I've never felt so alone in all my life."

"You can't reason with your father about the matter?"

"I've openly expressed my thoughts, but that earned me nothing but his wrath." She involuntarily lifted a hand and rubbed her cheek, her mind reverting to a distant memory.

The stress of Josephine's current predicament would be reason enough for her weight gain. Adding Lucille's nagging to the mix wouldn't make it easier on her.

"Men would lose their minds if we were to dictate to them as they do us. It's exhausting, how they think we are too delicate and weak to feel and think for ourselves," Whitney said with a disgusted huff. "Some womenfolk are made of sounder minds and greater strengths than the strongest of men."

Her opinion brought a laugh from Josephine. "One thing about Father's announcement that I'll delight in is the look on Lucille's face. She's unaware of my betrothal. I thought if I didn't breathe the words, then it wouldn't be true. The shock of the news will send her into a fit of rage. I'm sure of it."

Over Whitney's shoulder, I had a clear view of the front doors. Silas entered, looking dapper. He removed his hat and outer coat and gave them to the servant.

Lucille glided into the foyer. She clapped her hands in excitement at Silas's arrival.

"The mountain lion creeps in on its prey," Whitney said, as if reciting a script. "Wait for it…"

"Mr. Anderson, I'm delighted you've come." Lucille's voice carried like the unnerving squeal of hogs on butchering day. "I insisted that Josephine and Mrs. Abbotts extend an invitation to you. The evening simply wouldn't be as enjoyable without your attendance."

"Attack," Whitney whispered, throwing a triumphant fist in the air.

Josephine and I giggled.

"Always making a spectacle of herself! I'm embarrassed for her," Whitney said with a shake of her auburn locks. "The woman doesn't have the slightest clue how irritating she can be."

The three of us moved from the shadows to get a better view.

"Miss Carter, you are a vision." Silas charmed her with a smile.

Lucille placed a hand to her throat as she basked in his compliment. "I ordered this dress straight from Paris. The designer took the utmost care in designing this one-of-a-kind gown." She moved in and placed her hand into the crook of his elbow and led him away.

"One-of-a-kind gown," Whitney mocked, screwing up her face.

Josephine and I shared a glance, followed by laughter, as we went to join the rest of the guests in the parlor. Most of the furniture had been removed to open the space. Dressed in dark trousers and pressed white cotton shirts, men from the quarters formed the band of musicians in the far corner of the room.

Pleasant laughter stilled my breathing and turned my head toward Bowden, who stood with a beautiful petite blonde. The woman leaned in and was speaking to him. From across the room, the unmasked delight he took in what she was saying stirred a slow burn in me.

"Who's that woman with Bowden?" I asked Josephine.

"Why, that's Cora O'Brien. Her uncle is a general in the US Army. Word has it he was at the battle with the Mexicans along the Rio Grande..."

Josephine's chatter blurred as I became engrossed in the pair across the room. "I've never seen her before."

"I don't suppose you have. She's from Texas and recently moved here after the death of her father and brother. I feel for the woman."

"How so?"

"Why, her brother and father were taking a wagon train of settlers to California when they were attacked by savages. The heathens slaughtered the whole wagon train."

My heart went out to Miss O'Brien, but it didn't still the jealousy tunneling through me.

"It seems her uncle was an acquaintance of Bowden's grandfather," Lucille's voice whispered in my ear. My lips parted as I glanced at her over my shoulder. She stepped back with a pleased, smug smile. "I've seen Bowden and the stunning Cora O'Brien with her uncle around town a few times lately." Her eyes gleamed with pleasure as she added, "I see it's true, then?"

"What?" Narrowing my eyes, I turned back to the pair.

"That you did release him." Her hot breath steamed the skin of my neck.

"Lucille, not now!" Whitney hissed.

"I warned Willow this was bound to happen," she said with a shrug of her bare, flawless shoulders.

"Did Mr. Anderson tire of you already?" I glared at her.

"My father stole him away. But don't you worry, he will return." Her chin tilted up, and she turned to study Bowden and his companion. "He's obviously intrigued by Miss O'Brien. I mean, how could he not be, right? I heard she has the voice of a nightingale. Her pa sent her to Europe to learn opera. From what I hear, her voice surpasses Jenny Lind's."

"A wagon master rich enough to send his daughter all the way to Europe? Do you hear the ridiculousness of your words?" Whitney said.

Blocking out Lucille's ramblings, I allowed my eyes to be drawn to the woman who had captured Bowden's complete attention. My gaze moved to Bowden, trailing up his jawline to his neatly swept-back dark locks. The desire to be lost in his eyes and have him laughing with me instead of her overtook me.

I had no one to blame but myself. I'd done this. I'd set him free to all the women waiting in the wings to snare a man like Bowden. At this moment, I wanted nothing more than to push my way through the guests and swear my undying love for him. To have his arms surround me and to have the beautiful Cora O'Brien be a bystander while he lavished *me* in sweet kisses.

Bowden's eyes met mine, and I swallowed hard. His smile disappeared.

Miss O'Brien glanced to see what had stolen his attention, and uneasiness covered her soft, delicate features.

"I'm not feeling so well. I need some fresh air. If you'll all excuse me." Gathering the side of my gown, I pushed through the suffocating press of party guests.

Whitney's scorn followed me. "I hope you're pleased with yourself, Lucille."

CHAPTER
Thirty-Four

"Your wrap, Miss?" the servant said as I pushed past him and swept out the door.

I ignored him in my haste to relieve the constriction of my lungs. The cool evening air spilled over me, and I released a breath.

Descending the stairs, I slipped out of the light of the lanterns and away from the curious stares of guests fraternizing on the veranda.

Had I expected Bowden to wait for me? Hadn't he said there'd never be another woman for him? Selfishly, I'd clung to his words, allowing them to lull my mind and clot the bleeding of my heart.

"Willow," Ben's voice rang out.

I turned to find him moving toward me, shrugging into his frock coat with my wrap draped over his arm. He swung the wrap over my shoulders, and his fingers fumbled to clasp the button at my throat. I smiled at him trying to take care of me as a parent would a small child.

"I saw you leave." His face was taut with concern.

I rubbed the chill from my arms.

"I'm listening."

"I let a man I can never have steal my heart. I was the one to let him go, but to see him with her…" My voice shook with the despair and hopelessness that settled around my shoulders like a waterlogged cloak.

"You're referring to the lovely blonde on Bowden's arm."

"He—he has the right to court whomever he pleases, but it doesn't make it hurt any less. She is lovely, isn't she?"

He gawked at me, his lips parting, before a frown creased his brow, as if he was wondering if it was a trick question.

"Life can't always be this hard. If only things weren't so complicated. Why can't I be someone less complicated?"

"You can't wait for life to bring you happiness. You must go and find it on your own. I've spent a lifetime of living in the shadows while the woman I loved was with another. Don't make the same mistakes your mother and I did. Don't waste your life loving from afar."

"There is no way for me to change what is predetermined. Marrying Bowden would be like throwing away the key to my soul."

"Without him, will you ever be whole?"

"I don't know what I understand anymore. It's like I'm walking through life in a fog, a stranger to myself and everyone around me."

"Give it time. But don't push Bowden into the arms of another, or you'll come to regret it."

Feeling helpless, I shrugged. "It will be what it will be. I don't have the inclination to ponder such things. Let's get this night over so we can go home." I slipped my hand into the crook of his elbow as we walked back toward the house.

CHAPTER
Thirty-Five

THE PARLOR WAS ALIVE WITH VIBRANT TWIRLING GOWNS AS gentlemen gracefully led ladies around the dance floor. The band played "The Girl I Left Behind Me."

I stood outside the parlor, taking in the cheerful faces of the couples as they floated from one end of the room to the other. Under my gown, my foot tapped readily to the beat.

"May I have this dance?" Ben held out his hand.

I slipped my hand in his and followed him into the midst of the dancers.

The song ended and another began. The dance switched to the galop. Ben swung me briskly around the floor, and when the song finished I was winded, my face warm with exertion. The gaiety of the evening renewed my spirit.

Ben guided me to a nearby table of refreshments. A servant dressed in white and black held out a silver tray filled with glasses of punch. I greedily selected a glass and nodded my thanks as I took a long sip. The cooling liquid coated my parched throat.

I handed the empty glass back to the servant and moved to a corner of the room with Ben. I looked out at the dance floor and saw Whitney with a group of ladies, appearing bored at their topic of conversation. The Abbottses hadn't extended an invitation to Knox because he wasn't part of their social class.

Lucille's voice carried, and with a sideways glance, I saw her speaking to Silas. The poor man was still clutched in her talons.

"You own one slave?" she asked, her brow narrowed.

"His mama ran off when he was younger. He's become more like family," he said rather loudly. Over Lucille's head, his eyes pierced mine.

"Family!" she said with a slight curl of her lip. "Those lazy devils can hardly be family. My pa says that the slaves need to know who's master. He says that if Southern gentlemen keep cozying up with the slaves, it'll be the end of our pure race. Masters bearing children with the creatures…" Her face lost all prettiness with the disgust that transformed her features. "Why, it's an abomination. They may as well go out to the field and breed with the hogs. All these mulattos running around is unchristian."

Silas shifted his weight from one foot to the other. The stiffness in his body was evident, but like a gentleman, he listened without interruption. He was a saint. More than I could say for myself as I bristled with each word that came out of Lucille's mouth. My fingers curled in my gloves. Buttons sewed to Lucille's lips to muffle her belligerent chatter would ease all the bleeding ears in the room.

"A while back, my pa bought a new slave," she continued. "His eyes flash with fire like he's possessed. Pa says he just needs to be tamed and shown who his master is. The slave's endless chanting of 'I'm no man's slave' is permanently etched into my brain. He claims he's a free man."

Ben's and my eyes locked as our ears perked up. We moved closer to eavesdrop on the conversation.

Lucille, who loved to hear herself talk, went on. "But my pa will show him how the Carters take to slaves that don't understand their place. He'll be a prized bull by the time Pa is done with him."

"Mr. Anderson," Ben interrupted. "Would you mind if I danced with the lovely Miss Carter?"

"Oh…" Lucille blushed, and her hand went to her heart. More than pleased with the compliment, she said, "Certainly, Mr. Hendricks. If you don't mind, Mr. Anderson." She swept her lashes over her cheeks.

"Not at all," Silas said.

As she glided toward Ben, Lucille whispered to me, "Don't forget what I told you."

I bit my tongue.

"I don't believe I've had the pleasure of meeting your uncle," Silas said.

"No? I'll be sure to introduce you later. He has only recently returned. I've had him preoccupied since his return."

"It must come as a relief for him to take some of the burdens of running a plantation of Livingston's magnitude?"

"It does. Selfishly, I hope he doesn't have to leave on business for a while."

"Miss Carter mentioned to me that there was another attack by the masked men and that you and your uncle were their victims this time."

"I bet she did," I said. "The woman never ceases to amaze me with how she conjures up information." I only hoped she'd openly relay information about the slave she spoke about to Ben.

He dipped back his head and laughed. "She's a chatty one."

"Is that what you call it?" Indignation sparked in my chest.

"Did they harm you?"

"No, but they frightened us all and killed my driver. He was hardly a problematic slave, so that in itself is a loss. Not to mention the financial loss."

"It saddens me to hear of your misfortune. I'm at your service." He put a fist to his chest. "I assure you, I'll do whatever it takes to aid in bringing these criminals to justice." A single dimple etched his left cheek as he smiled down at me.

"Now, that's right neighborly of you. We'll leave the masked men to the constable and his men. However, I do appreciate—"

A couple bumped into Silas from behind. Irritation flashed across his face. "Do watch yourselves," he said in an even tone.

"I apologize for my clumsiness," Bowden said. He reached out to steady the blonde woman who gawked at us with huge, innocent eyes. From her precisely parted hairdo to the bottom of her periwinkle velvet gown, Cora O'Brien gleamed. She was the perfect accompaniment to any gentleman's arm. Just not Bowden's! Yet I wouldn't be lowered to quarreling over a man. Even if the sight of his hand on the small of her back had me wanting to shove her backward.

"Think nothing of it," Silas said graciously.

Bowden turned his hard focus from me to Silas. "How are you enjoying Charleston?"

"I'm liking it quite well. I'm moving forward with my plans to build a proper house on the property."

"The widow's place isn't suiting your fancy?" Bowden asked. He'd become so caught up in his analysis of Silas that he'd forgotten to introduce his companion. "I'm guessing you've managed to purchase some slaves of your own by now?"

"As I told Miss Willow, I don't intend to purchase slaves. I feel my money would be better invested elsewhere."

"If you bought a few slaves, wouldn't it move the building of a new home along?"

"I do not intend to have slaves build my home. The home I intend to build will be one that requires great craftsmanship."

"Some of the slaves have the best craftsmanship around these parts," Bowden countered. "Besides, why would you pay for someone to build your home when you can have your slaves build it for you?"

"Why do you care, Mr. Armstrong?"

"I don't! It was a simple question. You show up in Charleston and claim to buy out the widow's place and...poof." Bowden flicked his fingers in the air. "She disappears. It all appears to be a mite suspicious to me."

Bowden had voiced the thoughts Whitney and I had shared.

"I suppose I can see how that would appear. I don't know why the Widow Jenson wouldn't mention it to her close friends and neighbors. I wish I could tell you why she did what she did, but frankly, I don't have the answers you seek.

"I offered the widow a deal I guess she couldn't refuse. And within weeks, I found myself with the deeds to the property. I've never seen or heard from her since. Not that I would, seeing as we weren't acquainted outside of a business deal. If you think that I robbed the dear soul, you are mistaken. I assure you, I paid the widow what the place was worth, and then some."

"That's an interesting story you weave," Bowden said.

"I don't know what else I can say, Mr. Armstrong. I believe you've made your mind up about me. But something leads me to believe it has nothing to do with the widow's place and everything to do with Miss Hendricks." Silas drew himself up, challenging Bowden in a duel of words.

A twitch in Bowden's cheek proved Silas might have planted his sword. "I look out for people that matter to me. And Miss Hendricks has been my *friend* for many years."

Referring to me as a friend deepened the ache I carried over the demise of our courtship.

Cora O'Brien studied me with interest.

"Gentlemen, let's be done with this quibbling and move on to more pleasant topics. Like who your friend here may be." I held out my hand to her.

"Pardon me. Willow, I'd like you to meet Cora O'Brien."

"Welcome to Charleston."

"Thank you." She gripped my hand for an awkward moment too long. "How do you and Bowden know each other?" She touched his arm lightly.

"We grew up together," I said.

"I actually asked Willow to marry me, but she turned me down. But I have not given up on winning her heart," he said without concern for his lady friend. Either he didn't realize her fondness for him or he was withdrawing Silas's sword and going in for the victory strike.

Silas stiffened beside me.

Lucille joined us, and all of a sudden, I felt physically ill. "Mr. Armstrong is a fine and ethical businessman. I'm sorry I have to cut this short, but I must take my leave. Miss O'Brien, it was a pleasure to make your acquaintance. Lucille; Mr. Anderson." I offered a stilted curtsy. "Bowden."

They mumbled their goodbyes. I pivoted and went in search of Ben.

Ben stood talking to Mr. Carter and some other gentlemen from town.

"Uncle, I wish to go home now."

"You look pale. Are you ill?"

"I may be coming down with something." *The Lucille virus, in fact.* "I'll get the driver to bring the carriage around, and I'll meet you outside."

He nodded.

At the front door, I gathered my wraps once more and stepped outside.

A hand grabbed my elbow. "Willow, wait!"

I spun to look into Bowden's eyes. "What is it?"

"Let me speak with you before you take off in a huff."

"Why would I allow that? Were you trying to humiliate me and make a fool out of yourself in there? Because that definitely wasn't your most charming moment." I crossed my arms, walking across the veranda and out of the earshot of the other guests.

"Again, I've acted like a fool," he said with genuine regret.

"That's a fact," I said hotly.

"I seem to be doing that a lot lately."

I couldn't agree more, but I kept the thought to myself.

Since the afternoon by the pond, I'd tried my best to push him from my mind, but it was proving to be harder than I had even imagined. Ben's words of earlier played in my mind: Don't waste your life loving from afar.

"I want you to be my wife more than anything, and losing you is driving me mad. Obviously, I'm going around making a laughingstock of myself." He hung his head.

"Do you think this is any easier on me?"

"I'm sure it's not. I've tried to stay away from you to make it easier on the both of us. When I heard of the attack on the road, I wanted to ride over to Livingston to check in on you..." His thoughts pulled him away.

"You said in there that I was your friend. Do friends not check in on each other?"

"Yes. But I knew after seeing you in town that I wasn't in control of my emotions."

"We had a burial to attend to, and I'd have been preoccupied anyway." I dropped my eyes to my hands and picked at invisible lint on my gloves.

"Soon we'll have to face the reality that living so close by and running into each other isn't going to work."

"What do you suggest we should do?"

"I know what I'd like to do." He moved to rest his hands on the railing.

My heartbeat quickened. My eyes traced his profile, from the muscles of his biceps built by long, hard days on the plantation to the strawberry birthmark on his jaw. I swallowed hard. "What would you like to do?"

"Sell everything and leave it all behind. Lately, I've been thinking about moving to California to be closer to Stone."

A weight settled on my chest. The fragile string holding me together broke. It couldn't be. The end of our courtship had been devastating, but the thought of him leaving Charleston altogether was too much.

"Life is cruel and merciless," I said. An emptiness encompassed me. "Filled with so much pain, grief, and loss."

Bowden turned to me and placed his hands on my arms. I tilted my chin up to gaze into his eyes.

"I meant what I said the other day. You're the only woman for me. There'll never be another. I don't know how, but I have to believe that someday you'll be mine. I refuse to believe that this is all that was intended for us. To be drawn together, only to suffer a lifetime of torment."

"Aren't we causing our own heartache by holding on to something that's impossible?"

"Maybe. But life isn't livable without you by my side." He lowered his hands and placed a soft, light kiss on my lips before slipping by me.

He walked down the back steps and into the darkness.

I lifted my fingers and touched my lips. *I will always love you, Bowden Armstrong.*

I turned and walked back to the front veranda.

Whitney and Ben stood engaged in conversation, waiting for our driver to bring the carriage around. He arrived, and Ben looked from Whitney to me. "Shall we?" He offered us each an arm.

We nodded, descended the steps, and climbed into the waiting carriage.

ᴄᴏ CHAPTER ᴄᴏ
Thirty-Six

I WAS TOO DISTRACTED THAT NIGHT TO DISCUSS THIS CONVERSATION with Lucille with Ben. I retired to my room shortly after our arrival home, with a promise to Ben to accompany him on a morning ride.

The next day, dressed in my riding attire, I emerged from the house. Sunlight poured through the trees, and I closed my eyes, elevating my face to bask in its warmth.

Jimmy's whistling as he brought our horses into the yard brought a smile to my lips. "Good morning." I went to greet him.

"Ah, Miss Willie. Morning." Jimmy looped the reins over my horse's neck. With a gentle pat, he moved on to adjust the saddle.

We chatted for a moment or two before Ben joined us.

Ben leaned in and planted a kiss on my cheek. I noticed the holster he wore around his waist. It had become normal since the attack on the road.

Jimmy removed his straw hat and clutched it in his hands. "I got de horses all ready for you, Masa."

"A fine job, James."

Ben held out a hand and helped me onto my horse, and I took the riding crop Jimmy held up. Ben swung onto his mount.

We rode out of Livingston. A short way down the road, Ben reined his mount back to match the pace of mine.

"What did Lucille say that has us riding in the direction of her home?" I asked.

"A while back her father purchased a fine, unmarked slave. Fresh off the boat from Maryland."

"And you think it could be Toby?"

"I'm hoping. Last evening before my departure, I asked Mr. Carter if he'd teach me a thing or two on how a cotton gin runs. Appealing to his arrogance, I informed him that I went to medical school and didn't understand many things about running a plantation. He agreed and told me to come by today." He grinned, impressed with himself.

Great! An image of Lucille's face flashed in my mind. My stomach churned with dread at having to endure her company.

"Don't look so forlorn." He laughed.

I shot him a glare. "Easy for you to say. You don't have to deal with Lucille."

"From what I gather from Miss Carter, she isn't that much different than her father."

"Heaven help us both," I grumbled. "But if the man Lucille speaks of is, in fact, the free man, being forced to listen to her nonstop negativity for an afternoon will be worth it." I remained unconvinced by my weak attempt to infuse courage into myself.

He tossed back his head and chuckled. His mirth boomeranged around the countryside. "Was that falsehood for my benefit or yours?"

"Instilling courage, dear Uncle," I said. "The sooner we get this over with, the sooner I can be rid of this dreadful feeling that I'm going to a funeral—or that I'll be the one lowered into the ground in the pine box." I gave my horse a tap with the crop.

~ CHAPTER ~
Thirty-Seven

W E RODE INTO THE CARTER PLANTATION A SHORT TIME later. Lucille, having been informed of our impending arrival, waited conspicuously on the front veranda, painting on a canvas. A slave girl stood to one side, fanning her with an oversized palmetto fan.

Lucille glanced up as we drew near. She stood and made her way down the front steps before strolling down the pathway, dressed in a gown fit for an evening affair.

"Run," I whispered to Ben without moving my mouth.

He grinned.

Lucille's brow puckered at the amusement that passed between us. "Pa told me you'd be stopping by today. He's down by the dock. He's expecting you," she said to Ben.

Ben tipped his hat. "Much obliged." He left me to my demise.

"Are you going to get off that horse, or what?"

Biting down hard, I forced a smile and dismounted.

"Boy," I jumped when Lucille yelled, "get on over here and take Miss Hendricks's horse."

A slave boy around ten years old ran into the yard, and I offered him my reins.

"Now, make yourself scarce." Lucille flicked a hand in the air.

The boy vanished as fast as he'd appeared.

Lucille wrapped me in a dazzling smile. "I don't believe you've been here before."

Hopefully, I wouldn't be back anytime soon. "No, I believe not."

"Then let me show you around."

"Please do," I said, glad that I didn't have to request a tour of the plantation myself.

For the next half an hour, we covered most of the plantation while Lucille bragged about her family and their success. My face ached with the façade of smiles it wore and the laughter I showered her with. Like parched soil after a rainfall, she absorbed the attention, thinking nothing of the unusual warmth with which I doted on her.

"I've arranged to have refreshments served in the parlor."

"But you haven't shown me around the quarters."

Lucille stopped in her tracks and cast me a suspicious look. "Why do you care about the quarters?"

"I'm always interested in seeing how others run their plantations. One can learn much from others if one keeps an open mind." I lavished her with a smile.

Her shoulders rolled back, and she raised her chin. "I suppose so. With your uncle and you both lacking the knowledge of how to run a plantation properly, you could benefit from my family's skills."

How effortlessly I led the lamb to the slaughter. I smiled to myself.

In the quarters, the mood was solemn. Most of the capable slaves were in the fields or performing their daily tasks on other parts of the plantation. Children too small to work the plantation, underfed chickens, and a few hogs roamed freely in the quarters. An elderly slave woman who had to be creeping up on ninety sat on the stoop of a shack, holding an ailing infant. The overall smell of uncleanliness soured my stomach.

A door to a nearby shack opened, and I waited to see who came out. It wasn't until I heard movement that my eyes dropped to the slave man crawling down the two steps on his hands. His legs were stumps that stopped at the knees.

"That man," I said, "was he born that way?"

"No," Lucille mumbled from behind the handkerchief she held over her nose. "He's a runner. My pa and the overseer weren't quick enough, and the dogs had eaten away at his legs before they could call them off.

"Pa stormed the plantation for a week afterward. Said he may as well have burnt his money himself. Got so angry he shot his two best hounds on the spot. Mother said if he hadn't been drunk, he would've had the common sense to shoot the slave instead. He's good for nothing but to help the old woman with the children." Her upper lip curled with disgust. Her eyes followed the man as he wiggled his body like a snake to move.

I gulped at the ugliness contorting her face. No amount of surface beauty Lucille may have had could mask the deformity of her soul. She was the product of what had been instilled in her from birth. A belief that imprisoned her in a mindset that owning another human was her right for being born of a superior race.

"Pretty," a small voice said.

A tug on my gown drew my eyes down.

A girl not much older than three looked up at me with dark, awestruck eyes. Her wooly locks were matted with debris. Her Negro cloth shift, grayed with age, hung from her emaciated body.

"Away with you, you mongrel!" Lucille gave the child a shove backward and then rubbed her hand repetitively on her gown as if to wipe the plague from her hand.

The child tripped over her feet and landed on her backside.

Massive tears poured from her eyes, but not a peep or a whimper came from her. She pulled her quivering lip between her teeth.

I wanted to bend and swoop her up in my arms, to wipe away her tears and whisper that everything would be all right.

"Where's the child's mother?" I managed to say.

"Dead. One day she went crazy and tied a rock to her ankle and jumped off the dock." Lucille shrugged as if it were an everyday occurrence.

"And the child? Who watches her? Surely, she can't survive without a mother."

"She's simple-minded. Incapable of any task you give her. Wanders around the place, oblivious to the world around her. Pa says he's surprised an animal hasn't carried her off by now."

The casualness of her words cut through me. May God forgive me, but I wanted Lucille to suffer and suffer badly.

We moved on. With each step that guided me farther away from the child, the heavier my footfalls became.

I ambled through the quarters with my mind in a muddle. Lucille's chatter continued, but not a word she said registered with me. At the end of the quarters, she led me out and around the back side of the shacks.

"You should be thankful I brought you down here. I avoid coming here, with all the disease and germs these people carry. Mother would be enraged if she found out, so don't mention I brought you, all right?"

I wrung my hands on my skirt.

"Willow!"

"What?"

"Did you not hear what I said?"

"I'm sorry. I didn't. Let's leave this place."

"After you promise this remains our secret."

"I promise."

On the way to the house, I heard groaning from an outbuilding. "Did you hear that?" I said, coming to a stop.

She frowned. "What?"

"That noise. It sounds like it's coming from over there."

"I don't hear anything."

The groaning grew louder. "There it is again!"

She waved a hand in dismissal. "Oh, you mean the wails of that slave. He's been going on like that since last night. Even a pillow over my head couldn't blot out his whining."

"What's wrong with him?"

"Pa took him in hand last night. We had some gentlemen and their wives over for some refreshments after the banquet. The slave bolted into the house and frightened our guests half to death."

I raised a hand to my chest. "What caused the slave's lunatic state of mind?"

"He is unruly. He thought they'd listen to his pleas that he's free. But my pa has his papers. He bought him for top dollar down at the docks. You know these lazy niggers can't think for themselves. They're always trying to run off and find this promised land they chant about, but they don't know the first thing about taking care of themselves. Without us, they'd all be corpses in the fields." She walked on toward the house, leaving me no option but to follow her.

My mind swirled as I hurried to catch up. "I thought you had more control over your slaves," I said. "The last thing you want is for folks to start talking about how the Carters can't manage their blacks."

"That won't happen. My pa handled the situation right away. Whipped the ignorant fool right out in the front yard for all to see," she said.

"He didn't!" I shook my head in displeasure, then glanced

askance at Lucille as she sucked back a breath. Shifting my expression to mortification, I continued, "I mean, how did your guests regard such an act? After an enchanting evening such as the Abbottses put on, and then to come here to pay witness to bloodshed and be reminded of the daily drudgeries of running a plantation...to tarnish the evening in such a way is...why...it's downright nauseating. I do hope for your family's sake that the townsfolk don't turn that on your pa and refuse to accept future engagements. Especially after your pa was simply taking care of business." I stopped and turned concerned eyes on her.

"No, they won't...they mustn't." She chewed on the corner of her mouth.

That's right, Lucille Carter. Squirm in your shoes.

I touched her shoulder with fictitious amity. "If I hear any chatter of ill thoughts toward your family, I'll be sure to set them straight. Good Christian folk like you are simply doing the Lord's work." Bile rose in my mouth as I spoke the words.

"Maybe I've judged you wrong after all. Maybe you're someone I could consider a friend. You're different without that Northern girl trying to be your mouthpiece." Her lips twisted into a sulk.

Hours later, Ben and I mounted our horses and headed for home. Out of sight of disapproving eyes, I spurred my horse into a gallop. Maybe the wind would cleanse my skin of my shame at speaking those words that afternoon.

CHAPTER
Thirty-Eight

TWILIGHT HAD FADED OUT, AND A BLANKET OF DARKNESS engulfed the Carter plantation a few days later. Ben and I waited behind a massive oak at the tree line by the quarters, where smoke from the chimneys painted milky wisps across the sky. We studied the comings and goings on the plantation while Whitney tied the horses a short distance away. Murmured conversation came from a few slaves sitting on tree stumps by a crackling open fire.

"We must be careful," I said. "Carter's known to shoot without questioning."

The crunch of footsteps on undergrowth and branches launched my heart into my throat, and I clutched Ben's arm. We spun toward Whitney, who threw her hands up.

"It's me," she whispered.

"Lift your feet," I said. "If we'd wanted to alert the whole plantation, we would've ridden up the front lane." My nerves hummed.

"How can you be sure it's him?" she asked, crouching down.

"We aren't. But if this man is as determined as he's said to be, Mr. Carter will kill him before he breaks him. Therefore, he needs our help."

"Let's get this over with," Whitney said, jolting as a shiver ran through her.

"As we planned, straight in and straight out. No distractions,"

Ben said, and stepped out into the open.

Whitney and I shared a look. Her eyes mirrored the panic I'd fought to calm all evening.

We hurried to catch up to Ben. The quilt of stars and moon above stretched our silhouettes, pouring them like fluid across the ground as we raced toward the outbuilding. Our light, stealthy footsteps rumbled like thunderbolts in my ears.

At the outbuilding, we flattened against the wall. I closed my eyes and struggled to still my ragged breaths. Fear stabbed its blade into the pit of my stomach. *Please, help us get out of here.*

"Go!" Whitney whispered, giving me a shove.

I opened my eyes and turned to find Ben had disappeared. I moved to the corner of the building and peeked around. The door was slightly ajar, which meant Ben had to be inside. Whitney and I scurried inside after him.

Body odor mixed with the damp and moldy smell of the building, and visibility was minimal. Light from the night sky that pushed through the cracks of the walls would be our guide. I squinted, trying to get a feel for my surroundings. To my right were a carriage and some crates. Dark shadows enveloped other objects in the room.

"Over here," Ben said. Whitney and I moved in the direction of his voice.

Light seeping into the building revealed a man sitting on the floor, naked as the day he was born. A chain secured one of his ankles to the floor. Around his neck he wore an iron collar used to torture slaves. Three prongs poked out from the collar, making it impossible to rest. Slave owners used the collars to keep their slaves from running, as the prongs had hooks on the ends that would get caught in wooded areas. An iron bit designed for a horse was wedged into the man's mouth. The whites of his eyes were bright in the darkness as he stared at us.

"We're going to get you out of here," I said.

Ben dropped the knapsack he carried to the ground. He removed a file. Wasting no time, he knelt and began to file at the chain securing the ankle shackle.

"How are we going to get out of here with that contraption on his neck?" Whitney asked.

"Very carefully." Ben's words came out winded by the vigorous movement of filing.

Time dragged. Slow. Painful. My hands knotted with each scrape of the file. Every noise outside ceased Ben's movement, and our breath would catch. Then Ben would start to file again.

What had to have been an hour, maybe two, passed. Finally the chain gave way. "There," Ben said. "We're through."

"Let's—" Approaching footsteps cut off my words.

"I'm going to check and see if he's still breathing," a man said, his voice sounding slurred.

"I'll wait for you at your cabin," a woman said.

"You do that, darling. I won't be long."

A wave of fear pumped through me.

Footsteps moved further away before heavy footsteps advanced. A belch came from the man as he circled the building to the front door.

"What the hell…" His shadow darkened the doorway.

"Get down." Whitney pulled me out of sight.

Rustling in the corner by the door made my heart miss a beat. Before I could see what was scurrying around there, the door pushed open. I held my breath as moonlight flooded the interior, creeping around a man's bulk blocking the doorway. The man stepped inside.

The scurrying sound came again.

"Show yourself!" his voice boomed.

I clutched Ben's hand. *No, no, no.*

"What are you doing in here?" The man's voice hitched with surprise.

"Mama?" a tiny voice spoke.

I peeked from my hiding place behind some barrels and crates.

The orphan child from the quarters stood in front of the man. She'd been in here all along. Would she give us away?

"Get out of here before you find yourself in the river like your ma." His massive hand capped the back of her head and he sent her sailing out the door. She landed in a heap on the ground.

The man took another step, and I pulled back and crouched low. His ponderous steps scraped across the floor until he stopped in front of the man on the floor.

Please don't see the break in the chain.

He loomed over the man, so close I could reach out and grab the back of his coat without fully extending my arm. My lungs felt like they'd burst at any second. I slowly exhaled, then inhaled the fruity scent of liquor oozing from the man.

He grunted. An impolite noise fit only for the privy ripped through the building, followed by a foul odor that threatened to gag me. "I see you may survive this life yet. That's if the damn fool doesn't kill you first." He spun and walked toward the door while grumbling to himself, "The man never learns. Out cold on the back veranda already, and the night is still young. Can't handle his drink like some of us."

He closed the door behind him. A scraping noise followed by a thud made me gasp. Ben cursed quietly. He too knew the significance of the sound.

A plank now sealed the door shut.

When the man's footfalls faded, we rose to our feet.

"This is just wonderful!" Whitney said in a low snarl. "How are we getting out—"

A movement at the door stole her words.

No!

The plank on the door scraped.

My stomach dropped with dread. We dove into our hiding place, and I squeezed my eyes shut. This was it. We'd be found for sure.

As the light shuffling of footsteps moved toward us, I opened my eyes and peeked through the crack.

It was the girl from the quarters.

I rose to my feet. Whitney pulled at the hem of my skirt in an attempt to get me to stay down. "Hello, little one," I whispered.

The child tilted her head to look at me with big, round eyes before they flitted to Whitney and Ben as they slipped out of their hiding places. The child pointed at the man on the floor, then to us. Her fingers curled toward herself, summoning us to come.

Ben didn't hesitate. He grabbed his knapsack, scrambled to the man's side, and lifted him to his feet, keeping his head low to avoid being pierced by the hooks of the man's collar.

Outside, Whitney slid the plank back into place.

"Thank you," I whispered to the child.

"Let's go!" Whitney cast a look around.

Ben was already making his way toward the tree line.

"We can't just leave her. She has no one."

Whitney grasped my arm in a firm grip. "Do you want to endanger everyone?"

"Come." I held out a hand to the child.

She craned her head as if trying to figure out our intention, then scurried toward the cypress forest.

Don't go!

Whitney snatched my wrist and pulled me. "Come on!"

Ben was waiting for us when we arrived at the tree.

"One of you is going to have to help me. He's passed out."

Draping the man's other arm over my shoulder, I planted my heels in the ground for support.

"Got him?" Ben asked.

"Not for long." I felt the hook of a prong snag a loop of my hair.

With each step we made toward the horses, the hook ripped at my hair. Tears sprang to my eyes from the pain, and I stumbled under the weight of the man.

"You all right?" Ben said, breathing heavily.

Without answering, I steadied myself and adjusted the man's arm. Our steps now aligned, Ben's and my pace picked up.

At the horses, we managed to get the man on a horse. His naked body slumped forward, and Ben grabbed for him before his collar hooked the horse and sent the animal rearing. In one swift movement, Ben swung up behind him. Whitney and I mounted our horses. Out of the corner of my eye, I caught a movement. The tall grass parted, and the child stepped out.

"Look!" I pointed in her direction, then slid to the ground.

"Willow, get back on your horse this instant!" Whitney said through gritted teeth.

"Here." I shoved my reins at her hands.

Slowly, I edged toward the child. As I drew nearer, I held out a hand and dropped to my knees. She crept back a step or two, eyeing her surroundings.

"I won't hurt you."

Her eyes shifted from me to the others. She didn't move.

"We must hurry before the bad men get us," I said. "They hurt that man really bad."

Her body trembled.

A thought came to me, and I reached up and removed my

pearl earrings. "Pretty." I held them in the palm of my hand for her to see.

Her brow wrinkled.

"We must go!" Ben said.

The child looked from him to me. I thrust my hand at her. "For you."

She crept forward, and my heart hammered with anticipation. *Come on...*

Her fingers touched the palm of my hand, and in a flash, she scooped up the earrings. I didn't move, afraid a slight movement or breath would frighten the child.

Her eyes touched mine, and she said, "You good?"

I nodded.

"Help Toby?" She pointed at the unconscious man on the horse.

Toby? It was Toby! "Yes."

She inched closer and rested her small, warm hand in mine. Carefully, I pushed myself upright. "I'll take you to a safe place."

"Heaven?"

I smiled down at her upturned face. "No."

She appeared content with my answer.

As we approached the horses, I leaned down and picked up the child. Her body felt fragile and weightless as I sat her on my horse. She gripped at its mane while I hauled myself up behind her.

We rode hard toward Livingston without looking back.

CHAPTER
Thirty-Nine

As instructed, Mammy and Jimmy had waited for our return. Ben and Jimmy took the man to the stables where they removed the iron collar and bit. During the process, Ben said the man had groaned and cried while slipping in and out of consciousness.

In Mammy and Tillie's room, Ben tended to the man's wounds. Tillie had taken the child to the warming kitchen to feed her before they'd wandered upstairs to bathe the girl. I stood in the doorway of the room and watched Ben at work. On a trunk between the two beds, the lantern flickered and cast shadows around the room. Ben glided the needle through the skin on the back of the man the child had called Toby.

"Do you think he'll be all right?" I asked.

"Some of these lacerations are infected, but with proper care and rest, he should be fine."

The skin on the man's neck was raw and darkened from the chafing of the collar. His mouth arched back at the corners where the iron bit had once been.

"I'll sleep in here tonight to watch over him," Ben said. "Tomorrow we must move them before Carter and his men show up."

"Will he be stable enough to be moved?" I recalled the slave from a few months ago.

"It won't be easy for him, but if he has the will he's said to have, then he'll find the strength."

I sat in the warming kitchen, sipping at the tea Mammy had set out. Between sips, I gazed blankly at the brown liquid in the bottom of the blue-flowered china cup.

"Worries will steal your youth." Ben placed a gentle hand on my wrist as he slipped into the other chair at the small table.

"Worry and fear seem to be the only emotions I'm capable of lately." I studied the low-burning candle sitting in the middle of the table, then moved my hand to pick at the drips of wax rolling down the sides.

"It troubles me to see you like this."

"I find myself wondering if Father may have felt the same. Is that why he was distant and disconnected? I know I can't live in the past and keep questioning it, but there are so many unanswered questions I still long to put to rest."

Ben cleared his throat, and I shifted my gaze to observe his face. "What is it?"

"Charles was a complicated man."

"I'm aware."

"There are things you must know about your father. Things I've been waiting to tell you for some time but never felt the timing was right. I don't want to keep anything from you."

"Then don't."

"When we were in London, Sam found a ledger Olivia kept of slaves she'd given aid to, along with a journal. Charles's journal. The journal may help shed light on your father's deepest thoughts. It may help you find some peace. But it also may reveal things you don't want to know, or bring you more questions."

"Have you read this journal?"

"An excerpt or two, but that isn't the only thing I've wanted to tell you. In Charles's will, he mentioned a girl."

"A girl?" My pulse throbbed in my ears.

"A girl he says…is his daughter."

My throat tightened. "What?"

"He'd never mentioned the girl to me. But why would he? I had one purpose, and that was to watch you. Our bond as brothers was broken long ago." Bitterness lined his words.

Quiet settled over the room.

Father had a daughter. Tears welled in my eyes. But how? Why had he never mentioned her?

I shifted my eyes to Ben. The pain of the past was all too evident in his face. His jaw quivered with wavering emotions and became rigid as a memory or thought surfaced.

"Will it ever end?" I said, dropping my gaze to my cup.

"The secrets?"

"The secrets, the pain and the longing for…*them*. Will the day come when I find out that I'm not even a Hendricks? That, in fact, my parents aren't Olivia Shaw and Benjamin Hendricks at all." My voice fractured. Heavy droplets cascaded down my cheeks and plopped into my cup.

"Willow…" His hand clasped mine. Gently, his thumb stroked the fold between my thumb and index finger.

"I'm so tired of being tired. Tired of being sad and broken."

I heard him swallow hard. "We are in control of our own happiness."

"Are we?" I lifted tear-filled eyes to him, and his face contorted in the outpouring of my tears. "What about you? You emerged from the darkness to walk in the sunlight, but where's your happiness? You grieve for a woman who can never give us the comfort we seek. We love and detest a man that can never sit and tell us why he did the things he did. He can never set things right."

"We must put the past to rest. Only then will we find what

we are looking for."

"How does one do this?"

"I don't rightfully know," he said in all honesty.

"This girl you speak of; where is she? How old is she? What does that make her to me? A sister? A cousin?" My laugh sounded harsh in my own ears. "How much did you all think I was capable of handling?"

"I wish the facts weren't the facts. I wish I didn't have to add to the pain you've already endured, but I couldn't keep this from you any longer."

"Why did you?"

"I—I was afraid you couldn't handle any more disappointment."

"But look at me. Here I stand, Willow Hendricks, heiress of the empire built on lies and deceit." Bitterness soured my mouth. "Carrier of secrets and burdens so grand I may as well be the wearer of the iron collar and bit. I didn't ask for this life. You all laid it at my feet." I turned my blame and pain on the one person I needed more than I needed to breathe.

"A thousand apologies wouldn't right the wrongs we've done to you." He hung his head. A single tear slipped from the corner of his eye.

Shame and remorse yanked me from my wallowing. Was he not as broken as me? Had he not suffered? He'd survived a life sentence, and for what? For loving a woman who was rightfully his from the start. "I'm—I'm sorry."

"No need to be." Sorrow hollowed his eyes.

"Together, we'll find a way to move past all this," I said firmly. *It starts here...and now.*

He lifted his head and held my eyes with his. A pleasant smile softened the ache in his face. "We can't rob ourselves of a future. The past has stolen enough from us."

I stood and went to him. Leaning forward, I wrapped my arms around his neck. "I love you…Father." I placed a light kiss on his cheek, then stepped back.

Tears dampened his eyes as he reached for my hand. "You're the one good thing in my life." Emotion clotted his voice.

"And you mine." I wiped my tears with my free hand.

"It's been a long day." He stood. "Tomorrow will be upon us before we know it." He pulled me into his embrace.

For a moment we found comfort from the past and the present, escaping into the hope for a future that was within our grasp to change.

CHAPTER
Forty

I WOKE BEFORE DAWN TO THE DISTANT BARKING OF HOUNDS.

They were coming!

Fear exploded in my chest. I kicked back my blankets, and my feet hit the floor with a thud.

"Tillie, wake up!" I said, throwing the door to my closet open. "They're coming. Go wake Whitney and Ben. We need to get the man and the child down to the dock."

Tillie's nightcap peeked over the bottom of my four-poster bed from her pallet on the floor. My panic sent the child from the Carter plantation, who'd slept beside Tillie, into whimpers. Tillie stumbled to her feet and ran from the room.

I slipped on a pair of Father's trousers and a shirt. "Shhh, don't cry. It'll be all right." I tried to soothe the child as I tucked my braid under a dark hat and pulled it low on my head.

Moving to the girl, who sat clutching the blanket to her neck, I bent and lifted her into my arms. Placing my lips on her temple, I said, "Hush now. You mustn't cry."

I ran into the corridor and met a wide-eyed Whitney, also clothed in men's apparel. I blew past her and thundered down the stairs with her on my heels. Downstairs, I raced out the back door with the child bouncing in my arms. She buried her head in my throat, and her fingers dug into the back of my neck.

The howling of the dogs grew closer.

God in heaven, help us.

We raced past the quarters as folks stepped out on their stoops. Panic and worry spread across their faces. Not a soul would sleep with the danger of the dogs and slave catchers near. Murmurs rose. A threat to Livingston meant we were all at risk. Women and men raced to pick up appointed tasks they'd practiced for unexpected visits from outsiders. Children who were old enough and capable of understanding what was going on grabbed smaller children and hustled them inside, away from suspicious eyes.

Jones wiggled into a coat as he bolted for the dock with Jimmy and another black man right behind him.

"Where's Ben? Someone get to the house to help him," I screamed.

The black man charged for the house.

My legs felt weighted, and the dock seemed like it was miles away.

Reaching the end of the dock, Whitney jumped into the boat, her eyes bulging with fear as she extended her arms. I handed her the child as Jimmy untied the rope securing the boat.

I whipped my head around at the footsteps thundering along the dock. Ben and the black man I'd sent to the house half carried and half dragged the injured man. They stumbled across the dock to the edge of the water. The wounded man was alert and clenching his side as if in pain, his eyes wild with fear and determination.

Jones dropped into the boat and reached up to help the man. Once he was in, I climbed in after him. Jones threw back the tarp covering the crates of staged goods in the center of the boat.

"Lie down and take the child," Jones said. After they were lying on the floor, Jones wrapped the tarp around the supplies and secured it with ropes.

Jimmy and Ben pushed us out into the river. "Follow the

plan. No veering off track," Ben said, his eyes dark with worry.

I nodded and waved.

Ben swept his hands through his hair. "Be safe. I can't have anything—"

"Go!" I yelled.

He turned, and he and Jimmy bounded back down the dock. They split up as Ben raced to the house and Jimmy to his assigned position.

CHAPTER
Forty-One

THE THUNDERCLAP OF THE OARS SLAPPING THE WATER BLENDED with the baying of the dogs. I scanned the riverbanks. My gaze came to rest on Jones, who regarded me with inquisitive eyes.

"If you've something to say, say it." I held his hard stare.

His eyes turned to something over my shoulder, and his expression grew bland.

My body was strung tight with foreboding as we drifted down the river in the darkness. Fingers of panic circled my throat with each strike of the oars on the water. The chatter of the crickets and bullfrogs cut through the quiet entombing us, loud to our ears, sharpened to every minuscule sound.

We rowed until the landmark alerted us that we'd arrived at the next station. Branches and roots from trees above jutted out from the riverbank and formed what resembled a woman with long, flowing hair. As if guarding the river, a raised hand shielded her eyes. Hidden within the knotted twigs of her body was a rope ladder.

We pulled the skiff tight to the riverbank.

"I'll see if it's safe," I said.

Jones untangled the ladder and held it out for me. Grasping its sides, I swung my leg up with his help. My limbs burned with the struggle to advance up the ladder. Dirt speckled my face as the ladder slapped me against the riverbank. I used my forearm to wipe the dirt from my eyelids and spat out a mouthful of grit.

"Hurry. We're sitting targets out here," Whitney whispered from below.

I heaved a foot over the bank, dug my heel into the ground, and pulled myself up.

The sun slunk on the horizon like a globe of fire searing across the earth. I threaded through the trees toward the small farmhouse, pausing at the edge to scour the property for prying eyes. On the clothesline at the corner of the house, flapping gently in the early morning breeze, hung a quilt: the signal that all was safe.

Perched on a fence post, a rooster cocked back his head and crowed. Hens scurried around the yard, clucking. The clang of an object hitting metal drew my eyes to a nearby pasture.

"Blasted cow, stand still," Mr. Sully said. He'd been the first of my father's sources I'd met after discovering his involvement in the Underground Railroad.

Mr. Sully took off his hat and smacked the hindquarter of the cow before bending over to pick up the milk pail that lay on the ground in a puddle of fresh milk.

I cupped my hands and hooted like an owl. Mr. Sully froze and his eyes scanned the property. I pulled my hat low to shadow my face and stepped into view. Catching sight of me, he offered a low wave. He bent and climbed through the rungs of the fence and strolled toward me.

"It's you." Relief washed over his face.

"I have baggage," I whispered.

He cast a cautious look around and said through closed lips, "Carter and Thames have already been here this morning. But that isn't to say they aren't scouting the place out." He cleared his throat and said in a normal tone, "How many bundles of wood?"

"One small and one big."

We backtracked to the riverbank. I peered down to find Whitney and Jones keeping watch on the river. I picked up a pebble and threw it down. It cuffed the corner of the boat before hitting the water with a light splash. They looked up.

I gestured with a hand that it was clear.

Jones threw back the canvas and motioned to the man and child to come out. They stood on wobbly legs, the child clinging to the man's legs.

"The man's weak. He won't be able to climb the ladder." I bent by the pile of dead brush. Moving it aside, I withdrew the rope underneath.

Mr. Sully tied the rope to a tree. He made a loop at the other end and threw it down. Below, Jones circled the man's waist with the rope. A few words were shared between them, and the man nodded. Whitney lifted the child and placed her on the man's back. Pain rippled over the man's face. Jones pumped a fist in the air, signaling us to pull them up.

Mr. Sully and I dug our heels into the moss-covered earth and pulled. The rope chafed the flesh of my hands. Heat inflamed my muscles with each haul on the rope. Finally we heaved them over the bank, and they landed in a heap on the ground. Mr. Sully held out his hand and hauled the man to his feet. The child never released her hold around his neck.

"We believe this is the man I asked you to keep an eye out for," I said.

"Are you, in fact, the man?" Mr. Sully asked him.

For the first time, I heard him speak. In a deep voice, he said, "I'm Toby Adams of Maryland." His shoulders arched back, and his chin jutted out. "Born free. No nation or man or woman will take that from me."

He set the child on the ground, and a wince snatched at his breath. The child clasped his hand as she gawked up at him with trusting eyes. He smiled down at her. An angelic smile lifted the apples of her cheeks. Toby stroked her hair. "My protector."

"The next railroad line will assure your passage to *heaven*," I said, holding out a hand.

"Bless you." Toby shook my hand.

"I'll inform the *preachers*," I said.

He blinked his understanding.

The slave child stood huddled next to Toby. One small hand still tucked into his while the other formed into a fist at her side. I bent and took her free hand in mine. She tugged to reclaim her hand while adjusting what she clasped inside. Her dark eyes questioned me as I pried open her fingers one at a time to reveal my pearl earrings. They glistened with sweat from her palm. I smiled, closed her hand, and placed her hand on her chest. "Yours."

I rose. "The riverbank makes a mighty good road," I said to Toby.

"Godspeed," he said.

I nodded and turned and climbed down the ladder.

At the bottom, Jones caught me by the waist.

"Did you have tea and biscuits while you were up there?" Tension pulled at Whitney's temples. She didn't wait for us to be seated before she started rowing the skiff toward home.

Jones and I lurched forward. He steadied me before seating himself. Picking up his oar, he plunged it into the river. Together Whitney and Jones rowed with steady, even strokes.

Whitney's eyes skittered around, while Jones's, once again, fixed on me.

CHAPTER
Forty-Two

RUMORS OF THE GUARDIAN SWOOPING DOWN WHILE THE Carters slept and stealing Toby had swept through the countryside. Yet no mention was made of the orphan girl. It was as if she hadn't existed. Or maybe the Carters believed an animal *had* carried her off.

Planters had taken to chaining and locking the shacks in the quarters at night in hopes of protecting their investments. Guards were doubled. Paranoia spread as far as the Georgia and North Carolina borders.

Ben thought it was best for us to lie low with hopes the panic would blow over. We decided against writing Julia to let her know we'd located Toby. Fear of Toby and the child not making it to safety plagued us all.

Newspapers across South Carolina had dedicated their front pages to the Guardian. With each article I read, my worry intensified.

One evening, Whitney, Ben, and I sat in the library after the twins had gone to bed and the house slaves had gone to visit friends and family in the quarters. I read a recent edition of the *Charleston Courier*.

My heart raced as realization dawned on me. *How could I have been so stupid?*

I lowered the paper to my lap.

The Guardian surfaced each time we helped a slave escape.

Why hadn't I made the connection before?

"Of course. How could I be so oblivious?" I said aloud. It made perfect sense now.

"What?" Ben and Whitney said in unison.

"The Guardian."

"What about him?" Whitney said.

"It's us."

"Us?" She glanced at Ben as if he held the answers to my sudden madness.

His face didn't hold the same shock as hers.

"Each time we've transported slaves, folks mention this Guardian fellow."

She turned her eyes back to me as her mouth unhinged.

"You don't appear to be as surprised," I said to Ben.

He closed the medical book he'd been studying and leaned forward. His elbows rested on his knees as he clasped the book in his hands. "I had my suspicions." He rotated the book in a spinning motion between his knees.

"Yet you failed to mention it?" I frowned.

"My hands have been rather full since my return." His brow lifted. "But I'd wondered if the rumors had to do with the increase of escaped slaves over the last year in these parts."

I swallowed the lump in my throat as I stood and began pacing the floor. "We're amateurs at this. Trying to take on my parents' work as if we've any clue what we're doing."

Jaw clenched, Whitney eyed the doorway and whispered, "It's not like *they* left instructions on how to smuggle slaves in and out of plantations and around the country. We're doing the best we can."

"The best we can isn't good enough," I insisted, my hands on my waist.

"Until this dies down, we can't afford to stick our necks out.

Too many lives are in danger right here at Livingston." Ben stood. "All illegal actions are banned until further notice. We can't take any chances." I wrung my hands.

"Maybe it's time to consider disposing of all documents that could cripple Livingston if they were to fall into the wrong hands," Ben said.

"No!" I shrieked. Lowering my voice, I hissed through clamped teeth, "I've not had time to read through the ledger and journal you gave me."

What he was asking was out of the question. My parents' ledgers and journals were my connection to them. Reading their words gave me a sense of closeness…yet at times it made me feel so far removed.

"Charles kept them hidden for a reason. Ledgers with re-corded slaves' names instead of their tag numbers is a clue to anyone who comes looking. We must take every precaution. I urge you to read quickly and burn the rest."

Cold sweat prickled down my back as his words sank in. "But the ledgers could help reunite families when this is all over."

"An absurd dream that dwindles with the tightening of the South's grip on their wallets." Whitney sighed despondently.

"We need to be concerned with the present and surviving another day. If Livingston's cover is blown, the hopes of many will be lost." Ben's warning rang clear.

Later I tossed in bed, restless, finally flopping onto my back to gaze numbly at the ceiling. Ben's concerns over the ledgers and journals robbed me of sleep. As much as it would pain me to do away with the books, if keeping them meant risking lives and all we'd achieved so far, I'd do what had to be done.

CHAPTER
Forty-Three

Bowden

"I'LL HAVE THE REST OF YOUR SUPPLIES DELIVERED BY THE END of the week," Miss Smith said as we exited the general store and stepped out into the loading yard.

"Much appreciated." I tipped my hat while juggling the bags of goods I held in my arms.

"I hope you catch the persons responsible."

"With the tightening of security at the plantation, I'll nab the culprits sooner or later." My jaw clenched at the memory of the flames engulfing the kitchen house.

The cowards had waited until the plantation had settled for the night before setting the fire. The blast of a gunshot had awakened me. Whoever had started the fire had wanted me to bear witness to the calamity. They'd made their presence known and their warning clear.

Slaves and overseers had come together with me to save the kitchen house, but it'd been no use. Today the outbuilding lay in shambles. Nothing but cinders, smoke, and the chimney of the stone fireplace remained.

"Mr. Williams says de rest of de lumber be delivered tomorrow sometime," Gray said, running into the yard. I'd sent him to order lumber for the rebuild.

"The wagon loaded with what's available?" I asked.

He mopped the sweat from his brow with the cuff of his shirt. "Yes, Masa."

"Bring the wagon around and we'll be on our way."

Gray spun and ran back the way he'd come.

Under the seat of the wagon, I placed the bags of flour, sugar, and other goods I held in my arms. Miss Smith added the products she carried alongside mine.

Her eyes dropped to the holster on my waist. "You'd think it was Indian territory, with all you men carrying weapons lately." She smoothed back a wisp of her hair. "Sets me on edge with the jumpiness of folks. Someone is bound to get hurt. Or end up dead."

"Let's hope not." I climbed up to the wagon seat and untied the reins. I sat down and gave the reins a crack.

I guided the horses between the general store and the neighboring building to the main street. As I broke the shadows of the buildings, I spied a familiar face. Across the street, directly in my line of vision, he stood, watching me. When he was sure he'd captured my attention, he flipped back his coat to reveal his gun. A cocky grin broke across his face.

Collins!

I turned the wagon onto the street. My eyes chiseled through him. He moved his hand and let his coat fall. With a finger to the brim of his hat, he dipped his head in greeting. His eyes looked past me. The smugness vanished, replaced with loathing.

My ears tuned to the squeaking of wagon wheels behind me. I checked over my shoulder as Gray pulled his wagon onto the street. I swung back to look at Collins.

"It's a fine day for a little adventure, isn't it, Mr. Armstrong." His eyes turned to slits before he spun on his heels and stalked off.

I heeded his threat. When Gray and I were safely beyond

the town line, I pulled my team of horses to a stop and jumped down.

I walked up to Gray as he hauled back on his reins. "Whoa, boys." He turned worried eyes on me. "What's de trouble, Masa."

"You see Collins?"

"I saw him all right." Gray's mouth tightened.

"I don't trust the man. Keep a lookout."

"You suppose he's de one who set fire to de kitchen house?"

"It's a good possibility." I removed a revolver from my holster. "Keep this close in case we receive visitors."

"But, Masa, a slave ain't supposed to have no gun. Ef folks—"

"Take it!" I said, shoving the gun at him.

He took it without further questioning and placed it on the seat beside him, his eyes surveying the woods.

I walked back to the wagon and climbed up. My jaw ached from the clenching of my teeth. As I whipped the reins and the convoy lurched forward, Miss Smith's words from earlier played in my head: *Do you have enemies, Mr. Armstrong?*

One.

I was confident of that now.

I gave the reins another crack, and the horses sped up.

It all happened so fast. I didn't know what was happening until I was flying through the air and hit the ground with bone-crushing force. The reins snarled in my arms as the team tore down the road, dragging me behind them.

The weaving of the horses threw me back and forth like the waves slamming the sea wall during a hurricane. Rocks and debris chewed at my face and body, mangling my flesh, sending fire surging through every nerve. Never had I felt such pain.

Blocking out the pain, I twisted and tore at the reins, trying to slow the horses and gain control. "Whoa," I cried between mouthfuls of dirt, blinded by the cloud of dust kicked up by thundering hooves threatening to grind my brains into the ground.

This is it! This is how I'll die.

Her face entered my mind seconds before my face slammed into the rock that catapulted me into a tunnel of black.

Willow.

∾ CHAPTER ∾
Forty-Four

Willow

B EN HAD ARRANGED A MEETING WITH SAM AT HIS OFFICE TO
review my father's will for the second time.

Reading the will with my own eyes, I slumped back
in my chair.

Her name was Callie. She was the daughter of a dressmaker
in London. She was my father's heir. Yet he left her the town
home in London and nothing more.

"Why would he not leave her part of his businesses and es-
tates here in America?"

"That remains a mystery to us all."

"So far his journal says nothing of her existence."

"It was a secret he wanted to keep hidden," Ben said.

"Did my mother know?"

Ben stared down at his hands. "Another mystery."

I looked at Sam. "Did she?"

"He never said. She'd passed by the time he had his will re-
done. Your father and I'd been friends since we were boys. He
never mentioned the girl until the day he came to redo the will."

"When was that?" I said.

"About a year before his death," Sam said. He grimaced as
his mind drifted.

"What is it?" I asked.

"I was thinking back to our conversation that day."

"And?"

The eerie stillness that fell on the room chilled my blood.

"He said he'd thought someone was watching him," Sam said.

Ben and I sat up straighter.

"What exactly did my father say?"

"He said he'd noticed a man observing Livingston on horseback. I'd questioned him, thinking maybe it was you he'd spotted," Sam said to Ben. "But then he went on to say on a few occasions he'd seen a man around town that hung back, watching him."

I leaned forward. "Did he ever confront the man?"

"Not that I'm aware of."

"Do you believe my brother was concerned for his life?"

Elbows on his desk, Sam rested his hands under his chin in thought. "There's no way of knowing that now." Regret pulled at his face. "I dismissed his concerns at the time. Chalked up his paranoia to working too hard and the amount of stress he was under."

"Did Father say what this man looked like?"

"No." Sam fumbled with some papers at the edge of his desk.

"Did he ever mention to you that he thought he was being watched?" I said to Ben.

"Never. But he did seek me out one day after the Barry fire. His mood was none too pleasant. Told me if I let you out of my sight for a second, it'd be the last time I'd lay eyes on you. I'd thought it was a precaution due to the madness of the townsfolk and he didn't want you getting in the way."

"And now?" I said.

"I'm not sure." He stood and went to the window. "Let's say

Charles *was* being watched. What was the man's motive? Where is he now?"

"I've seen no one," I said. "Have you?"

"No," Ben said. He straightened, shoulders back, feet rooted to the floor.

Was someone out there watching us? Why hadn't they revealed themselves? What did Ben intend to do?

A commotion outside beckoned us all to the window.

A man on a horse galloped at full speed down the road. "Clear out of the way," he yelled. People dove in every direction to avoid being trampled. The rider flashed by the window.

Silas?

Behind him, a colored man drove a wagon loaded with lumber as if the rightful owner were hot on his trail. Slouched on the front seat beside him was a man. His clothes were torn and covered in blood and filth.

Gray?

What in heaven's name was going on?

"It's Gray." I dashed for the door. "Someone's been injured."

Footsteps pounded behind me.

On the boardwalk, I peered down the street in the direction they'd gone. The wagon had stopped outside of the doctor's office. I gathered my skirt and ran.

"Willow!" Ben called behind me. I didn't stop.

Gray pushed by me into the doctor's office. People flocked around the wagon. They murmured and gasped in horror at the slouched figure on the front seat.

I pushed through the observers to get a better view.

"Get out of the way. Move," the doctor's voice bellowed. He pushed by me and climbed up on the wagon.

Gray moved closer. "Gray!" I grabbed his arm. "What happened? Who's injured?"

Gray turned stunned, worried eyes on me. "Masa Bowden. De horses gave way and dey dragged him clear down de road. Ef et warn't for Mr. Anderson, Masa be dead for sho'." Tears thickened Gray's voice.

What? No! It can't be. My eyes flew back to the man behind the people crowding the space around the wagon. My hand slipped to my forehead. The voices around me muffled and blurred.

Strong arms reached for me and closed around me.

"Gray…" My sobs were absorbed by his chest. "I can't lose him." His hand stroked my hair. I sobbed harder. My fingers clenched the fiber of his shirt. The sweet scent of his—

I pulled back. "Mr. Anderson. I thought…" The blood drained from my face. "I'm sorry, I didn't mean to…"

His face filled with concern. "No need to explain, Miss Hendricks. Let me find you a place to sit down." He reached for my arm.

I yanked it away. "No. I need to see Bowden." My eyes searched the smothering bodies until I located Sam in the crowd.

"Sam!" I plowed my way toward him.

"Come on now, people, move out of the way," Silas's voice boomed.

The sea of bodies parted and I hurried to Sam. "Where's my uncle?"

"Inside with the doctor." Sam's face was taut with concern.

"I need to see Bowden."

Sam swallowed hard and took my elbow to turn me away. "I don't…I don't think that's best right now."

"I don't care what you think!" I spun and pushed my way to the front door of the office. I needed to see him. I had to.

"Miss Hendricks, you mustn't go in there," a woman said.

Paying her no mind, I opened the door and stepped inside

and closed the door behind me.

"Those horses messed him up pretty bad," the doctor was saying. "If he lives, he'll be scarred for life."

I walked down the hallway to the room their voices were coming from. Gray stood just inside. At the doorway, I shut my eyes and inhaled a deep breath before opening them.

Scissors in hand, the doctor cut open what remained of Bowden's shirt. A gasp escaped me at what I saw. I lifted a fist to my mouth. My teeth bit into my knuckles.

The doctor and Ben turned to me. Ben's face paled, and he closed the distance between us. "You shouldn't be in here." He shielded my view with his body.

"I must see him." I peered up at him through bleary eyes. "Please don't stop me," I said softly.

Ben's mouth set in a grim line. He rested an arm around my shoulders and guided me toward the table where Bowden lay. Each step grew heavier as I took in the extent of Bowden's battered body. His shirt now lay open. Layers of his chest had been peeled back, the flesh mangled like pulverized meat. I lifted a hand to stifle a sob. Creeping closer, I shifted my gaze to his face. Bruises and gashes with the accompanying swelling made him almost unrecognizable.

"From what the slave says, he should be dead," the doctor said. "If it hadn't been for Mr. Anderson, he would be."

"What does Anderson have to do with this?" I said.

"Gray says Anderson was headed to town when he saw the team charging down the road. Anderson managed to stop them," Ben said.

Bowden stirred on the table. A low groan came from him before horrifying, agonizing cries deafened the room. His back arched and his body thrashed wildly.

"Hold him down. He's coming to," the doctor ordered,

gesturing to Ben and Gray. The doctor reached for a cloth and a bottle labeled *Chloroform*.

I leaned down and whispered in Bowden's ear, "Fight. You mustn't give up."

"Will…" a hoarse rasp came from him. "W-Wi—"

"I'm here. I'm not going anywhere until you're back on your feet."

His body convulsed and a scream of pain parted his lips.

The doctor placed the cloth over his mouth. Bowden's legs kicked and then grew still. His head dropped to the side.

"Now, young lady, I need you to leave. You take her." He motioned to Gray. "Mr. Hendricks, I could use your help."

Ben removed his coat and rolled up his sleeves. "Take her home, Gray," he said.

"I won't go home."

"Willow, not now," Ben said as he washed his hands in a basin.

I followed Gray from the room.

On the boardwalk, I avoided eye contact and turned to walk down the street.

"How is he?" Silas's voice stopped my departure.

I turned to face him. "I don't know."

"Can I do anything for you? I could take you home."

"I'm not leaving here until I know how he's doing. But thank you, Mr. Anderson." I turned to walk away but stopped. "I want to personally thank you for stopping those horses."

"I only did what any decent fellow would do," he said. "I hope he pulls through. I have business to attend to, but if you need me for any reason, please don't hesitate to ask. I'll be back to check on Mr. Armstrong." He gently touched my elbow.

"Good day." I reeled and continued down the boardwalk.

CHAPTER
Forty-Five

OVER A WEEK HAD PASSED SINCE BOWDEN'S ACCIDENT. BEN had returned to Livingston to help Whitney while I remained in Charleston at our townhouse. Ben had sent Tillie to attend to my needs.

Our Charleston home was managed by a freed black family in our absence. Though their faces were familiar from their years of service, they were practically strangers, as time spent at our home in town was limited to the odd summer and during social season. I missed the comfort of Livingston and all the ones I held dear.

Bowden was recovering at Knox's until the doctor thought it was safe for him to be transported home. Ben and the doctor had spent hours repairing the damage to Bowden's body. It wasn't the broken ribs or leg that concerned me, but how Bowden's mental well-being would be affected by his physical appearance. The doctor had said in time Bowden would heal, but the damage from being dragged by the horses would leave permanent scars. The first few days the doctor had administered laudanum to manage the pain. I'd sat by Bowden's bedside while he'd drifted in and out of reality.

After the doctor gave his approval for Bowden to be moved to Knox's, Ben and I'd gone to pay him a visit. The woman Bowden hired to aid him in his recovery while Knox was at the docks turned us away at the door, telling us Bowden had requested no visitors. Each day I tried to see him, but to no avail.

Ben would be returning today to take Tillie and me home. My time was needed at Livingston. Before my departure, I wanted to speak with Knox about Bowden's condition. Tillie and I made our way down the dock in search of him.

We spotted him as he left a merchant ship and crossed the gangplank to the pier. I called to him. Once he located the sound of my voice, he waved and strode over to us.

"What brings you down to the docks?" he asked. The usual good cheer that enveloped Knox was absent.

"I've been filling my time at the warehouses with Captain Gillies. He's been teaching Parker, a boy from the quarters, all the ins and outs of being a sailor in the Hendrickses' employ. I needed something to keep my mind off of Bowden."

"I see."

"How is he today?" I asked, over the squawking of the seagulls above.

"Out of bed, finally. That busted leg has him foaming at the mouth."

"Only the leg?"

"The leg keeps him from riding on out of here. Wants nothing more than to hide from the world. Lucky for him his chest and legs got the worst of it."

"You consider that lucky?"

"Guess not. But clothing will hide most of the scars once he heals."

"I want to see him."

"You can forget that idea. Above the rest, you're the one he wants to avoid."

"Why?"

"Says you won't want half a man," he said.

I gaped at him a moment before I said, "I care not a whit for what anyone's appearance may be."

"I know that. But tell that to Bowden." He shook his head. "He's as stubborn as they come and he's got it in his head that you won't ever look at him the same again. He's in a real dark place. Maybe that'll change in time. Don't tear yourself up over it. Only Bowden can change what's going on in his head. Besides, until he figures out who did this—"

"Who did what?"

"I suppose you wouldn't have heard. The accident was no accident."

My heart missed a beat. "What?"

"The harnesses were cut. Someone intended to take Bowden out or leave him near death."

"But who...why?"

"Gray came to tell me right after it happened. Said that a man by the name of Collins, who was employed by Bowden, may be responsible. After Bowden caught him mistreating Gray, he let him go. Gray said Collins was spitting mad. On the day of the accident, Collins was in town. Doesn't prove much, but after speaking to Bowden, he's almost certain he's the one responsible for the accident and the kitchen house."

We'd seen the fire at the Armstrong Plantation from Livingston, but by the time Ben and Jones got there with help, the kitchen house was gone.

Nausea roiled in me. "What does Bowden intend to do?"

"That's the problem: until he recovers, there isn't much he *can* do."

"Collins can't get away with this. We have to tell the sheriff."

"And risk Bowden's wrath? I think not."

I expelled a deep breath.

"And don't you go getting yourself involved. The last thing

we need is Collins centering his vendetta on you and Whitney," he said.

"Mr. Tucker, you're not employed to lollygag. Now, back to work." The foreman smacked Knox's shoulder on the way by.

After leaving Knox, Tillie and I made our way back to the house in time for Ben's arrival.

CHAPTER
Forty-Six

AFTER MY RETURN TO LIVINGSTON, I SAT IN THE STUDY LATE ONE night, poring over my father's journal. The chatter and pattering of feet around the house had dwindled hours ago. Even the quarters had grown still. Besides the crickets and an occasional owl hoot outside, I heard only the groaning and creaking of the house.

The candles in the candelabra on the desk burned low and sputtered, threatening to immerse me in darkness. I shut the book and lifted a fist to stifle a yawn. The comfort of my bed called to me, but I picked up my mother's ledger and opened it.

Names and locations of slaves she'd helped free were recorded back to a few years before her death. I envisioned my mother hunched over this very desk. I could imagine the tautness in her shoulders and neck as she moved the quill across the pages and inscribed the freedom seekers' details in the ledger.

Page after page I read, trying to burn each and every name and location into my memory until the writing all became a blur of letters and numbers.

Just one more page. I pushed on, scrolling the tip of my finger over the entries.

My tired eyes almost passed over the name.

My breathing stopped.

No.

It couldn't be.

It was impossible!

I sat up straight, shook my head, and rubbed the sleepiness from my eyes before moving the candelabra closer.

The entry read: *Mag; age 3–6; last location, ship headed for New York; year 1832.*

Goosebumps peppered my body. The roots of my hair sprang awake.

Could it be?

No.

But what if...could it be her?

My heart flipped into my stomach. I looked from the book to the painting of my mother on the wall. "Is it her?"

Is it... Tears compressed my throat. I slumped back in my chair.

Jimmy had stated Mag was around that age when she was sold. But she'd been headed to a plantation in Virginia. How could she have ended up here?

I had to tell him.

I raced from the study with the ledger clasped under my arm. Through the French doors I bounded. Gathering the sides of my skirt in my hands, I raced toward his cabin.

I beat on the door with a fist. "Jimmy! It's Willow. I must talk to you." I leaned against the stoop post, gasping and trying to catch my breath. My limbs trembled.

Shuffles and murmurs came from inside. Through the cracks of the plank door, the faint yellow hue of a candle flickered. The door creaked open, and Jimmy's sleep-laden face came alert with concern as he looked around it. "Evvything all right?"

"I must speak to you. Please meet me in the study. It's urgent."

His eyes widened, and he nodded.

I returned to the house and met Mammy in the corridor,

blinding me with the light of a lantern. Tendrils of her wooly mane peeked out from under her nightcap. "What you up to? Running 'bout in de middle of de night, making all dis racket?"

"Mammy, could I trouble you to bring some coffee to the study, right away?"

"At dis hour?" she grumbled, but she was already turning to head to the warming kitchen. She waddled down the corridor, her mutterings trailing behind her. "Dat gal's going to be de end of me."

In the study, I paced the floor with the ledger clasped in my white-knuckled grip. Jimmy arrived, his face drenched with concern. I laid the ledger on the desk and flipped pages until I came to the entry. "Look what it says." I traced my finger under the name.

Silently, he read the line my finger indicated. The anguish I'd come to recognize over the loss of his daughter saturated his face. "What are you trying to say?"

"This is the ledger containing every slave my mother helped."

Mammy returned with a tray of coffee and set it on the edge of the desk. She poured a cup for me, and I handed it to Jimmy.

"Sit," I said to him.

He obeyed, sitting on the edge of the chair in front of the desk. "But dere ain't no way of telling ef dat be my Mag." His eyes fell to a stain on his trousers.

"You're right. But this child would be the same age as your Mag, and the date is around the same time she was sold. With Mother and Father gone, I'm afraid we don't have much to go on. But the ledger says she was put on a ship to New York. I'll have my contacts focus their search for the time being in New York. My friend Ruby has helped many slaves to freedom. I know it's a bleak hope, but it's more than we had before."

A shuffling of feet in the corridor followed by a cough alerted me of Ben's approach. He appeared in the doorway dressed in his nightclothes, his eyes heavy with sleep, his blond hair tousled. "A staff meeting in the middle of the night?" he said with a yawn.

"Come in. Maybe she mentioned something to you."

His eyes widened. "Who?"

I picked up the ledger and carried it to him.

"Gal has done gone and lost her mind." Mammy handed Ben a coffee.

He took a sip and squinted at the ledger I held up.

"This child—do you know anything about her? Did Mother ever mention her?"

"I remember her, all right. Your mother almost got herself and the child killed, along with you."

My heart pounded harder. "Me?"

Jimmy rose to his feet and crept to my side.

"Olivia found the child hiding on the plantation. Somehow, she'd escaped the slave traders. By the time Olivia found the child, the dogs had picked up the child's scent. Your mother panicked and headed straight for the swamps. She knew it was their best bet at shaking them off their trail.

"Your mother was due with you any week. But as she often did, she acted with her heart and didn't stop to think what it could mean for the three of you. I wanted to take her over my knee and spank her myself for her carelessness. However, she used her wit and escaped the traders. The next morning, I ran into her as she and the child were doubling back." His forehead creased as he tried to recall the day.

"What else do you know of the child? Did she tell you anything?" I pulled on his arm and sloshed the coffee in his cup.

"I never got to speak to her much. We disguised her as a boy. I rode into town and put her on a ship headed for New York."

"On our ships?"

"Yes, but it was back when Charles wasn't involved in Olivia's efforts, and before their ships employed the crew we do now. Unfortunately, the child was hidden on board the vessel by a dockworker Olivia knew, and we were forced to send the girl on her own. I held out hope that she'd outsmarted the traders, and just maybe she'd be able to sneak around for food and keep hidden for the most part."

"Is there anything else? Did the child say anything to Mother? Like where she came from? Her parents? Anything?"

"Slow down." Ben put up a hand. "Why do you want to know so much about this child?"

"I've reason to believe she may be Jimmy's daughter."

Ben glanced at Jimmy with round eyes. "Father…wait a minute. Olivia did say the child said her papa had been sold. Didn't say anything about her mother. Let me think." He circled the room, still carrying his coffee. "Virginia. Her father was sold to a plantation in Virginia. No, it was her. She was to be sold to a plantation in Virginia." He whirled around.

"Mag…" A groan escaped from Jimmy. He stumbled forward.

I grabbed for him. Ben set his coffee down and hurried to help. "Help me get him to the chair," I said, looking over Jimmy's head into Ben's eyes.

Jimmy's body trembled, and a whimper came from deep within him as we lowered him into the chair. Kneeling in front of him, I clasped his hands in mine. A tear shed from his eye splattered on my hands and trickled between my fingers.

"She escaped." I tried to soothe him. "Ben got her on a ship. There's a chance Mag is alive and living in New York or somewhere in the North."

He shook his head. "Stop."

"But it has to be her. You said she was a clever girl. If she managed to outsmart the traders and make it to Livingston, then I know she got to New York safely."

"No!" His voice rose before falling to an empty, pain-filled moan. "Please...don't. My gal's gone. I know your heart is good...but I can't take dis." He pushed to his feet and wove by me to the door.

His footsteps were light and almost soundless as he walked down the hall. The click of the door closing behind him shattered me.

I'd hurt him. Placed a branding iron on his soul. Never would he look at me the same way again.

Never.

CHAPTER
Forty-Seven

S LEEP NEVER CAME TO ME THAT NIGHT. BEN HAD TRIED TO console me, but it only made my tears come harder. He'd left my room, and soon the floorboards in the hallway groaned with Mammy's weighted steps. She'd sat on my bed with her head resting against the headboard until I'd fallen asleep, as she'd often done when I was a child.

The next morning I woke later than usual, and after dressing for the day, I sat at the stationary desk in my room and scripted a letter to William Still, updating him on the new information before I began writing a second letter to Ruby.

Charleston, January 1853

My dearest friend,

I'm writing to ask your and Kipling's assistance in locating a slave child that I have reason to believe may have passed through New York. She was placed on the vessel Olivia I in Charleston in the year of '32, heading to New York.

She would have been four to five years old when she escaped. Her given name was Mag. I know I'm grasping with so few facts, but if you could aid me in any way, I'd be forever in your debt.

I look forward to your upcoming visit.

Your friend,

Willow

I slipped the letter into an envelope and sealed it with our family crest. I'd see to it the letter was on the afternoon train. It was urgent that the message reach Ruby. Jimmy would never forgive me, but I couldn't let the discovery of Mag's passing through Livingston rest, and I'd keep my continued search a secret.

"Tillie, please go to the stables and have a carriage readied. I'm going to town."

"Yessum." She curtsied and left the room.

She'd no sooner left before Whitney sailed into the room and plopped down on the edge of my bed. "I've been thinking…"

"Why does that scare me." I rose to my feet.

She scrunched up her face. "You said that Silas came to Bowden's aid, right?"

"Yes."

"And he was offering his comfort to you in your distress?"

"What are you getting at?"

"Silas just happens to be on the road to rescue Bowden. Then he's there for you to fall into his arms. It's all so convenient, don't you think?"

"Are you suggesting that Silas is responsible for the accident?"

"That's exactly what I'm suggesting. He planned it all out. So that you would be in town and he could be the hero in all of this when he's the reason for it."

"Honestly, Whitney, listen to yourself. There's no possible way Silas could know I was in town. Besides, Knox said Bowden believes Collins is responsible. I told you this."

Whitney hit the bed with the palm of her hand. "I know what you told me. You all are missing what's right in front of your faces. I know you're overwhelmed with everything that's been going on, but wake up before it's too late."

The earnestness in her eyes caused me to consider the possibility. "But why? What would be Silas's motive in harming Bowden?"

"Because there's one person that stands between Silas winning you for himself and that's Bowden."

"I can't do this." I rubbed a hand over my face. The pain behind my eyes increased with every word she spoke.

"You're smarter than most but you are blinded to who Silas Anderson really is. I hope you realize it before it's too late." She stood, ran her hands over the bodice of her blouse, and left without another word.

I sighed, disheartened. Was I blind? Had I missed something? Whitney had openly expressed her dislike for Anderson on multiple occasions, and Bowden hadn't been overly fond of him either. I'd believed it was because he might be jealous. Had I not felt the same threat over Miss O'Brien at the Christmas ball? Whitney didn't like many people, and her instant dislike of Anderson was evident from our first encounter months ago.

"Pete's bringing de carriage 'round straightaway." Tillie stood in the doorway grasping her side as if she had a stitch, trying to catch her breath.

"Ready yourself for town and meet me downstairs."

Outside, Ben mounted the steps as I was descending. He looked from me to the holster belted on my waist. "And where do you think you are going?"

"Town. If you think you're going to stop me, I'll save you the trouble. I'd suggest you come with us if that is your intent."

"I see why Charles's temples pulsated with the very mention of your name. You, my darling, are your mother's daughter for sure."

"Meaning we won't be pushed around?"

"Precisely."

"Does it offend you?" I arched a brow in defiance.

"On the contrary. It was the one thing I admired about your mother. And it was what got her killed," he said. "I can't stop you any more then I could her. But if you think I'll allow you to run around the countryside, unprotected and equipped as if you're a hardened criminal, you're mistaken."

My mouth twisted and I bit the corner of my mouth to hold back the words I wanted to unleash on him. "Understood," I pushed out.

"Good morning, Miss Hendricks." The driver bowed with a hand placed on his waistline.

I grumbled a reply and climbed into the carriage.

CHAPTER
Forty-Eight

Kipling

"PAPERS FOR THE SLAVE." THE CHARLESTON HARBORMASTER held out his hand.

I removed the documents from my pocketbook.

Taking the papers, the harbormaster eyed Ruby suspiciously over his spectacles. Ruby hung back, holding our satchels with her head bowed.

"Looks like the rain is coming," I said to the man.

He grunted as he scanned the documents. Not the friendly sort. I held my breath.

"How long will you and your manservant be in town?" the man asked.

"Until the end of the month."

"What brings you to Charleston?"

"Here to help my sister's husband. He's taken a fall from his horse and needs help managing his plantation."

"Got no overseer?" He laid questioning gray eyes on me.

I rolled back my shoulders. "He does. You see, they aren't rich folk and can only offer the man employment a few days a week. Surely you can understand the hardship of putting meat on the table," I said.

"What makes you think I'd know?"

"A harbormaster can't make that good of coin, can he?"

His gaze hardened. My pulse geared up a notch.

"Times are hard." He folded the papers and handed them back to me. "Next," he said and waved for me to move on.

I could feel Ruby's breath on my neck as we hurried along the dock.

"I'll hire a carriage, and we'll be on our way to Livingston," I said. A raindrop hit the brim of my top hat.

As we'd drawn closer to Charleston, Ruby's jitters grew. It wasn't the first time she'd been disguised to suit a purpose. Her quietness had puzzled me. When questioned on it, she'd said it was the worry of being found out that troubled her. Traveling unaccompanied with a woman was one thing, but with a colored woman would bring unwanted scrutiny. A master flaunting his bedmate around respectable, civilized folks was unacceptable. Sexual acts done behind closed doors were between the master and his property. Beautiful mulatto and colored women went for top dollar at the market. More than a skilled slave.

The immoral ways of these men turned my stomach. They hid behind the spoken word and sinned without shame or remorse. All because they didn't see the Negroes as human. People didn't treat their livestock as poorly as they did the blacks. In the North, it was no different. Chains might not hang around the coloreds' necks and ankles, but they were disregarded and treated as less than the whites. The Irish and blacks congested the Five Points. Ruby's and my work in the slums gave us a perspective most chose to turn a blind eye to.

The oppression and discrimination placed upon one for being different drove my passion, and I'd aligned my voice with many across the country.

By the time we left Charleston behind and the countryside came into view, the skies had let go.

I regarded Ruby where she sat across from me. "The threat

of discovery has passed. Yet your smile has not returned. Are you not happy to be seeing Willow and Whitney again?"

"Yes. Quite." She stopped picking at the edge of the windowpane with the tip of her gloved finger.

"Then why the solemn demeanor?"

She smiled brightly, for my sake; the smile never left her mouth.

I'd never understood women and had given up trying. I smiled back at her, acting as though I believed the show she was putting on. Resting my head back against the seat, I closed my eyes.

The crackling of paper told me Ruby had withdrawn the paper I'd caught her reading more than once; each time she'd shove it in her pocketbook whenever I drew near. How many weeks had I wondered what was written on the paper that captivated her every thought? I'd lost track.

Ruby might be preoccupied with whatever went on in women's heads, but I for one was thrilled to be able to catch up with Willow and Whitney and meet Willow's uncle. The thought of Willow made my heart race. Some days I caught myself daydreaming about what our lives might've been like if she'd been open to our fathers' proposal. Then I told myself it would never have happened. Willow had a mind of her own. No one could tell her otherwise. I smiled to myself as I recalled the day she'd stormed out of the house after her father had revealed his intention of joining our hands in matrimony.

God, she was beautiful, even when she was mad. Yet it was Willow's heart that held the beauty I admired most. Within her burned passion. I suppose I'd loved her from that moment. Perhaps I always would. But I'd learned if I wanted to be part of her life, friendship was all that would ever be between us. With that understanding, I'd convinced myself I was content.

When we pulled into Livingston, I peeked out the gap between the curtain and the window. Raindrops trailed down the glass. My heart ached as I caught sight of Willow standing on the front veranda. Her hair was flattened by the rain and cupped her face. She'd wrapped her arms around her torso to ward off the chill. I thought of opening my coat and her walking into my arms and finding warmth in my embrace...

"Sir," the driver said.

Lost in the fantasy, I'd not noticed him open the door. I glanced at Ruby and saw sadness mixed with worry. Confused by the emotional battle she seemed to be in, I opened my mouth to inquire about the turmoil, then reconsidered and stepped out.

❧ CHAPTER ❧
Forty-Nine

Willow

FEBRUARY BROUGHT WITH IT THE BLOOMING OF MAGNOLIAS AND the budding of pink, white, and red camellias. The plantation sprang to life, renewed in glorious colors and beauty far more stunning than the greatest artist's painting.

The day of Ruby and Kip's arrival, the heavens mocked me with heavy rain clouds. I'd stewed with displeasure before setting out to finish last minute touches. I'd wanted everything to be perfect. To lavish Ruby with Southern hospitality and provide her with a refreshing view of the South. Show her there was beauty and good beyond the bad.

In preparing for Ruby's arrival, I found a distraction from Bowden's rejection and the guilt I felt over inflicting pain on Jimmy. A pain I intended to make right. Some way. Somehow, I'd do right by him.

Kip's family refused to allow a colored to stay in their home and I'd been more than happy for Ruby to spend her time at Livingston. Despite my feelings on the matter, I'd prepared the marriage cabin in the quarters for her arrival. I couldn't take the chance of wagging tongues by putting her in the house. Putting her in the cabin had caused enough trouble in the quarters. Tillie had reported coming back from the river on washing day and overhearing one woman claim, "She's colored. 'Cause she's a freed woman don't make her no better dan de rest of us. My man's coming in two weeks' time and I'd hoped to ask de missus for de cabin."

No matter how hard I tried, I couldn't please them all. I heaved a sigh.

Mary Grace, who'd been enthralled with Ruby since our trip to New York, had been chattering all morning while we cleaned the cabin. The lull of her humming was the only thing that'd kept me from sitting down and weeping.

The hearth now gleamed after being raked, swept, and oiled. Wood was stacked neatly in the corner. Shelves were organized, and the floor scrubbed. The window sparkled like new glass. A hooked rug lay on the floor in front of an oak rocker. I glanced around the cabin before going to the small wooden table by the stone fireplace and adjusting the glass vase of pink and mauve wildflowers.

"How many times are you going to rearrange that vase?" Mary Grace laughed. She stood fluffing the recently stuffed straw-tick mattress on the bed in the corner. Against the wall sat my mother's vanity I had brought down from the house.

Dread had chased me for weeks about telling Ruby that she'd have to sleep in the quarters during her stay.

The door burst open. Jack strode in, blinking the rain from his glee-filled eyes. "They're coming."

With the threat of a storm, Whitney had confined him to the house, and he'd been none too happy about it. Sourly, for most of the morning, he'd sat at the window in the parlor that had the best view of the lane leading up to the plantation.

I looked around the small one-room cabin. It would have to do.

"No need to fret. Miss Ruby will understand." Mary Grace tugged on my hand and smiled knowingly.

Grasping at the belief and understanding in her eyes, I headed for the door.

"You best put this on to save your hair." Mary Grace handed me my shawl.

I smoothed back the hair escaping my pins and combs. Then I shook my skirt to expel the dust and took one last look around. Everything was in order. Surely my guests would excuse the appearance of their hostess. "A little rain won't hurt anyone," I said with a hopeful smile. *Besides, could I look any worse?*

"That ain't what ya'll been saying all day!" Jack said.

"That *isn't*, Masa Jack," Mary Grace corrected, steering him toward the door.

"Ain't. Isn't. It's all the same," he muttered, allowing Mary Grace to lead him.

Mary Grace opened the door. She removed her shawl and covered her and Jack's heads as they ran for the house.

At the front of the house, Mary Grace hustled Jack inside as the closed carriage pulled to a stop. Drenched and chilled, I sought cover on the veranda.

The driver jumped down, popped up an umbrella, then strode over and opened the door. A top hat poked out. Then my heart swelled with happiness at the sight of Kip's face. Kip spotted me and smiled, stepping down. I waved and rose on tiptoe, trying to look past him for Ruby.

The driver stood holding the umbrella over Kip. A movement behind him brought a smile to my lips, but it slipped as a colored man stepped out and closed the door behind him. My heart dropped with disappointment. Had Ruby forgone the trip?

Kip splashed through the puddles as he hurried to find cover on the veranda. The driver ran to keep up with him, followed by the colored man.

A man from the quarters came and took the driver and

horses around back.

"What happened? Where's Ruby?" I said, unable to hide my disappointment.

"I give you Jacob," Kip sidestepped and the colored man removed his hat and bowed graciously.

"It's a pleasure," I said to the man, and eyed Kip. "That's all well and good. Now, answer my question. Was she ill?"

Kip tipped back his head and laughed. His amusement was completely lost on me.

Mary Grace and Tillie stepped out onto the veranda. "Mary Grace, please see to it that our guest is fed and made comfortable until Kip is ready to leave," I said to her.

"Sending me on my way already?"

"I thought you'd want to get to your sister's place before nightfall. I haven't prepared the guesthouse," I said as Mary Grace led the man away.

"It'll do for one night."

"My uncle's home, so I suppose it'll be all right," I said. "Tillie, please have the guesthouse freshened up." Tillie curtsied and left.

Kip dipped his head respectfully. "Much appreciated."

I smiled. "Then welcome to Livingston. I hope your journey wasn't too tedious."

"The view at the end of the journey will always be worth it," Kip said with a wink, offering me an elbow.

Heat infused my face at his remark. I placed my hand in the curve of his elbow as we turned and walked inside.

∽ CHAPTER ∽
Fifty

"WELCOME, MR. KIPLING," MAMMY SAID WITH A toothy smile.

"Miss Rita, you look divine."

"Aw, hush now. Dat sweet talk may work on de young'uns, but not me." Mammy swatted a hand in the air, but as she took Kip's coat, pink tinged the tops of her cheeks.

Kip had a way of making everyone feel important, a quality I admired in him.

Whitney and the twins joined us. "Where's Ruby?" Whitney asked after the twins settled their excitement.

"Oh, Mary Grace took her around back to get cleaned up." Kip laughed as my mouth dropped open.

"But he…her disguise was so deceiving." I pushed down the foolishness I felt over not realizing the colored man was Ruby.

"We've become good at trickery. But I must say, Ruby was a saint this time. She willingly cut her hair to avoid being detected. Not a lot of women would do that," he said with admiration.

Ben made his way down the staircase.

"Kip, I'd like you to meet my uncle, Benjamin Hendricks."

Kip extended a hand. "Sir."

Pleasantries were exchanged before we moved into the parlor.

"Your niece was to be my betrothed, but she refused in the most hurtful way. I've yet to get over it." Kip placed a hand to his wounded heart.

I laughed at his reminder of my outright rage at Father's attempt at an arranged marriage.

"Kipling has been talking like a lovestruck woman about this trip for months. Nothing would stop him from coming." Ruby, clad in a simple peach skirt and ivory blouse, stood in the doorway.

"Now don't be telling Willow stories of my affections when she's already spoken for." Kip's neck above his collar reddened, and a boyish grin broke across his face.

I didn't miss the sadness that darkened Ruby's eyes, and I quickly brushed off Kip's remark. "I'm so happy you came." I crossed the room and gathered Ruby in a quick hug.

She stiffly returned my embrace.

I pulled back and did my best to hide my confusion. Was she not as happy to be here as we were to have her? "Children, please go play," I said.

"Yes, Miss Willow," they chimed and dashed from the room.

"Ruby, if you'll follow me."

"I intend to hold the child you were carrying when you were in New York," Ruby said as we passed Mary Grace in the corridor. Mary Grace beamed and nodded.

I turned to Ruby and took her hand in mine, beside myself with worry. "There's something I must speak to you about."

Ruby glanced past me to a servant as he walked by.

"I hope you'll understand, but we've set up a cabin in the quarters for your stay."

"That will be lovely," she said, clearly distracted.

"Unless you'd prefer the kitchen house?" I tried to get a reaction.

"Sure." Her eyes slid to the servant polishing the staircase.

I glanced at Whitney. She shrugged, obviously as baffled as me.

"Have I done something to displease you?" I waved a hand in front of Ruby's face.

Ruby set confused eyes on me. "What? No."

"You seem disconnected or upset," I said.

"It's just...it's..."

"What is it?" I touched her arm.

"Is there a place we can speak in private?"

"Certainly." I led her down the corridor to the study. Whitney followed. I opened the door and gestured for Ruby to enter, then followed—only to collide with her back.

Whitney tumbled into me. "What in the name of—?" she muttered in exasperation.

Ruby stood frozen. "The woman in the picture, who is she?"

I rubbed the cheek that had collided with her shoulder. "My mother." I stepped past her into the room and smiled proudly as I turned to look back at Ruby. My smile faded at the shock on her face and the building panic in her dark eyes. "Is something wrong?"

"Your mother..." Her voice fractured, her eyes never leaving the picture.

I looked from the picture to Whitney, and back to the portrait. "Olivia was her name."

"Olivia..." She rolled the name over her tongue.

"You're frightening me." My limbs tingled.

"I know her."

"That's impossible," I sputtered.

"I assure you it's not."

What was she saying? My mother was dead. Wasn't she? Had they all lied to me about that, too?

No. They wouldn't be that cruel. Would they?

"What Willow's trying to say is, her mother is dead. But you knew this already...?" Whitney's forehead furrowed.

Ruby turned to look at us, her dark skin pale. "Forgive me. I didn't mean to confuse you." She reached for the edge of the desk to steady herself.

Whitney took her by the elbow and guided her to a chair. "Sit," she ordered. She turned to me. "You too. You look ready to faint."

The vibrating in my heart made me feel like the walls were pressing in on me. I shuffled to a chair next to Ruby and sank into it.

"That's the woman," Ruby said. "The one in my vision. Her eyes are...your eyes." Her eyes wide, she glanced at the portrait, then back to me. "As sure as I'm here now, she's indeed the woman."

She's mistaken. It isn't so.

"When I received your letter, I'd dared hope, but the impossibility of it all gave me cause to doubt."

"Stop." I held up a hand. My heart thumped in the base of my throat. "You're talking in riddles. What are you saying?"

"I believe...I believe I'm Mag."

She became a tiny speckle in my vision and as she continued to speak, her words all jumbled into one.

Mag?

Could...God be righting a wrong of the past? Or was the world playing a twisted prank on us all? The unlikelihood of it all was like capturing a star in your hand.

"Willow!" Whitney said before going to shut the study door.

I shook my head. Rubbed my hands over my face and pulled them down, staring at Ruby. "What makes you think you're the Mag I mentioned in the letter?"

"I remember the ship. I remember landing in New York. And I remember the name *Mag*. Like a whisper in the wind, it's always been there in my head."

I couldn't stop the tears that sheeted down my cheeks. Ruby's voice again became a murmur as my mind wandered. *Is it her? Could she be Mag? But what if she isn't? I can't give Jimmy false hope.* Nausea rumbled in my stomach.

"What do you know of this Mag you wrote about?" Ruby asked.

"My mother found the child hiding on the plantation. She'd escaped the slave traders. They'd hidden in the swamps until Mother thought it was safe. Then they doubled back, and Ben disguised the child as a boy and put her on a ship to New York. You see, we don't even know if Mag reached New York."

"Why are you so insistent on finding this child?" Ruby asked.

"Because...because I believe her to be the child of someone very dear to me."

Ruby's back straightened, and her eyes sharpened with yearning. "Who is this person?" She swallowed hard.

"His name is Jimmy. He's a blacksmith here at Livingston."

"James," Whitney corrected. "His given name is James. His wife's name was Nellie."

"Do you recognize the names?" I asked.

"No," Ruby said. Her face fell. "I'd hoped...I..."

"We all did," I said, releasing a deep breath.

"Perhaps I can meet your blacksmith."

"No!" I gasped, and my eyes flew to her face.

Her eyes grew round, and her lips parted at my outburst.

I hurried to explain. "When I told Jimmy about the name in the ledger and Ben revealed the details of the child, Jimmy was distraught. Told me never to speak of her again."

"Yet you continue to search for her?"

"Yes."

"But why?"

"Because I can't give up. If you could only see the ache in his eyes. Losing her broke him."

"You care for the blacksmith."

"Like a father." For the first time, I spoke the feelings in my heart.

Dangerous words. Words that were my truth. Feelings that could bring harm to Jimmy and me both.

"He must be quite a man, to bring on such feelings."

"He's extraordinary. Wise. Intelligent. Good at whatever he puts his hands to. He's been there for me through many dark times in my life. Guided me…and, I like to believe, loved me."

"Will you introduce me to this man?"

"If you promise not to mention my letter. We must also be certain you are Mag. I can't risk breaking his heart again."

"Understood."

"Very well, then. Let us show you to your quarters," I said.

🙠 CHAPTER 🙢
Fifty-One

OVER THE NEXT DAYS, RUBY MINGLED WITH THE FOLKS IN THE quarters. Some welcomed her into their cabins, and others stood back and scrutinized the Northern freed black in her fancy clothes with her educated speech.

Ruby, if aware of their rebuff, hadn't allowed it to deter her from helping them. I'd stood back, mesmerized by the way she handled and soothed a sick child. She'd moved from cabin to cabin, gracing people with her time and kindness, playing nursemaid to those who needed tending. She radiated beauty far greater than the beauty one sees at first glance. Kimie became her shadow, and Ruby devoted her time to teaching her the skills she'd learned from years of helping the sick in the slums.

Nights for Ruby were spent sitting with the folk and listening to their stories. I yearned to sit amongst them and shed the burden of being the Lady of Livingston. From my window, I'd watched them gathered around the fire and imagined them sharing with her the memories of their lives before coming to Livingston. I wanted to feel their pain and rejoice in the pretense of happiness they projected. For it didn't matter how I tried to make life better for the people of the quarters, they could never be happy in a life where free will didn't exist.

One day, from the doorway of the forge, I watched Ruby coming back from the river on washing day. She fit in where I'd never belonged amongst the people I'd loved since I was a little girl; where my heart pulled me, but society would never permit me.

"Dat one be quite a woman," Jimmy said, coming to stand beside me. He wiped his hands on his heavy apron, looking out over the grounds.

I shifted my gaze to Ruby as she and the washing women strolled past the forge. Her mouth moved with the words of the black spiritual the women were singing. I envied her.

"Bin helping in de quarters evvy day since she came here."

I snuck a sideways glance at Jimmy. Admiration shone in his face as his eyes followed her across the yard. Fear gripped my chest. What if she was Mag? Would she replace me in his heart?

"What's dat luk on your purty face, Miss Willie?"

"What look?"

"Lak you done gone and lost somepin'."

Had I?

I searched his face. He'd spoken, yet his eyes were glued to Ruby's retreating back. He wasn't waiting for my reply. The admiration had slipped away, replaced by a look of puzzlement.

"Have you spoken to Miss Ruby?" I asked.

He didn't answer. He lifted a hand to scratch his head as the line between his brows deepened. "Dat girl never bin here before?"

"No. Why?"

"Ain't nothing." He turned away.

"Are you certain of that?"

"Et's jus' somepin' 'bout her makes me think I've seen her before."

My breath hitched.

I glanced at Ruby as she bent to retrieve a linen from the basket to hang on the line. If she was Mag, I could never keep her from him. But how did I tell him that the very girl he was marveling at might be his daughter? And if I did, where did that leave me?

Stop. Willow Hendricks, you are a selfish, horrible person.

Heat flushed my cheeks and I dropped my eyes to the piece of straw I'd been fraying with my fingernail. Emotions swelled my throat. Losing him would be the end of me. Could he find room in his heart for the both of us if, in fact, Ruby was his daughter? I squeezed my eyes shut to cut off the tears crowding the corners of my eyes.

"Miss Willie, you all right?"

I opened my eyes to find him regarding me with concern. My lip trembled. "Yes."

"You don't luk fine."

"There's something I want to say, but I don't know how—"

"Willow!" Whitney's call turned our heads.

Whitney stood on the back veranda, summoning me with her hand.

"I'd best go see what she needs."

"Sho' thing, Miss Willie."

I touched his arm. "I'll speak to you later." I smiled softly.

"Ol' Jimmy be here. Always." He smiled back.

You promise? I wanted to throw my arms around him and make him swear his words were true. To tell him never to leave me. Because without him…I'd wilt and die…crumble like petals to become dust in the wind. Forgotten.

Broken and uncertain, I turned and strolled toward the house.

His sweet tune drifted out of the forge, the melody that soothed my sorrows. It swirled around my heart and captured me in the warmth of his embrace.

Fly, my little angel,
spread your wings and soar

Above the trees may you find freedom,
a slave no more.

"What is et, Miss Ruby?" one of the women said.

I froze and looked in their direction.

Ruby stood unmoving, her posture stiff, the soggy linen clutched forgotten in her hands. Dazed, only her eyes moved, seeking the source of the tune.

I looked from her to the forge.

Awareness captured all my senses. I recalled Ruby's and my conversation in the café in New York. She'd said, *"It's the same visions over and over. In other dreams, a man appears to me—like the woman, always the same man. He pats my head affectionately, and his infectious laughter makes me laugh. Then when my dreams turn to nightmares, he rides in like a black knight and hums a tune that soothes all my fears."*

The infectious laughter…the black knight's tune.

My gaze returned to her.

It was her. Here in the flesh, she stood. Jimmy's Mag. We'd found her.

Happiness blotted out all my fears.

I moved toward her. "Ruby." I pulled at the linen in her trembling hand.

Her stunned eyes turned to me. "That tune—" Her voice shook.

"I know."

"It's…the tune that's haunted me." Her eyes glistened.

"Come with me." I handed the linen to a woman who stood gawking at us in confusion. I took Ruby's hand in mine and pulled her toward the forge.

"Where are we going?"

"To meet the one you've been searching for," I said.

Her steps halted, and she grabbed at my arms, her face a

mixture of fear and worry. "I don't know. I can't do this. I need more time," she pleaded.

I lifted a hand to cup her cheek. "Life has stolen enough time from you." Tears pooled in my eyes as I stood looking at the woman who'd captured Jimmy's heart from the moment of her birth; the daughter who'd always have his heart.

"I can't."

"You must."

Fear and uncertainty shone in her eyes. She glanced from me to the forge and back to me.

I slipped my arm around her waist and slowly guided her to the forge. My heart hammered. My stomach churned.

As we stepped into the forge, the desire to flee and lock Ruby away, to secure my place in Jimmy's heart, darkened my heart. I blocked out the morbid fear tainting my conscience. "Jimmy," I said quietly.

His whistling ceased as he turned to us. "Ah, Miss Willie. Somepin' I can help you wid?"

"I–I wanted you to meet Ruby." I swallowed a time or two before I said, "I believe...we think..." I looked at Ruby, and my fingers tightened on her waist. Her trembling clashed with mine. "This is Mag."

He dropped the tool he held in his hand. His face drained of color.

"I thought...we suspected she was your Mag. But we are certain of this now."

"How?" His gaze turned from me to her.

"The tune you were whistling—I remember it...it's haunted me every day of my life." Ruby's voice quivered. She glanced at me. "I remember Olivia's eyes. Her voice. The swamps. The dogs. The ship. All of it." She returned her gaze to him. "And you."

"Miss Willie, I asked...I tole you..." He turned and leaned his hands on the workbench. "Et ain't possible. My gal is daid... gone, I tell ya." Tears thickened in his voice as his shoulders slumped forward. His eyes closed and silent tears etched his cheeks.

I wanted to go to him. To offer him comfort. To tell him I loved him, and that I had done this all for him. But it was their moment. A moment between a father and his daughter. I gave Ruby a gentle nudge forward.

She moved hesitantly, casting a glance over her shoulder at me. I gave her an encouraging nod.

She stopped and stood beside him. She lifted a hand and touched his shoulder.

He stiffened.

She flinched.

Then the courage I'd known she possessed overtook any doubt of his love.

"Father..." Her soft voice was that of a little girl seeking the comfort of a parent.

He straightened, his face never lifting.

Ruby's hand rose to stroke his cheek. A gasp came from Jimmy. Deep. Painful. Raw with the agony from years of loneliness and longing for the girl that now stood before him.

"Is et you..." he said, lifting eyes to her that welled with tears.

"I am Mag."

As she said the words, all of our hearts knew she spoke the truth. She was Mag, daughter of James of Livingston Plantation.

With this realization, I slipped unnoticed from the forge and up to the house.

"What happened? What is it?" Whitney asked. She and Mammy stood in the corridor when I entered the house.

I brushed past them as the tears burst from me. I raced up the stairs without a word. A sob, followed by another and another, battered my soul. I fell onto my bed and wept.

Tears of loss, happiness, bitterness, and self-pity soaked my coverlet.

CHAPTER
Fifty-Two

WEEKS HAD COME AND GONE SINCE RUBY HAD REUNITED with her father. Her and Jimmy's joy was evident on their faces. My feelings of sadness and loss faded, for the most part. I found myself smiling as I watched their interactions. Gentle and nurturing by nature, Ruby would engage with Jimmy by placing a hand on his arm, and out of social awkwardness he'd cringe from her touch, drawing tears of frustration from Ruby at what she thought was Jimmy's rejection of her. But after I and many around the plantation reassured her, Ruby began to understand the ways of her father. I found myself giving her advice on how to sneak into his guarded heart, a task that had seemed impossible at times. Jimmy wasn't an easy man, but he was a man worth loving.

As I'd discovered in my relationship with Ben, only time would form a bond between father and daughter.

"What's whisking up in that head of yours?" Ben asked as he strolled into the music room one morning.

I smiled up at him from a chair by the window. He sat down in the armchair next to me, separated by a small Victorian walnut table. He lifted the coffee urn from the silver tray and poured himself some coffee.

"Nothing, really. I was thinking about Ruby and...us."

"Us?"

"The awkwardness of realizing a complete stranger is your

father. Learning how to accept that and form a relationship at the same time."

"We are doing all right, aren't we?"

"I believe so," I said as I beheld the face of the man I loved more with each passing day. "The ease of having you in my life when I've known you scarcely a year is something I never had with Father. Though I understand why he did the things he did, I somehow feel cheated of a father."

Ben's breath caught. "Many times over the years I've questioned if we did right by you. Some days I think we failed you. If we'd done things differently, maybe your mother would be alive—"

"You mustn't torture yourself. If we could step back in time, I'm sure we'd all change a lot about our past."

He chuckled lightly. "How did you become so wise?"

"I'm a thinker." I laughed. "My mind is ten miles ahead of even me. It's rather exhausting sometimes."

"Maybe with our departure for the summer you will find time to relax your mind. However, something tells me you'll find things to keep you occupied in the North."

"Always spinning." I placed a finger to the side of my temple.

"I knew a woman who was like that." His eyes gleamed.

I smiled at him as I refilled my coffee. "So I keep hearing."

"She'd have found your ways amusing."

"You think?" My hands swaddled the warmth of my cup.

"Certain as my next breath." He crossed a leg and set tender eyes on me.

His words were like an embrace to my soul. Since he'd become part of my life, he'd tried to etch his memories of my mother into my mind.

"I noticed on rounds of the plantation there was a new grave in the cemetery, but I was unaware of anyone's death; nor did I recognize the name of the person scratched into the cross marking the grave," he said.

"With all the craziness lately, I forgot to mention it. I had the grave dug, and the ledgers buried."

He straightened in his seat. "I thought we agreed on destroying them."

"Those journals are the reason Ruby was reunited with her father. Think about the others we could help. No one would go looking in a slave cemetery for anything of value. Therefore, the ledgers are safe."

He considered my words for a moment before a smile broke across his face. "If you were a man, you would be dangerous."

"And as a woman, I'm not?" I said, tipping my nose up while a grin crept over my face.

"Noted." He chuckled.

"I'll be in the fields for most of the day," he added. "If we intend to have the ground turned to start sowing the cotton seed mid-March, it needs to be finished by the end of the week."

"Is that doable?"

"Jones and the men believe so."

"Look at you, becoming a planter," I said with amusement.

He stood. "Not my choice of work, but we do what needs done, don't we?"

"I suppose so."

"I'll see you this evening," he said.

"You won't be back for dinner?"

"No time." He turned to walk away, but turned back. "I've noticed Knox visiting Whitney; any mention of how Bowden is faring?"

"Physically, he's recovering, but Knox says he's angry. I guess Bowden paid Collins's folks a visit. His parents said he wasn't living there. When asked where he was, they said they were unsure of his whereabouts. Said he informed them he'd taken on another job close by but left out the details."

"That's a bit bizarre, isn't it?"

"I thought so."

"And what's the sheriff doing about Bowden's accident?"

"Nothing more than what we already knew. Said that troubles outside the town of Charleston are the problems of the constable and the country folk to handle. But he went on to say Bowden's suspicions aren't just cause to accuse the man. Knox says Bowden isn't holding out any hope of getting justice on the matter."

The sheriff and his few deputies were stretched thin, handling the law in town and the demands of the citizens that the masked men be found. And law officials outside of Charleston were scarce. In our rural area, Mr. Sterling was an appointed constable and the country folk, vigilante groups, and posses were often left to apprehend those guilty of a crime. Advertisements had been put into local newspapers by the law and citizens asking for the assistance of the vigilante committees in finding the men guilty of larceny.

"Unbelievable. Who has to end up dead in order to get justice?" Ben said.

I let out a heavy sigh. "On another matter, Anderson came by the other day."

"Oh? And what did he want?"

"You're never going to believe this. When I told Whitney, she spat her mouthful of food across the table and splattered poor Kimie."

"Indulge me."

"He asked if I'd be fine with him asking your permission to court me." Heat brushed my cheeks as I recalled the discomfort of the moment.

"Really? That's interesting."

"How so?"

"Surely he's aware of your and Bowden's affections?"

"I believe so. Bowden made it quite clear at the Christmas banquet."

A groove formed between his brows and his jaw tightened. "I'll see you tonight."

After he was gone, I gathered the tray and headed to the warming kitchen. Inside, I found Tillie washing the morning dishes.

"Just the person I wanted to see. I've got a question for you."

She continued scrubbing the plate in the basin of water. "What is et, Missus?"

"When you were at the Anderson farm, did you ever get the feeling that Mr. Anderson may not be who he appears to be?"

Her hands stopped moving. "What you mean?"

"He came here the other day and asked me about approaching my uncle with a proposal to court me—"

"No, Missus!" she blurted.

"No, what?" Her bold response gave me pause.

"You can't court Mr. Anderson."

"Why?"

Her hands scrubbed fiercely. Water splashed on the counter. "You can't consider him. Mr. Bowden be better dan dat man."

"But you said you never noticed anything out of the ordinary while you were there."

"But in the quarters—"

"Empty quarters and his late-night visitor are no cause to think he's unfit as a suitor."

"I jus' got a feelin'…"

"You and Whitney both," I said in exasperation. Not that I'd consider Anderson's request of courtship, but a niggling at the back of my mind had troubled me since he'd made his thoughts known.

"Maybe you bes' listen to Miss Whitney dis time."

I left the kitchen, but not before the swinging door revealed Tillie's soft-spoken thought. "Ain't good at all."

Were they all right? If so, what was Anderson's motive?

CHAPTER
Fifty-Three

Plantation down the Way

THE ONSET OF LABOR PAINS STARTED LATE IN THE EVENING AFTER the young woman's parents had retired to their chamber. Hours had passed, and her handmaid's snoring came from her pallet in the corner. The woman buried her face in the linens and gripped them between her teeth to muffle her cries as the pain intensified.

God, please help me, she silently prayed. But she knew He wouldn't hear her prayers. God didn't condone wickedness. She was certain a hard birth would be her punishment.

A gush of wetness soaked her linens, and she trembled with the realization that had plagued her body all day. The baby was coming, and nothing could stop it. Rachel from the quarters had said, "When you feel lak your bladder let loose, you run lak de devil is after you."

Throwing back the covers, she grabbed her red silk shawl that lay on the window seat and covered her blond locks. Another pain came, and she rested her forehead against the post of her bed.

The woman made her way to the back stairs. Each step seemed to creak under her weight, and she winced with apprehension. If her secret were found out, her pa would see to it that Jethro never saw another day.

In the darkness she crept toward the parlor, thankful for the dim light of the moon shining through the windowpanes. She threaded around the furniture until she reached the back door. From there she hurried toward the slave quarters.

She paused a few yards from the house as the pain surged through her again. "Sweet Jesus, please don't leave me," she whispered. She picked up her pace in hopes of reaching Rachel's family's shack before the next birthing pain hit.

At the door, she knocked, and when no one called out, she pounded louder. She searched for intruding eyes over her shoulder.

"I'm coming," a sleep-thickened voice mumbled from inside. The door swung open, and a skinny slave girl poked her head out. "Missus, what you doing here—"

"It's time, Rachel." The woman leaned against the stoop post as a groan escaped her trembling lips.

"Oh, Lard have mussy. Git in here 'fore someone sees you." Rachel pulled the woman inside.

Inside the shack, the family stirred as the master's daughter entered. "Pa, go git Jethro. De babe is coming." Rachel's father left for the big house.

Once the door closed behind him, Rachel turned panicky eyes on her ma. "Heat some water."

Rachel showed the woman to the bed. "Don't fret. We'll do as planned and no one will find out."

The woman's next birth pain hit. She rolled and hit the straw mattress with her fist. Tears streamed down her plump face. The pain left her gasping as it passed. She flopped onto her back.

Her weight gain had camouflaged her pregnancy. She'd feigned an interest in cooking. Much to her mother's distress, she'd developed an appetite and sampled dishes until she thought her insides would burst. It had been the only way she'd known how to hide the circumference of her middle.

One day her father had rubbed his rotund stomach at her mother's nagging. "Leave the girl be. She can't help it that she's inherited my structure. Besides, the women in my family are known for their healthy appetites."

Her mother had huffed and gone on about her daughter's refusal to wear a corset.

"It cuts into me," she told her mother. "Besides, not all women wear them."

Her mother had almost discovered her secret a few months ago when she barged into her room. Only quickly dashing behind the privacy screen had saved her. After that she'd told her mother she was too old for her to come into her room unannounced.

The day her handmaid became aware of the hardness forming under the fat expanding the woman's middle, fear had gripped the woman. "You must never tell!" Her teeth clenched. "Or I'll see to it you're sold so far away from your children you'll wish you had kept quiet." A reality all too likely.

Her handmaid had said in a fear-infused voice, "I promise, Missus. I ain't gonna tell nobody." And she'd kept her promise.

Now the woman lay bursting with child. The child eagerly tore at her insides, demanding to be set free into a world the woman worried would not accept the child because of the Negro blood that would run in its veins. Though desperate to get the child out of her, she couldn't bear the thought of giving up the baby. Jethro had never revealed the details of his plan to save their child. He'd said he was taking the child to someone who'd care for the baby. But to who, she'd never know. Maybe…it was for the best.

"You lay back, Missus, and no matter how much you want to scream, don't." Rachel gently pushed the woman back against the mattress.

The door burst open, and a man of color darkened the doorway. Rachel's pa stood in the man's shadow.

"Jethro!" The woman held out a hand, and the man went to her and awkwardly knelt by the bed. He placed a tender hand to her forehead. "I can't…I don't know if I can give the baby up."

"If the babe is to survive, we must do this." His voice quivered.

"We can hide it. Here in the quarters!" Tears cascaded down her cheeks.

"We already talked about this. The master—"

The pain came again.

"Ma, you get me some clean cloth. Pa, you go now, so de missus has some decency when dis is all over," Rachel said and, without waiting, she pushed up the woman's white cotton nightgown.

"Dis right here is de end of us. Ef de masa finds out, we all be whipped until our flesh lays raw," Rachel's ma said as she went to get the fresh cloths and her pa left the shack.

"You need to hush dat grumbling ef you expect me to take care of dis gal," Rachel said.

Her mother returned with the cloths.

"Wipe her brow." Rachel gave instructions to Jethro before she twisted a cloth into a tight rope and placed it in the woman's mouth. "You bear down on dis ef you feel de need to scream."

The woman's eyes were large and her vision blurred with pain.

During the night, a squalling, red-faced newborn informed the world he'd arrived.

"Et's a boy. A beautiful, healthy boy." Rachel grinned, mopping the birth from her nephew.

The new mother sank into the bed. Her eyes squeezed shut

as tears soaked her sweat-speckled face. Jethro kissed her cheeks and pushed back the wet hair framing her face.

"Let me see my son." She held out shaking arms.

Rachel stared at her, hesitant. "You got to be careful. You can't go gitting attached to de boy."

"I know," she said, her voice tattered.

Rachel placed the infant in his mother's arms. "He's a real fine boy, Miss Josephine. A real fine boy."

Blinded by tears, Josephine became engrossed in her son. Small. Helpless. Innocent. She lightly brushed his head of tight, damp curls. Alert and silent, he squinted up at his mother as if studying her. "He's perfect. I shall call him Samuel after the prophet. May the Lord not take out our sins on our son." Fear and remorse engulfed her as she looked at Jethro.

For a few precious moments, they celebrated the life they'd created with their love. A forbidden love. An act that was sinful before God and society. All too soon, the realization of what they had to do replaced their happiness.

"I must take him before the sun comes up." Jethro reached for the baby. A moan escaped Josephine as he pried the boy from her fingers.

She couldn't do this. Her heart shattered. She knew she'd never love another child like she did Samuel. Her heart would never heal from the longing for him. In the reality life was forcing her to face, she glimpsed the pain and suffering the Negroes had endured. And in this realization, she felt great, unbearable shame.

Jethro headed for the door. "Wait! Wrap him in this." She held out her shawl.

Jethro returned to the side of the bed.

The invisible fingers around her throat squeezed the air from her lungs. She planted a tender kiss on her son's head. With her thumb she stroked his cheek and whispered, "May God bring you to my arms once more." Broken and exhausted, she fell back against the bed and turned her head to face the plank wall. "Go now before I change my mind."

The door opened, and Jethro fled with his son into the night.

With the baby clenched against his chest, Jethro bounded through the woods toward the Livingston Plantation, leaping over fallen trees and bushes. The pounding of his heart blocked out the mewling of the infant. Within hours the sun would rise, and he'd be missed as the slaves set out to perform their daily tasks.

On his trips running errands for his master, he'd memorized the path he'd take when his child arrived. Keeping a mulatto child at the plantation would mean death. Josephine's pa didn't bed the slave women, and he'd spare nothing and no one to figure out who the baby belonged to. Slaves were to be registered with the town of Charleston and tagged. But some masters avoided registering their slaves to evade paying taxes. Mr. Abbotts was not that sort of man. He wanted every slave's tag number recorded in his books and the town's files. If the master found out the child was his daughter's, he'd have the infant sold off or drowned in the river. He would not allow the shame of his unwed daughter giving him a grandson by a slave.

If the child stood a chance at life, it was at the Hendricks woman's plantation. Jethro had never met Miss Hendricks himself, but his mama said the woman's father had helped a slave or two in his time. Word was the Hendricks man was dead. Jethro had overheard the master and his friends talking about the Guardian, and how the planters in Charleston County were assembling in homes, deciding what was to be done if they could catch the man.

A while back Jethro had been hired out to Mr. Anderson, and he'd crossed through the woods near the Livingston Plantation just before dawn. At the sound of the hounds, he'd crouched low in the weeds along the riverbank. He had seen it all. The Hendricks woman running with the child, followed by another white woman. Then the Hendricks man exited the house dragging an ailing slave. He'd watched as Livingston's slaves stumbled from their shacks and spread out across the work yard. The white women, along with another man, boarded a riverboat with the slave and the child and hid them under the tarps before pushing off down the river.

They'd barely pushed off before some white men, one he recognized as Mr. Carter, arrived at the plantation and chatted with Mr. Hendricks. Soon after, Mr. Hendricks mounted a horse and rode off with the hunting party.

He'd kept the Hendrickses' secret, but in doing so, he'd contrived a plan. A plan to save his child from an inevitable fate.

As the plantation came into view, he paused and leaned back against a tree to catch his breath. He peeked at his son, who wailed with displeasure at the jostling of their escape and his hunger.

"Shh, little one. We're almost there," he soothed, caressing his son's cheek with the back of his long finger.

When the infant's cries had quieted, he examined the grounds. The plantation was still. He moved with haste across the backyard to the front steps. His eyes roved the vicinity as he mounted the steps. In front of the double doors, he knelt and laid his son on the veranda.

"They will take care of you here. It's a good place for boys like you," he said, swallowing back tears. He patted the silk shawl and rose to his feet.

Then he heard her move. His eyes darted to the rocker and the Hendricks woman sitting there. Fear yanked at his heart. He turned, and his bare feet thrashed down the steps.

"Wait, don't go!" she called after him.

Only when he reached the woods did he glance back. He saw the woman bend and lift his son. Her gaze turned to the woods. She stood unmoving, as if pondering what to do, and then her hand grasped the door handle, and she vanished inside.

Jethro tilted his head to look at the sun that spilled across the sky. A warning: morning was upon him.

If you are up there, watch over my boy, he prayed through the tears burning his eyes.

He reeled and raced toward the Abbotts Plantation.

CHAPTER
Fifty-Four

Willow

I WIGGLED MY ARMS INTO A DRESSING ROBE AND TIED THE ROPE ABOUT my waist before wandering downstairs. The early hours of the morning while the plantation still slept were when I cleared my mind. They had become my favorite hours of the day.

In the warming kitchen, I found day-old biscuits and slathered one with freshly churned butter and cherry preserves. With the biscuit in hand, I opened the front door and sauntered outside.

Sinking into a rocker, I curled my legs up under me. In the distance, the sun was awakening. The master of the skies parted the darkness, brushing strokes of bright orange and red across the sky with His promise of a new day.

From the corner of my eye, a movement caught my attention, and I turned my head to see a colored man slink around the edge of the house. He looked over his shoulder and around the plantation, unaware of me. He ascended the stairs with a red bundle in his arms.

I squinted to get a better look. He wasn't from Livingston. I sat unmoving, not daring to breathe. He knelt and laid the bundle carefully on the veranda. He mumbled something and affectionately touched the package.

It moved.

I leaned forward. The man noticed my movement, and jerked his head in my direction. Our eyes locked. The agony pooling in his dark eyes was quickly replaced with shock and then fear. He leaped to his feet and his slave tag flashed as he fled.

"Wait, don't go!" I jumped to my feet.

The man never stopped. He vanished into the woods.

A muffled wail drew me to the red bundle. From within a small, dark fist thrust at the heavens.

My hand flew to my breast. A baby.

The cries grew more frantic, and I awkwardly bent and lifted the bundle. I tightened the blanket around the baby, sealing his arms and legs securely as I'd seen Mary Grace do with Evie when she was a newborn. Still, the child wouldn't calm.

Once more I looked to the woods before opening the door and going inside.

"I'm not good at this," I said, bouncing the baby up and down, which only made his pitiful cries grow louder.

I was about to burst into Mammy and Tillie's room when Mammy, doing up the last buttons on her dress, opened the door. Her face was lined with concern.

"Where did you git dat babe?" She held out her thick arms. Not waiting for my reply, she said, "Hand de chile to me."

I passed her the baby. "Someone left him on the veranda. What's wrong with him?"

Tillie, still in her night clothes, ambled over to us to sneak a peek at the baby.

Mammy pulled back the blanket and gasped. "De child ain't barely born."

"How do you know?" I edged closer to get a better look at the baby, now that his squirmy body was safe in Mammy's arms.

"Got de birthing still on him." She placed her pinkie to the baby's mouth, and he turned his head into her finger and tried to gnaw it off. "He's hungry," she said.

Oh. I sighed with relief as the baby's cries turned to fever-ish whimpers when Mammy's finger proved to be an insufficient food source.

"Tillie, go git Mary Grace. She can feed de chile."

Tillie slipped past us and down the corridor.

"You say you found him at de front door?"

"A man dropped him off."

"You git a luk at dis man?"

"Briefly. I rose early and was on the front veranda when he came up the steps. The darkness made it difficult to get a good look at him."

"You know de man?"

"No. But I do know he was a slave."

"Why would he bring de boy here?"

Her questions were my own. I recalled the agony in the man's eyes. "I believe the man is the boy's father, or related some-how." I touched the blanket the baby was wrapped in. "This cloth is made of silk. Not something a slave would have."

Mammy nodded her agreement. "Maybe he's a house slave, and he stole et from his missus."

"It's possible."

"What will you do wid de boy?"

"We'll care for the child. The man trusted this house with the life of the baby, and we must see he receives the best care."

Wild-haired and rubbing the sleep from her eyes, Mary Grace trailed in behind Tillie. Without questions, Mary Grace held out her arms and Mammy placed the baby in them. She entered Mammy and Tillie's room and sat down on the edge of the bed. Unbuttoning her top, she revealed her breast and placed the infant to it. Soon the baby ate greedily.

My body relaxed. "Will you care for him until we can figure

out what to do with him?"

"I've got plenty of milk for Evie and him both," Mary Grace said.

"You're relieved of house duties until I can figure this out. Please care for the boy and help Sara with the children." I left them to get dressed. Tillie shadowed my steps.

My thoughts returned to the man who'd fled. It was evident he thought the child would be safe at Livingston. But how had he come to that perception?

CHAPTER
Fifty-Five

ONE EVENING I SAT IN THE CABIN MARY GRACE SHARED WITH Sara and the others, holding the infant. Over the weeks since the baby was left at Livingston, I found myself drawn to him. Unlike Mary Grace's daughter, who had screamed until she was purple in the face, day in and day out, this baby was content.

Beautiful and peaceful, I thought as he held my finger in his small fist.

So far no one had made mention of a missing slave baby. I suspected that maybe no one knew of the baby's existence.

"The child needs a name," Mary Grace said from where she sat on the floor playing with Evie and Noah.

"I thought...we could call him Sailor?"

"Sailor?" Tillie's mother, Sara, said from her rocker. "Dat an odd name for de boy."

"Miss Willow is an odd one herself," Mary Grace said with a light chuckle.

I wrinkled my nose at her. "I don't know why, but that's the name that came to mind."

"It's quite a sight, seeing you sitting there all mother-like," Mary Grace said. "You'd get all squirmy whenever I tried to get you to hold Evie."

"Babies make me nervous. They're fussy, and I don't know what they want. If they could talk from birth, maybe I wouldn't find them so scary."

"Yet you don't seem to find him scary," Mary Grace said.

"I do…but for some reason he likes me. And I feel the need to protect him."

Mary Grace stood and hovered over the baby and me. "Because someone left him in your care?" She gently touched his cheek.

"Maybe. His father brought him here for a reason. He trusted we'd care for him."

"How you know he's de boy's father?" Sara said as she lit her pipe.

"The way he handled the child, as if he was the most precious thing. He appeared to be going through agony, but it was obvious he loved the infant. He felt he had no choice but to leave him. I saw it in his eyes. I felt his pain." My voice succumbed to the sadness I carried for the father.

Mary Grace caressed my shoulder with a hand. "You have a big old heart. Since we were girls, you couldn't help yourself. Can you believe once she brought a dead snake that was shedding its skin to Mama, asking her to fix it?" Mary Grace directed her question at Sara with a shake of her head.

Sara removed her pipe and smiled. "Always bin a tender-hearted gal as long as I knowed her."

"Mammy had worked miracles before. She fixed the broken leg of that chicken I brought her," I said.

"Hogwash. She went and found another chicken from the hen house and made you think she'd fixed it when in all actuality that scrumptious chicken pie you had for your evening meal was your little friend." Her eyes gleamed with glee.

"You are mean-spirited." I frowned, feigning displeasure. Shuffling to my feet, I moved to the cradle Jimmy had fashioned for the baby. I kissed his velvet cheek and laid him down and covered him with the blanket he'd arrived swaddled in. "Sleep well, Sailor," I whispered. After bidding them all good evening, I left for the main house.

The voices of Whitney, Ben, and Kip drifted from the front veranda, and I went to join them.

"Evening," I said, mounting the steps.

Whitney moved over on the porch swing and patted the open space. I seated myself beside her.

"How's the baby doing?" Ben asked before taking a sip of his brandy.

"His name's Sailor, and he's doing well," I said.

Ben's hand jerked, and he lowered his glass. "You've given the child a name?"

"We can't continue to refer to him as 'the baby,' now can we?" I smoothed my skirt while avoiding his gaze.

"I suppose not. But you do seem to be spending more time in the quarters lately."

"It's all over her face." Whitney was not going to miss the chance to jump in with the opinion she'd stated countless times since the baby arrived. "She cares for the baby, and not only because she feels responsible for him."

Traitor.

"Is this a fact?" Ben lifted the glass to his lips and took a rather long sip.

"I don't know…I feel he's alone in the world. That he needs me."

"He's hardly alone. He has every woman in the quarters doting on him. The boy will be spoiled rotten before you know it," Whitney said.

"Sailor. His name's Sailor," I reiterated.

"Be careful. You'll only set yourself up for heartache if you get too attached to the child," Ben said.

I knew that he spoke the truth. A white woman and a mistress of a plantation coddling and showing affection to a black child would set people to talking. "You're right, of course."

"But that won't stop what's already in your heart." Kip crossed his ankle over his knee, and his caring brown eyes fell on me.

I shrugged. Tilting back my head, I let out a sigh as I peered up at the glistening stars sprinkled like grains of sugar across the rich black sky.

He was right. Sailor had wiggled into my heart. The desire to protect him had been aroused in me when I'd first held him in my arms. *Is this what mothers feel when their infant is placed in their arms for the first time?* "I do care for him," I said, lowering my head. I wasn't willing to share with them how deep-rooted my feelings were for the baby.

A blanket of silence fell.

Whitney rose to her feet. "I'm going to head in for the night." She gave me a hug and said her good nights before wandering inside.

"If you two don't mind, I'm going to do a final round of the property before I retire." Ben stood and descended the steps and disappeared.

After they were gone, I turned to Kip. "Sorry I chased them away."

He chuckled. "You have strange effects on people. If I didn't know better, I'd say you take pleasure in chasing people away."

I grimaced at him. We sat for a moment in quiet bliss. Effortless and comfortable was the way it was between Kip and I.

"You know, I don't regret the day Father tried to marry me off to you. If he hadn't, maybe life wouldn't have brought us together."

"If he'd succeeded, maybe you wouldn't be creeping up on

spinster age now." His eyes gleamed with amusement.

I snickered. "Maybe."

He fell silent. His eyes captured an insignificant object in the distance.

"Kip?"

"Hmm."

"You don't hold my choice against me, do you? I mean...you understand, right?"

"What's there to understand?" He looked at me with serious eyes that burrowed into mine. "You can't make anyone love someone they don't. If God had aligned our paths differently, maybe you would've looked my way." He laughed in an effort to brush away his true feelings, and the ache that shadowed his face hurt me.

He was my friend and I loved him.

How different would my life be if my heart had fallen for him? I'd be living in New York with Kipling, and together we'd be making a difference in this dark world. The weary question that often rampaged through my mind surfaced. Why had life placed me here? Bound by law and country, the owner of slaves, and a mockery of myself in all I believed.

"You'll marry one day. She'll be a lovely creature who will sweep you off your feet and make you forget what you think should've been your life," I said.

"Perhaps." He leaned back in his chair and glided it back and forth with his feet.

If only things were different...

Kip had gone to the guesthouse. After his departure I took a stroll along the path by the pond. The hot weather was coming, and the humidity in the air made my skin sticky. Tomorrow Ruby and Kip would return to New York. I'd miss them terribly, but Ruby had promised to return soon.

Soon my household would make the journey to the North for the summer, and this year more than any other distressed me. Jones and his men would oversee the plantation while we were gone. The threat of the masked men attacking plantations while the owners were away was on everyone's mind. Then there was Silas Anderson. What was I supposed to think of his suggestion of courtship? When I'd declined his offer, his expression had been that of a rejected man, hadn't it? Recently, my nightmares were sprinkled with his face, and it wasn't the pleasant one I'd known, but bitter and demonic. I told myself my overactive mind was taking Whitney and Tillie's foreboding and making up a script of its own to play with my head.

Then there was Bowden. The thought of him pained me. Knox had said he was healing and I had to find peace in that. We'd called our courtship off, and being friends had proven too painful for the both of us. The accident had only pushed us further away from each other. I'd given up trying to see him and came to terms with the realization that where life had brought us together for a short time, it had now divided our paths. In this understanding, I focused on making it through another day and protecting all that I loved here at Livingston. I'd find ways to keep busy by helping my friends and sources in the North in the cause.

Hearing footsteps behind me, I spun around and lifted my lantern. Ben strolled toward me.

"I wanted to speak to you."

"Everything all right around the grounds?"

"Yes. All is good. I've been thinking…"

My pulse quickened. "Why does that concern me?"

"When you all go North I'm going to remain behind to

make sure things don't go awry here. With all that's going on, I think someone of the household needs to watch over things."

"I've been mulling that over in my own head. There are too many uncertainties to leave. Maybe Whitney and the twins should stay in Charleston, and you and I remain here."

"There's no need for us both to risk the sicknesses and diseases. But it may be a good idea if you stay in town this season. I'll be in and out of town, and I'll keep you informed on the running of the plantation. You can see to the warehouses and manage the shipments. If you relieve that from my mind, I'd be able to focus on this place and keep an eye out for anything of concern."

"Like the masked men?"

"Among other things."

"It's for—"

We swung our heads toward the pounding of horse's hooves coming up the lane.

"Who could that be? Are you expecting anyone?" I said.

"No. But whoever it is, they appear to be in a hurry."

We hurried around the pond and reached the front walk as the riders drew close enough to get a clear view. Against the darkness of the night, a vision of a woman dressed in pale blue fabric and the cream Negro cloth of a man's shirt flashed toward us.

Josephine? What could she want?

She sat in front on the horse with a strapping slave man mounted behind her. His thick arms surrounded her middle as he held the reins. Josephine's eyes were wild. She sent a glance back down the lane before her eyes fell on Ben and me. "Willow!" she called out. Panic gripped her face.

The man reined the horse to a stop.

"Get down," Josephine instructed the slave.

He jumped down and turned and held his hands up to her. She rested her hands on his shoulders, and he wrapped his hands around her waist and swung her with care to the ground. As soon as Josephine's feet hit the ground, she strode toward me. She winced as her hands moved to hold her lower stomach.

Was she injured?

"I need your help!" Tears shook her voice. "I don't know who else to turn to." Her face was strained, and it appeared as if she hadn't slept in weeks. "Please—he knows."

"Who? Who knows?" I clasped her wrists with my hands.

"Father." Tears welled in her fear-filled eyes.

"What does he know?"

"He knows...about us." She motioned to the slave. "You may see wrong in what I've done, but I know you have more heart than anyone I know." Her words tumbled over one another.

"Josephine!" I shook her. "You aren't making any sense."

"Mother tricked my handmaid into revealing my secret. Father had Jethro chained up until his return from town. He's expected back from town any hour, and he promised on his return he was going to hang Jethro." She became hysterical, and shook her arms free of my grasp. "I need you to get him out on your ships. Please help us. Please..." She collapsed against me; her fingers dug at my flesh through my sleeves. "I'd rather know he's far away and safe, even if I never see him again, than to see what my father will do."

I regarded the slave, who hadn't stood still since he got off the horse. I flinched as memory hit me. He was the man who had left Sailor at the door. *Oh, God. No.*

My mouth agape, I pulled her back and looked into her bloodshot eyes.

"We'll help you," Ben said, stepping forward. "You get on home, and we'll handle things from here."

Through tears, she said, "I'll never forget your kindness."

"Josie, you must go now!" the slave said. His eyes darted nervously.

She buried her face in her hands, and her whole body shook with sobs. The slave encased her in his arms. "Don't cry, my love. All will be fine." He rested his chin on her head.

"You put us all in danger. You must leave," I said, my jitteriness turning to panic.

Josephine turned to her lover and wrapped her arms around his neck. His hands circled her waist. She smiled softly. "Until we meet again."

"If not on earth, may it be in heaven." He planted a tender kiss on her lips. Then in a swift movement, as if she were weightless, he swung her back up on the horse. Her tears flowed freely as she looked at me and nodded in gratitude.

The slave slapped the rear of the horse, and it took off toward home. We waited until the last glimmer of Josephine's white petticoats and blue dress faded into the darkness before we sprang into action.

✦ CHAPTER ✦
Fifty-Six

"SLOW DOWN. WE MUST THINK THIS THROUGH," I CALLED out to Ben, who was in an almost full-out run toward the dock.

Hidden from view of the front lane, we stopped.

"You're him," I said to the slave. "The baby's father."

Ben and Kip examined the man with interest.

"That is correct."

"I saw you at the Christmas banquet at the Abbottses. You're a domestic slave." I recalled how Josephine had looked at him.

"Yes." The cords in his neck tightened.

"Josephine's his mother, isn't she?" I said, already knowing what his answer would be.

His stare was bold and almost pleading. "She can't know."

Had he come unhinged? I'd witnessed Evie's birth, and it wasn't a pretty sight. It was impossible for a woman to forget she'd given birth after the horror it took to get a child out. My womb clenched at the memory. "Know what?"

"That you have the boy. For your sake and for hers."

"Why?" Ben said, his face darkening as he draped a protective arm around my shoulder.

"She'd be tempted to come for the boy. We all know what Masa Abbotts would do if he found out the child lives."

"He thinks he's dead?" Kip said.

"Josie told him he was stillborn and she threw him in the

river to hide her shame. Masa Abbotts doesn't want anyone knowing, and he'll silence whoever he needs to, to keep the truth from coming out. He'll have my Josie married within the month. He said so."

To the dreadful old man Josephine had mentioned at the Christmas banquet. All of this was making sense. The nonstop eating, the weight gain, the change in attitude.

Oh, Josephine, my heart cried. The agony she had to be going through!

"With my disappearance, I fear for my ma and pa and my sister." Jethro's shoulders slumped.

"No more dillydallying. He leaves tonight," Ben said, marching toward the dock. "If Abbotts doesn't wait for morning, he will come by horse."

"What's the plan?" I hurried to match his pace. Kip and Jethro's heavy footfalls pounded behind me.

"Get him to the next station," Ben said over his shoulder.

"We must proceed with a different plan. Moving him to the next station won't work this time. Stop!" I grabbed at the back of his arm.

Ben halted and turned to me. "What do you suggest?"

"Jethro won't be regarded as a runaway slave. Abbotts will hunt every inch of the country seeking him out. No homestead will be left unturned. He must be on the next ship out."

"I agree with her," Kip said.

Not waiting for Ben to agree, I turned to Kip. "You'll be leaving for town tonight."

"Me?" Kip's brow rose.

"Get your things and meet us at the dock," I said.

"I'll grab Ruby," Kip said.

"No need. Ruby won't be going with you. You will have a new manservant for the journey. Jacob, wasn't it?" I referred to the name he'd forged on Ruby's papers.

Understanding spread over Kip's face. "Jethro will take Ruby's place."

"Brilliant." Ben smiled grimly. "Now, let's go. Kipling, get your things. We'll inform Ruby in the morning of the change of plans. I'll see to it you both make it to town tonight. A night in the warehouse won't be the most comfortable, but it's the best I can think of for now."

"It'll work. I've had worse sleeping arrangements." Kip waved a hand.

"You may not be saying that soon," Ben said.

"Why is that?"

"You will set sail on a cargo ship as soon as I can arrange it." Ben clapped him on the shoulder. "I'll get Jones. Meet me at the dock."

Kip ran back to the guesthouse. Ben barreled off toward Jones's cabin.

"Come," I said to Jethro.

On the dock, we waited for the men to join us.

"Your son—"

"I can't take him with me. I'll be on the run. I can't care for an infant, and he needs a wet nurse." Tears welled in his eyes.

Relief rushed through me, washed away as quickly as it arrived by a wave of sadness. "I promise you, I will care for Sailor like he was my family."

"You called the boy Sailor?" He raised his head to look at me.

"Why did you bring him here?"

"I know what you do for the slaves."

I felt my face drain of blood.

"My folks—can you help them? With my disappearance, I fear for their safety."

"I can't. It's too risky. I'm sorry…" I swallowed back tears.

He nodded; his shoulders drooped.

We turned at the hammering of footsteps vibrating the dock. Ben raced by me and climbed down into the riverboat, and Kip jumped in behind him. Jones untied the rope and gestured to Jethro. "Come on, move along."

I grabbed Jethro's hand as he moved past me and squeezed it. "I will tell him of you." My voice trembled. "And…her."

A tear dropped down his cheek. "Bless you."

"Willow, we must leave. Now!" Ben said with growing irritation.

"Go with God," I said.

"You are hope for us all," he whispered as a shudder ran through him. He broke away and charged down the dock and leaped into the boat. Jones jumped in after him.

The boat drifted out into the river and soon vanished from sight. Without delay, I made for the house to prepare for the arrival of Abbotts and his posse. They'd come. If not tonight, tomorrow or the next day, but they'd come, and of that I was certain.

❧ CHAPTER ❧
Fifty-Seven

Ben

W E MOVED ALONG THE RIVER AS QUICKLY AS BANDITS ON the run from the law. On the floor of the boat, the man lay covered by a tarp. My grip on the oars tightened as the one question that had repeated in my head since the man's arrival took precedence.

The man had brought his child to Livingston because he believed the boy would be safe there. Who else had he told?

I kicked back the edge of the tarp with my boot to reveal his face. "How did you know to bring the child to Livingston?"

Only the whites of his eyes could be seen in the darkness encompassing us. "Slaves say your brother helped slaves. Folks called him the Guardian."

Charles was the one they call the Guardian? "Go on," I said, craning my neck side to side to ease the tightness in my neck and shoulders.

"With his death, folks lost hope. Until slaves started disappearing again and they started saying he was the phoenix rising from the dust."

Phoenix, I thought bitterly. *If you're the slaves' savior, where are you now?*

Jones watched me intently as I fought to maintain a bland expression. We'd all been under overwhelming pressure since

Charles's death. I grew weary of walking in his long-faded footsteps and dreamed of a life of my own. One that wasn't surrounded by memories of Charles.

"I never told another soul what I witnessed that morning," Jethro said.

"What are you talking about?"

"The Carters' slave you helped."

"How do you know about that?" Jones beat me to the question.

"I was making my way through the woods to Mr. Anderson's farm when I heard the dogs. I hid, and from there I saw it all."

A cold knot settled in my stomach as I exchanged a look with Jones and Kipling. I turned my eyes back to the man. "What was your business with Anderson?"

"Masa Abbotts hired me out to him."

I shifted in my seat. "You were hired by Anderson?"

Jones's back became erect, and he eyed the slave with a hooded expression.

"Several times," Jethro said. "It'd do folks well to pay attention to Mr. Anderson and his comings and goings."

"Make yourself clear," I said.

"I overheard Mr. Anderson talking to someone down by the river on my way to the quarters one evening. He was carrying on like someone had wronged him. Curiosity got the best of me—"

"That seems to happen to you a lot," I grumbled.

Jethro grew silent. In the moonlight I could see his sharp eyes assessing me. "Well, go on." A muscle twitched in my cheek as I suppressed my impatience.

"I crept in to take a look," he continued. "Only thing was, he was by himself."

Jones and Kipling appeared as confused as I was.

"Then who was he talking to?" Kipling said.

"Don't rightfully know. He was acting all crazy, flailing his arms around and saying you will pay. Then he lifted his hands and started hitting the sides of his head with his palms."

Kipling's frown deepened. "What else?"

"A man called to him from his cabin asking him if he was all right. After Mr. Anderson told him to mind his own business and go back inside, Mr. Anderson wiped his hands over his eyes as if to clear his vision and went to the house."

"The man? You mean Caesar?"

"Not the black man, the hired man."

"I wasn't aware Anderson had a hired man," I said.

"Name's Collins," Jethro said.

Collins. The man Bowden had fired? The one Bowden thought was responsible for cutting the horses' harnesses?

Jones and I rowed harder, our gazes locked on each other. The sound of the oars hitting the water mimicked the pounding in my chest.

∾ CHAPTER ∾
Fifty-Eight

Willow

"I TOLD YOU!" WHITNEY LEAPED FROM HER CHAIR THE NEXT morning at breakfast when Ben filled us in on what Jethro had revealed about Anderson. "He's no good. Crazy, in fact, by the sounds of it." She paced the room.

Jack's fork clanged on his plate, and his face paled. Kimie's eyes followed her sister around the room as she chewed faster to empty her mouth.

"What is it?" Kimie said to Whitney's back when she finished her bite.

"Children, everything is fine," Ben said, patting Jack's tight fist where it lay on the white-draped table. "Tillie, please take the children outside."

Tillie moved from her position in the corner. "Come along, chillum; let's go see if Dolly had her calf yet." She pulled back Kimie's chair.

"But James says the baby isn't to be born for at least another few weeks," Kimie said as Tillie took her hand.

Jack rose. Fear and worry shone in his eyes. The boy, like his sister, had seen and dealt with things no children ever should. "Calf could've come last night." He encircled his sister's shoulders with an arm as they left the room.

My stomach roiled with worry as I looked at Ben. "What do

you think? Is Anderson a threat to Livingston?"

"Well, he doesn't seem all together. Certainly not the neat little package he has presented himself as."

"The question we need to be asking ourselves is why did he take over the widow's homestead and whom does he intend to make pay? And pay for what?" Whitney mumbled, more to herself than us. I swear, if she kept up her pacing, she'd wear the floorboards down to splinters.

"For the love of God, Whitney, take a seat." Her pacing had carved through my last nerve.

She plopped down beside me. "Do you think we have reason to be concerned?" Stress and worry pulled at her pretty face as she sought reassurance from Ben.

"No one really knows for sure. It all seems a mite suspicious. Until Jones and I can figure out if Anderson is up to something or is just some poor bloke touched in the head, I think it's best if you two pack up the children and move to town earlier than expected."

I wanted to dispute him on the matter, but I kept silent. We were all under an abundance of stress, and my challenging him on his decision would only put unnecessary pressure on him. Haggard and tired, he'd returned home as we came down for breakfast.

"We'll go." Whitney rose to her feet. "I'll start packing the twins' trunks."

When she was gone, Ben pushed back his chair and stood. "Do you think you can get yourselves together by the afternoon?"

"I'm sure we can."

"Good. I'll have Jimmy prepare the carriages. I'll arrange for some of Jones's men to accompany you to town."

"You aren't coming with us? At least to say goodbye?"

"We'll say our farewells here. I intend to pay Bowden a visit and let him know where Collins has found employment. Maybe we'll pay Anderson a visit as well."

Fear exploded in me like the firing of a cannon. "No. You can't." I jumped to my feet. "I can't bear the thought of something happening to either of you."

"We'll be fine."

"You can't promise that."

"Only a fool would poke at a buzzing hornet's nest."

"But if you show up with Bowden, that will only fuel up Collins and Bowden both."

"Very well. You speak reason. I'll take Jones with me."

Not that I liked the idea any better. "Be careful," I said.

In the early afternoon, a caravan of carriages and a wagon filled with trunks pulled out of Livingston headed for Charleston. Mary Grace and Mammy, along with the other house slaves, were left to manage the house until our return in the fall.

"You leave it in capable hands." Ruby smiled with encouragement.

I shifted my gaze from the window to rest on her where she sat across from me. Her bonnet, accented with peach and ivory flowers, brought out the rosiness in her cheeks. The hat sat cock-eyed on her head, its ribbons tied securely under her chin.

"I shall miss you when you are gone," I said.

"And I, you. My time went too fast, and I feel like my father and I were only beginning to get to know each other. I hope you'll have me back someday. I quite liked being in the quarters. It gave me a sense of what my life might have been like if it weren't for your family."

"My family?"

"I'm indebted to your family and gratefully so. If your father hadn't brought you to New York, we might have never met.

Who knows what would have happened to me if it wasn't for your mother and her bravery. Then there's you—if your love for my father hadn't guided your steps, all of this would never have happened." Her beautiful face gleamed with happiness and rosiness caressed her high cheekbones.

I studied her for a moment. "I'm not sure I deserve that gratitude."

The softness in her face faded and a puzzled expression took its place.

I dropped my eyes to my hands, folded in my lap, and hurried to explain myself. "For so long he'd been *my* Jimmy—the father I always longed for—so when I found out he had a daughter, I searched for you. I was determined to find you, but when I discovered you were Mag, I feared you'd take him from me."

She snorted and her eyes glinted. She grinned. "Aww, Miss Willie, dere ain't nobody dat ever gonna steal de affections I have for you," she mimicked before convulsing in a fit of booming laughter—his laughter.

When she straightened and her laughter ceased, she said, "He bonds us together. We're sisters, in a way."

I smiled. "I like the sound of that."

My mind drifted to another girl an ocean away, the rightful daughter of Charles Hendricks. *Callie.* What was she like? Did she know of me?

⟡ CHAPTER ⟡
Fifty-Nine

WHITNEY, THE TWINS, AND I SETTLED INTO THE TOWNHOUSE in Charleston. Papers were drawn up, and Ruby returned to New York accompanied by a female companion and conductor of the Underground Railroad. Over the summer, Ben came to visit and brought word of things at home. He'd gone by the Anderson homestead and reported that Silas was building a new house. Though only a frame of a home stood, Silas's mention of this intention at the Christmas banquet rang true.

Silas informed Ben that Collins had ridden up looking for a job a while back and, needing the help, he'd hired him. Ben said that Silas was cordial and invited Ben and Jones in for some whiskey. Silas hadn't joined them in a drink, but spent his time speaking about the masked men. He told them that someone had recently come by his homestead when he wasn't home and ransacked the house. Besides the desperate need for a housekeeper, Ben thought all appeared normal. However, he wouldn't dismiss Jethro's insight so easily.

Mr. Abbotts put up posters all over town for his runaway and doubled the reward for the Guardian. Word in the quarters was that slaves on the plantations across the country sang the praises of a man said to be outsmarting the planters. Talk that riddled me with fear.

Today I sat in the front garden, engrossed in *Uncle Tom's*

Cabin, the novel that was all the buzz lately. The hustle and bustle of the street just beyond the wrought-iron gates melted away as I read how Eliza crossed the Ohio River on a floating piece of ice to escape the slave traders. Eliza's profound courage was an inspiration in itself.

Whitney's raised voice pulled me from the book, and I lowered it to my lap. Whitney was storming up the street, her arms swinging fiercely. Knox trailed slowly behind her; his expression was one of total bewilderment. She charged through the gates, and they rasped on their hinges. "Willow. Just the person I wanted to see," she said as she strode up the stone walkway. "He has lost his mind."

"What is the problem?" I said.

"Can you believe the nerve of that man?" she scoffed, crossing her arms over her chest.

"What has got you so riled up?"

"That man is the reason." She jerked her head at Knox as he reached the gate. "He thinks he can show up here proposing marriage and think I—"

"That's what has you so angry?" I laughed.

Her sourness amplified. "You bet it does. I told him from the start I wasn't the marrying kind. If he were looking for a woman to mother a herd of children, he'd best keep on looking. It isn't just me he would have to care for. There are the twins too. Besides, his apartment over the general store just wouldn't do. Jack would never be happy in town. The funds I've saved up from the wage you pay me is enough to purchase a piece of land, but a house would take months to build. He'd go from caring for one person to four."

"Sit down and calm yourself." I poured her a glass of punch.

She dropped into the white rocker with a thud. Her eyes fell on Knox as he strolled cautiously toward us.

"Mind your manners." I plucked the words from her book of vocabulary titled *Jack Barry*.

She scowled and leaned back in the rocker, and it began to rock furiously. *Squeak...groan...scrape,* the rocker sang.

Knox clenched his tan hat in his big paws. With the sleeve of his shirt, he wiped the sweat dripping down his forehead as his shadow engulfed us. His warm brown eyes shifted from me to Whitney.

"Is that a no?" he asked.

"It's a hell, no." She shifted her body away.

"Whitney Barry! You better get ahold of yourself," I said, astonished at her rudeness. "Don't mind her none. Whitney doesn't take kindly to people showing their feelings."

Whitney turned her flashing eyes on me with a *you-better-watch-it* look.

"Now, ladies, I didn't mean to cause all this fuss. I'll be on my way." Knox set his crumpled hat on his head. "At least think on it." His eyes fell on Whitney.

She tilted her nose in the air.

"She will," I answered for her and offered him a smile of encouragement.

"Good day, ladies." He tipped his hat and left.

After he was gone, I said, "I know you love him. So what's the trouble?"

"And what makes you think that?"

"A woman like you wouldn't allow Knox to call on you if you didn't care for him."

"Care and love are two gravely different things." Her posture relaxed somewhat, the best Whitney Barry was capable of.

"You deserve to be happy, and I believe Knox would be the person to do that. He'd be a good father to the twins."

"Are you suggesting I marry to lighten my burden?"

"Of course not. It's just—"

"It's just you think I'm too headstrong to see what I need in life."

"Maybe," I said, blushing, knowing I was not one to give advice on love. Look at the horrible mess I'd made of my own life.

She thought for a minute and then, as if overcome by too many confused emotions, she rose. "I know you mean well, but you should get your love affairs in order before you give insight into mine." She marched toward the front piazza and up the steps and into the house, slamming the door behind her.

"Did I not just think that?" I shook my head in annoyance.

I reached out to steady the empty rocker beside me and heaved a sigh as I slumped back in my chair. "So much for a pleasant day," I said to the ruby-throated hummingbird that hovered at the coral-colored trumpet vine entwining the wood archway.

∽ CHAPTER ∽
Sixty

"**Y**OU KNOW YOU HAVE PAID STAFF TO DO THAT," WHITNEY said from the doorway of the carriage house a few days later.

"I enjoy coming out here. Mindless hours of wondering how things are at Livingston are making me crazy. It's best to keep busy." I brushed the coat of the sixteen-hands-high bay.

An elderly silver-haired man polished the enclosed carriage that sat in the middle of the building.

Whitney ambled toward the two-horse stall. She stroked the nose of the horse I groomed. I took a sideways glance at her and smiled to myself. Something was troubling her and knowing Whitney as I did, she was struggling to find the words to speak what was on her mind.

Expelling a long sigh, she said, "I'm sorry. I behaved poorly. Can you find it within your big old heart to forgive me?" Redness crept into her face as she looked at me through lowered auburn lashes.

I stopped brushing the horse and balled a fist on my hip. "I did that the day you acted so ghastly. Well…by the next day, at least." I broke into a big smile.

Her laugh echoed throughout the building. A light chuckle came from the man polishing the carriage. "I appreciate your generosity." She dipped low into a curtsy, but not before I caught her roll her eyes.

I held out my hand, palm down, for her to kiss.

"I'm not kissing that! You've been playing with horses all morning." She swiped my hand away. "I've been thinking, and I think maybe I should consider Knox's proposal."

"It's about time you started making sense. Knox loves you and the twins. You'd be very happy."

"I suppose we could make his apartment work until we could build our own place."

"I've got a better idea. You may think it's selfish on my part, but I've had some land cleared close to Livingston. Before we came here, I rode out to check on how things were coming along. By the time we return home, the house will be almost finished. I'd love for you, Knox, and the twins to have it. My wedding gift to you."

"But why?"

"Why not? I guessed marriage was in your future. Jack would have the countryside for a playground, I would have my best friend near, and it's the least you deserve. We all win." I beamed.

"I don't know what to say."

"Say nothing. I count it a blessing, the day you were dumped in my lap. Without you, these last years would've been bleaker than they've already been. I can't thank you enough."

Tears dampened her eyes, and her lip quivered. "I-I can't begin—"

"Then don't." I leaned over the half wall of the stall and placed a kiss on her cheek.

"You're too much, Willow Hendricks...too much." She grabbed my hand and gave it a squeeze. "You know it doesn't come easy for me...but I love you."

"I might love you a little too."

Carefree laughter passed between us and for the first time in a long while, I felt almost content—like stepping out and breathing in the fresh air after a rainstorm. Laughter was indeed the remedy to soothe the soul.

"I suppose this means we need to plan a wedding." Whitney looped her arm with mine and led me toward the house.

CHAPTER
Sixty-One

SQUEALS OF DELIGHT CAME FROM KIMIE AND JACK WHEN KNOX AND Whitney shared with them the news of their upcoming marriage. It was decided that the wedding would be a small, quaint affair and take place on our return to Livingston in October. Whitney sent a letter to Aunt Em in New York informing her of the wedding. Invitations were ordered and delivered by a hired man on horseback to the list of invited guests.

During the next few weeks, we made multiple trips to the dressmaker's shop, and dresses were ordered and plans for the wedding were put into motion. In the months that followed, I was grateful for the distraction the wedding planning provided from my longing for Livingston.

One morning in September, while we were visiting the general store, Miss Smith said to Whitney and I, "With Knox leaving, I'll have to find a new renter for the apartment. Without his heavy tread, I'd never have known anyone lived above." Her eyes followed the only other customer in the store as he made his exit.

"I'd think you'd find it more convenient if you lived upstairs." Whitney ran an appreciative hand over a bolt of silver fabric.

"I've considered it over the years, but my house is out of the way of prying eyes." She removed her spectacles and rubbed the bridge of her nose before replacing them.

"Always watching. Always on edge. We understand that all

too well. I think a wedding is exactly what we needed. It's a time to celebrate," I said.

The door opened, and we all turned as Mrs. Abbotts and Josephine entered.

"Good day, ladies," Miss Smith greeted them in her monotonous voice.

My heart pounded at the sight of Josephine. Over the months since we'd attended her wedding, she'd lost more weight. Her cheekbones had taken over her face and dark circles formed under her eyes. The rose muslin gown she wore failed to add color to her cheeks.

Mrs. Abbotts spoke to Miss Smith at the end of the counter. Josephine ambled aimlessly around the store, never making eye contact with us. I moved toward her, my throat thickening.

"Good morning, Josephine," my voice squeaked.

She turned to look at me with glassy, empty eyes. Her brow wrinkled in confusion, as if she were trying to place my voice. Then recognition lit her face. "Willow, how are you?" With a trembling hand she smoothed her blond tresses.

Guilt devoured me. I wanted to pull her aside and whisper in her ear that I had her son and he was safe and loved. That I'd received word Jethro was settled in a town called Chatham in Lower Canada. But nothing I could say would take away the ache of the walking corpse she'd become. It was clear she used laudanum to forget her pain.

"I'm well. When we all return home, I'd be pleased to have you over for a luncheon."

"That would be lovely." Her arm moved like a mechanical piece as she touched mine. "Why don't I bring Lucille along?"

Hadn't she rid herself of that woman by now? I bit down hard. "I'd rather it just be you. It'd be nice to just be ourselves for a change, wouldn't you agree?"

"That would be nice." Her words stretched.

Whitney's steps made the wooden planks creak as she moved in beside me.

"Hello," Josephine said. Her eyes centered on the narrow gap between Whitney's face and mine. A smile formed on her lips. "Word has it you are to be married."

"I am."

Sadness spread across her face. "Do you love him?"

"I do."

"I loved someone. It seems like so long ago now—"

"Ladies, it appears Josephine is tired." Mrs. Abbotts pushed her way between Josephine and us. "She hasn't been herself lately, as you can see. Married life has her quite busy. She simply puts too much pressure on herself to be a loving, doting wife. Isn't that so, dear?"

"Yes...busy. Very busy." Josephine fluttered a gloved hand in the air, and her set smile landed on her mother. A hardness no strength of medicine could numb or hide contorted her face. "Shall we go," she said in a deadly cold tone that made the hair on my arms stand on end.

I stared out the window long after they disappeared down the boardwalk.

"Are you all right?" Whitney whispered.

Tears threatened to overwhelm me. "She's hurting...and I could ease her pain. I could tell her—"

"Don't," she said in a low voice, sending a look Miss Smith's way. She stood dusting the front display window. "You did as Jethro requested."

"I fear I've lost my desire to shop. Do you mind if we go home?"

"Of course not. I'll pay for our things and meet you outside."

I nodded and strode to the door, and the silent tears flowed.

Closing the store door behind me, I turned to walk to our waiting carriage and ran headfirst into someone. A firm grip prevented me from toppling over.

"I'm sorry. Please accept my a-apology." I brushed away my tears with the fingertips of my gloves, but to no avail.

"It pains me to see your distress." Silas said in his deep voice. "Is there something I can do?"

I jerked from his grasp and stumbled back, wiping my hands over my clothing as if to cleanse myself of his touch. "No. I'm fine. Good day, Mr. Anderson." I maneuvered past him and scrambled into the carriage.

Whitney exited the store, and her eyes regarded Mr. Anderson with disdain as she moved past him, but she kept her lips sealed and took the hand the coachman offered her. Arranging her skirt, she sat down beside me and veiled my hand with hers, where it lay wadded in a fist on the seat. The tender smile she offered me said *everything will be all right*. Despondency enveloped me because soon she'd be moving on as a married woman, and the comfort of her daily presence would become a distant memory.

The coachman took his position, and the carriage lurched forward. From the corner of my eye, I saw Silas standing studying us. And for the first time, his façade faltered, and the murderous and harrowing look that transformed his handsome face froze my blood.

⌒ CHAPTER ⌒
Sixty-Two

Silas

I WATCHED WILLOW HENDRICKS'S CARRIAGE PULL AWAY.

Under my fingers, her body was trembling when I'd caught her. As she bolted toward the carriage, the usual irritating way she threw her shoulders back with pride and determination had faltered. Today her shoulders stooped forward in defeat, and the crack in her demeanor sent a ripple of pleasure through me. Moments ago she'd stood before me, and her cheeks, like succulent summer peaches, had caught her tears. My breathing had stilled with the urge to flick out my tongue and savor the sweet nectar of her pain.

Her beauty blinded men. She was a woman not yet broken. The pathetic Bowden Armstrong had fallen victim to her womanly ways, and in doing so, he'd failed to remind her of her place. She needed taming, and I was just the man to do it.

Such a task took patience. Willow would become my possession and my wife. When we were married, I'd teach her to bow to me. Her becoming suspicious of me would ruin everything, and all would be lost. Each word I said or move I'd made was calculated.

I'd moved into position and secured the widow's homestead. From the beginning, two obstacles had hindered me in swooping in and rescuing the grieving daughter of the tycoon Charles

Hendricks, and that was Armstrong and the Barry woman.

I wasn't past sending the redhead to the bottom of the Ashley River. The thought of her lifeless form, silenced once and for all, decayed and bloated as it surfaced on the water thickened the saliva in my mouth. No woman humiliated me and got away with it. But chance had taken care of the Northern woman for the time being and removed her from the top of my list, with her marrying the dockworker. Soon she'd be gone from Livingston and no more an immediate threat.

Armstrong was another matter. I wanted to rip his beating heart from his chest. Taking him out had proven to be no easy task. I'd intended to sweep in after the horses had made hog slop of his head, but the bastard wouldn't die. He'd clawed and fought to live—a sight that on any other day would cloak me with warmth, but not that day. Well, he might not be dead, but the accident had caused him to slither away like a wounded animal.

Collins reported Armstrong had a buyer come by his place the other day, an artist from Liverpool. Selling out only meant one thing, and that was that the hideous, disfigured man would run.

Run, little birdie, run, the voices chimed.

Had the gods finally shone their favor on me? Was the string of curses on my family over?

Challenges had risen at every turn. Ending Charles Hendricks's life had been too easy. The unexpected arrival of his brother had put a twist in my plans. I had yet to figure out what to do with him. But he'd moved to the top of my execution list. Showing up at my place with his suspicious eyes roaming over every inch of my land and his endless questions of where I drifted in from and what were my intentions in asking to court his niece. It wasn't the final words he'd said as he swung up on his horse and tugged the reins that steamed my blood, but the warning in his eyes.

No one threatens the McCoy men and gets away with it!

The burn of my fingernails biting into my palms pulled me from my thoughts. I glanced down at my fists and flexed my fingers. Lifting a hand, I rubbed the iron grip of the muscles in my jaw.

"Excuse me, sir," a gentleman said.

I stepped aside to let him by. Turning, I leaned against the post out front of the general store and studied the folks of Charleston as they went about their business. The stink of wealth some exuded sickened me. Did any of them know what it was like to be so poor your stomach convulsed until only dry heaves came? A few...maybe. How tired I grew of their upturned noses and gold-lined pocketbooks. Watching them shake and tremble when I emptied them was intoxicating.

A carriage pulled up in front of me, and a blond woman disembarked followed by a young boy around six or eight.

"But Mother, must we go to the bank first?" the boy asked.

"Yes, Albert darling," she said, adjusting his collar. "Then I promise we'll go next door to the general store." She patted his dark locks before kissing the tip of his nose.

The boy grinned with pleasure, succumbing to her affection. She circled his shoulders with her arm and mounted the stairs, offered me a smile in passing, and walked down the boardwalk.

Nauseating, I sneered. But even as I thought that, the voices rose, gibbering—

"Eat this slowly, or you'll be sick." Mother stands over me at the table, her hand on my shoulder. I feel its warmth; her warmth.

I look at the bowl of stew and lift my spoon. I want to scarf it down. My hand shakes. I haven't eaten for three days, not since Pa locked me in the outbuilding. Mother said he's off on another drinking binge in town. I fear for her. He will be angry that she freed me, but it was so dark, and cold, and I am so hungry—

The door flies open. The spoon falls from my fingers. I hear Mother gasp, and her hand jerks away from my shoulder. Pa darkens the doorway. I cringe back into the chair, wanting to follow Mother, wherever she went, wanting to feel her at my back. We should have heard him, why didn't we hear him?

His eyes are on me. His face is red, and the vein in the center of his forehead pulses as rage overtakes him. My heart is hammering, too fast—I can't hear anything but its pounding.

His eyes turn to Mother, and his hand moves to the gun tucked in his waistband.

No! my mind screams.

"You will defy me no more!"

The crack of the gun seems to ricochet around the room. I scream. Blood and brain matter splatter my face. I hear a groan from Mother, and she falls on me. Heavy and wet. In my terror, I push her weight off of me. Her head cracks on the table before hitting the floor. I jump from my chair. Horror fills me. I see the hole where Pa has parted her skull.

I can't breathe. Can't think.

I drop to my knees beside her. The knees of my trousers grow damp in a crimson pond of blood spilling over the floorboards. "Mother..." I sob, reaching for her limp hand. Her lifeless eyes stare at me.

Who will protect me now?

My head snaps forward, the blow nearly toppling me over. "Go get a shovel, boy, and get her in the ground before she starts smelling up the place." He spits on her body before raising his jar of whiskey to his lips.

I run out the door. On the porch, I spot the slave boy, shaking at the corner of the house.

"Come on, Caesar," I say.

"What happened?"

"He killed her," I cry. Blinded by floods of tears, I plunge through *mother's prize rose bushes, feeling the bite of the thorns on my trousers. The pain is so small compared to the crushing inside my chest.*

Together Caesar and I dig the shallow grave, bathing the ground in our tears. Hours later, we haul my mother's body across the floor and down the rotting porch steps. The crack of her head hitting each tread makes me wince and brings tears I thought long spent. Her body leaves a burgundy stain as we struggle to pull her to the grave.

Later in bed I try to block the sounds and sights of the day from my mind. I drift off to sleep only to awake screaming and digging at my ears. I cry out for her, but she doesn't come because she is gone.

Stop! I grabbed the sides of my head. A guttural grunt vibrated in my chest, and my body trembled. To feel made one less of a man. To remember the pathetic tears, the pain, the anger and emptiness of the lost boy I once was, was a weakness I'd carved out.

Loving my mother had earned me nothing. My brother and father had used her tenderness toward me as a weapon. Love was for the weak and with it brought pain and suffering.

No one would ever have power over me again. Pa had made sure of it. And my brother…that night on the road back from Charleston…

I stare down at the woman—Olivia Hendricks. She's sitting within the rumpled circle of her skirts, reeling from the blow. Pa'd hit her hard. She shouldn't have stood up for that slave woman. Didn't do any good anyway, I note, registering the screams as Pa and my brother and his friend Yates have their fun.

The screams stop. I hear Pa chuckling, and look up. He's got that nigger by the arm, half dragging her over to me and the woman at my feet. His eyes gleam with the lust to inflict pain. I know that look all too well.

He throws the nigger down next to her fool mistress. "Get a rope. We're going to have ourselves some fun," Pa shouts, eyeing me. I step back. "Mama's boy," he sneers. My brother goes for the rope.

When he's securing the noose around Olivia's neck, she screams, "Curse you! Curse you all! May you suffer painful obscurity!" and I go cold. Those words have weight.

But Olivia dies like anybody else. And when her and the slave's bodies are wiggling and fighting for life, I look into Olivia's bulging eyes and a thrill charges through me beyond anything I've ever experienced. Sweat dampens my hands, and my heart races with exhilaration. I cock my head and watch her take her last breath.

It was after that the voices in my head awoke.

Never had the body of a woman beneath me filled me with the same sensation as ending a life. Women were a curse to men. As the weaker sex, they fed off the desire of men to penetrate the warmth between their legs. I'd never been such a man. But when I bedded Willow Hendricks, and bed her I would, would she be the first to give me the same ecstasy?

"Helpless little boy." Olivia's voice rose above the rest of the murmurings.

"Go away!" I shook my head to rid myself of her taunting.

"Sir, is everything fine?" An elderly man stood in front of me on the boardwalk, his fossil face saturated with concern.

I dislodged the voices from my head. "Quite well." I tipped my hat and dodged past him.

You're the king and Willow will be your queen, the voices whispered. *You'll secure her fortune and then she'll meet the same fate as her mother.*

After all, weren't humans merely pieces on a chessboard, to be discarded as they outlived their usefulness?

❧ CHAPTER ❧
Sixty-Three

Willow

"MISS HENDRICKS, GOOD AFTERNOON," SAM BENNICK said with a broad smile when I walked into his office one afternoon in mid-October. "To what do I owe the pleasure?" He indicated an empty chair in front of the desk.

Seated, I smoothed the fabric of my skirt before clasping my hands in my lap. "My uncle will be returning tomorrow to take us home. I wanted to stop by and see if you have found anything on my father's daughter."

In the midst of the chaos going on in my life, I'd never stopped thinking of her. How old was she? What was she like?

He took a deep breath. "Nothing that will provide you with the answers you seek. His friends in London say they don't recall Charles with any woman. At least none that stood out as someone of interest to him. However, our sources say they'd seen him over the years with a child down by the docks."

"And the child: did they say if it was a boy or girl? Maybe a full name. Anything?" My trotting heart quickened to a gallop, and I pulled at the suddenly restricting high collar on my blouse.

He dropped his eyes to the brass magnifying glass on his walnut desk; his fingers had repeatedly turned it since I'd sat down. "The child was a girl, but they couldn't recall a name. There's no way of telling if it was her—"

"Do you remember my father at all?"

The spinning of the magnifying glass stopped. "You've lost me."

I leaned forward, resting folded hands on the desk. "He wasn't the type to waste time on children. If he was carting a child around with him, there has to be a connection. Was there anything they remembered about the girl? Like her hair color... eyes?"

His grave expression gave me pause. "What is it? You know something."

"She was a mulatto," he said.

His lips continued to move but his words became a murmur as my thoughts mashed into one jumbled mess.

A mulatto. Did Father have a love affair with a colored woman? And was this why he'd kept Callie a secret?

"We need to find her." I cut him off in mid-sentence. "I must know. If things weren't awry here, I'd go myself. If this girl is Callie, I want to meet her. Surely if she had a relationship with Father, she's been wondering what happened to him."

"Your father's influences reached far, and folks in London know of his death."

I nodded and sank back into my chair. "Do you think he told her about me?"

"One can never know. I've known you all your life, and I consider you like a niece. If I can find her, I will." He made no effort to suppress the sadness over the loss of his friend as he regarded me. Since my father's passing he'd shown palpable reverence in the handling of my father's affairs and answered my ledger full of questions. He'd even sat through many of my breakdowns and awkwardly offered a gentle pat of reassurance on occasion.

"I hate to do this, but I have an appointment soon." He stood and circled the desk. "I'll keep digging, and I'll be sure to inform you about anything I come up with."

I rose and held out my gloved hand. "Thank you, Sam."

"We'll find her." His fingers gripped mine.

I left his office holding onto his belief. Someday...somehow, Callie and I would meet; even if I had to set sail myself, I'd find her.

CHAPTER
Sixty-Four

"MAKE SURE THAT CRATE DOESN'T GET SENT ON THIS shipment. It's to be delivered to James Island the day after tomorrow." I pointed to a crate labeled *Fragile*.

"Yes, ma'am." The worker signaled another man. They moved the crate out of the way of the others being loaded into a wagon to be taken to the ship leaving the harbor today.

I wove through the workers to the door that led to the small shipping office.

"Everything under control?" Ben asked, his eyes still pinned on the records he was filling out when I entered.

"It appears to be." I strolled over to the window overlooking the harbor.

"We'll head for home momentarily."

The word "home" warmed my heart. Soon I'd embrace my loved ones and slip down to the quarters to spend countless hours holding Sailor. I'd found myself thinking of him and how much he'd grown. He had to be crawling, and his empty gums might hold a pearl or two by now.

Through the crowd on the dock bridge, my gaze fell on the familiar silhouette of a man who stood a few feet away, speaking to Knox. His dark waves slipped forward, covering the sides of his face as he dropped his head and peered at the ground.

Bowden.

My heart surged at the sight of him.

Knox gripped Bowden's shoulder with a hand, his body conveying the conviction with which he spoke. If only I could be one of the seagulls perching on the posts along the seawall, I'd tune an ear into their conversation and hear what drove the passion behind Knox's intensity.

Bowden lifted his head, and they turned to look toward the warehouse. I leaped aside to avoid being caught spying.

Ben glanced up from his work, and he frowned at me pressed against the wall beside the window. His eyes moved to the window, and a knowing look spread across his face. "What are you waiting for? Go speak to him."

"But...I—" I stammered.

"You must seize an opportunity when it arises. Tomorrow isn't promised. And life holds no guarantee that you'll get another chance."

Taking strength from his encouragement and the support I saw on his face, I walked to the half glass-paned door. My hand hesitated on the handle. Squeezing my eyes closed, I gusted a sigh.

"It's now or never," Ben said.

"I'm going," I grumbled, pulling the door open.

On the dock bridge, Knox had turned to speak to another worker while Bowden waited.

Ben's words echoed: *It's now or never.* I forced myself forward.

"You're back," I started.

He spun around in surprise. "W-what are you doing here?" He ducked his head, letting his wavy hair veil his face.

"I've been filling the months working here. But I could ask you the same."

"I had business with Knox." He shifted his body away from me, and his eyes flitted around for an escape.

"Don't!" I grabbed his arm. "Please don't run away. Not this time. I won't allow you to." Months of mixed emotions shook my voice.

Knox told Whitney and me that Bowden had gone to Texas for the summer months. He'd also informed us that Bowden had been in contact with an artist who was interested in purchasing his plantation. Upon hearing the news, I'd taken to my bed for days and cried enough tears to fill the harbor as Tillie had sat and stroked my hair.

"Willow…please. Don't make this any more difficult than it needs to be."

"On you? Or me?"

"Both."

"All I ask is for a few minutes of your time. Then I'll let you be," I said to the back of his head.

"Where?"

"In the office," I said, turning to walk back the way I'd come.

Ben exited the office at our approach and I wondered if he'd been watching us. I gestured for Bowden to go first.

As I passed him, Ben leaned in and whispered, "Tell him what's in your heart." I smiled grimly, fighting down the nerves coursing through me.

Inside, I tilted my ear to the soft click of the door shutting behind me.

Bowden stood in the center of the room with his back to me. He tossed his hat on the desk before clasping his hands in front of him. My gaze roved over his broad shoulders, which usually arched back with pride but were now lowered in defeat. I wanted to go to him, lay my cheek against his back and wrap my arms around him, and tell him I understood he'd suffered and suffered greatly, but no matter the scars that'd demoralized him, I loved him.

"Why are you doing this?" His voice came out pained and forced.

"Doing what?" I circled to stand in front of him. "Not allowing you to run anymore?"

He averted his eyes, and his jaw tensed.

"You can't keep running," I said.

"I'm not. But I'm also not willing to be a pity case for you or anyone else in this godforsaken town." His voice was bitter.

"You think I came to you all those times out of pity. Do you know nothing of who I am?" I retorted.

"I'm not a vain man. But the accident...you deserve a man you can stand to look at."

"Because beauty is all I see," I said harshly.

"No—"

"Have I not proven I care not for what one looks like, but what is in their heart? That the fight for the ones I love comes from here?" I placed a hand to my heart.

He moved away, never looking me in the face. His fingers wrung through his hair, revealing the pink raised scar that ran up his jawline, over his birthmark, and disappeared into his hairline. "We've discussed this until I can't see straight. We are two different people."

"Are we?" I turned from him and stifled a scream of frustration. Walking to the desk, I placed my palms on the top to steady myself. "Or are you too stubborn to see what stares you in the face every day you walk your grounds?"

"Not for long," he said.

I stiffened.

"I'm selling the plantation..."

I turned and found him standing at the window, his eyes on something far off in the middle of the harbor.

He continued. "But you need not worry. The buyer isn't

interested in the way things are done here. He sees the world through the beauty of colors and visions."

"And where will you go?" Hearing the words from him solidified the end of the daydream that'd occupied my mind for months—the hope that time and a near-death experience would change him. Immense sadness settled in my chest with the realization that I'd lost him for good.

He leaned his forehead against his arm resting on the window frame over his head. "Texas."

He was going home. Tears escaped the corners of my eyes. Our love story ended here. A tragic...pathetic disaster. He'd find a beautiful woman who'd manage his homestead and give him a family. They'd have a lifetime of happiness. The thought of him in another woman's arms...

"Willow..."

Lost in my misery, I hadn't heard him approach. Tender fingers lifted my chin. I gazed into his eyes, the gems that had stolen my heart all those years ago. I'd been spellbound since setting eyes on the prankster boy in his youth. For the first time in almost a year, our eyes held each other.

The accident had left a slight droop to one eye, and a few pink scars marked his chin. The most troublesome injury was the one colliding with the birthmark I'd come to treasure. It was part of him.

He caressed my bottom lip with a finger, and a grimace contorted his face. His hand dropped, and he stepped back. "I've ensured the buyer won't be a threat to Livingston and the secrets you hold."

"What do you think you know?"

"You're involved in things that could have you jailed," he said. "I considered turning you in to save you from yourself."

"You wouldn't." I crossed my arms.

He shrugged and shook of his head. "Loving you drives a man mad."

"Then release yourself from loving me," I challenged. "Maybe I should consider Silas's offer to court me and put us both out of our misery."

A hard glint entered his eyes. "Ben said he asked."

I turned away. "Maybe I should reconsider. After all, he's handsome and making his way up in the world." Sarcasm poured from me. "We'd be happy, you know."

"You stay away from him, you hear me?" His hand gripped my arm and spun me around. "He isn't who he says he is."

"Of course he isn't." I shook my arm free and moved from his shadow. "An idle mind has time to think and being stuck in town has given me nothing but time. The masked men have been silent, and only after his arrival did they become active again and start making their attacks. Mrs. Jenson vanishes without a goodbye."

He picked up where my thoughts led. "Then someone messes with my wagon. I suspected Collins, and I suppose revenge could be motive enough, but why not both wagons? If Collins charged off because he was enraged by me firing him over something he believed Gray caused, why didn't he come after us both?"

"It doesn't make any sense." I fiddled with the quill on the desk as I spoke the disturbing thoughts that had gnawed at me. "And as if by divine intervention, Silas is there to stop the horses and play the hero. What if Silas wanted you dead to get to me? What if he is behind the masked men? What if he did away with Mrs. Jenson…" A tremor shook me as I spoke the words that I'd mulled over in my mind since the day on the boardwalk. The day the façade I now believed Silas hid behind had faltered.

"But why? Why go to so much trouble to get your attention?

Going to such drastic measures to court a woman seems desperate, when he's got the charm and looks to sweep all you fickle women off your feet."

I ignored his jab. "There's one thing he doesn't seem to have."

"Money."

I nodded. "He dresses and carries himself like a man of fine quality. Right down to the expensive bay he rides. He gives off the air of coming from elite society. Yet if he is financially secure, why buy a homestead? If he wants to portray himself as a gentleman of substance, you'd think he'd buy land with a grand home, not a small farm."

"Precisely my point. It all leads to the same motive. He wants to be close to Livingston and you."

"Sometime back I ran into him when I was coming out of the general store. I was distraught over running into Josephine and seeing her deterioration after her marriage to that man with one foot in the grave," I said, not hiding my irritation. "When our carriage was pulling away, I glanced back at him, and the look on his face left me unsettled. It was as if he hated me."

Bowden's face darkened with concern. "You must be careful. Until we can figure this all out, you mustn't go off alone."

My hand rubbed over the nape of my neck. Fear pounded in my chest.

"Are you listening to me?" he said.

"Yes. Ben has already told me this."

"As if that matters!" he said in exasperation. "Listening isn't one of your admirable qualities."

"You'd be pleased to know it's something I've been working on."

"Is that a fact?" The corners of his mouth quirked and I caught a glimpse of the old Bowden.

I tilted my chin up. "It is."

He laughed and walked to the door. Pausing with his hand on the knob, he glanced back, and his expression reflected the regret spilling from my heart. "If only...I..."

"I understand," I said. "It was never meant to be."

He dropped his eyes and heaved a sigh. "Take care of yourself."

I was still staring at the empty doorway when Ben darkened the threshold several minutes later.

"I know a lot of eager folks waiting on your return," he said. "Shall we head for home?"

"As fast as we can get there." I walked past him and pecked his cheek on the way by.

CHAPTER
Sixty-Five

WE RETURNED HOME, AND THE FINAL PLANS FOR WHITNEY'S wedding occupied our time.

On the day of the wedding, I stood back, mesmerized by the beautiful bride clad in an off-the-shoulder dovegray dress with long, flowing sleeves that stopped at the elbow. She tipped her head to hear what her new husband was saying. Whitney laughed, and a lopsided grin spread across Knox's face. He had a way of bringing calmness to her with his endless lines of nonsense. They had a promising future.

In Whitney's twenty-one years she'd met challenges with as much grace as possible for a woman like her. I admired her strength and perseverance. Now she'd finally have the life she deserved. Oh, how I'd miss her. But marrying Knox was her chance at happiness. Besides—I smiled to myself—with the location of her home, she was barely a quarter-hour's trot away.

"She's beautiful, isn't she?" Julia tilted her head toward me as she loaded her plate with barbecued meat, red beans and rice, and sweet cornbread. Mammy and the kitchen staff had prepared the dishes that often filled our tables, from recipes passed down generation after generation that wove Southern and the slaves' cuisine together.

"And happy," I said, letting my eyes fall away from the couple. "I'm glad you could come."

"Jeffery wasn't keen on the idea of the journey, with our

soon-to-be arrival." She rubbed her belly affectionately. Her expanding middle was hidden beneath the layers of her gown.

"I'm afraid I've become the spinster of us all," I said with a laugh, then took a sip of my currant wine.

"Don't fret; you'll be married before Lucille. That I can promise you."

"Whatever happened to her insisting she'd marry Mr. Anderson?"

"Josephine says Lucille tried plenty of times to secure his hand, but her father wouldn't give in to her pleas to propose a marriage between the two. He believes Mr. Anderson dips on the scale of the lower class. Mr. Carter would prefer a planter for her husband. After all, a homestead without slaves or cotton or rice isn't what one would consider a profitable property," she said as we seated ourselves on white wooden chairs in the shade of a magnolia tree. "Whitney mentioned that she and Knox won't own slaves." She turned admiring eyes on the couple. "I knew I liked the woman within minutes of meeting her."

"Her heart is good. Even if she's an unrefined gem, I owe my sanity over the past few years to her, among others. Along with…" I leaned in and whispered in her ear, "the folks in the quarters."

She pulled back and regarded me with inquisitive eyes. "How so?"

I cupped her ear with my hand. "They are my heart."

"No…truly? You too?"

I placed a finger to my lips and smiled.

She turned her gaze to the newlyweds, and her hand squeezed mine. "I should've known."

"Why is that?"

"A woman with a heart like yours can't abide such barbaric beliefs," she whispered through closed lips.

"You're too sweet."

"I took your advice and learned to tame my emotions," she said smugly, jutting out her chin.

"Brilliant." I laughed.

Bowden walked by. He looked dashing in his black long-tailed coat and trousers with an ivory cravat. Offering us a half-bow, he continued on.

"That's why!" Enlightenment shone in Julia's light blue eyes.

"What?"

Between closed lips, she said, "You and Bowden. Your love for each other has been the envy of all the young ladies, even me at times. One thing keeps us all from witnessing the wedding of the century. Am I correct?" Her voice was somber.

"Never more right," I said. "But that's a chat for afternoon tea. Let's not let Bowden's and my shortcomings dampen the beauty of Whitney's day. What do you say?"

As the afternoon skies darkened and the evening closed in, Ben brought around the carriage. Bowden had gone ahead with the luggage to secure the newlyweds' passage at the train station to wherever the couple's journey was taking them. I surmised that Whitney had some grand plan. Though not knowing picked at me, it was improper to inquire where they'd be heading.

The couple finished their final goodbyes, then moved toward the waiting carriage to head off on their wedding journey. The guests sprinkled fistfuls of rice before them, showering them with well wishes and luck for the future. Whitney had strictly banned the throwing of shoes. She'd fought me on the wasting of rice, but I told her she owed me. If I had put up with her for this long, she was going to follow traditions and at least allow the sprinkling of rice to send her off.

She squeezed my hand on the way by. "I'll be back before you know it."

I smiled through my tears while my heart cried, *Hurry back.*

After their departure, a stream of carriages rolled down the lane as the guests started to leave.

"When do we set sail for New York?" Jack asked Aunt Em.

She walked toward the house with her arms around the twins' shoulders. "First thing in the morning. Mr. Hendricks has asked Mr. Jones to take us to the Hendrickses' townhouse this afternoon so we can meet the morning train."

The sense of loss and change cloaked my shoulders and heart with a great loneliness.

Mammy stood inside the door when I walked in. She took one glance at my tear-stained face and said, "Come on, gal, let me cut a big slab of dat cake and fix you some tea. Ain't nothin' lak a heap of sugar to heal all de pains of de heart."

CHAPTER
Sixty-Six

DAYS HAD UNRAVELED INTO WEEKS SINCE WHITNEY LEFT ON her wedding journey and the twins had left for New York. I missed them terribly.

One lazy Sunday afternoon, I straightened the jars of spices on the shelves in the kitchen house, lost in the misery of my loneliness.

Mammy hummed as she stood over a simmering pot of fish stew. It was a recipe her Big John had shared with her from his country in West Africa. A tender smile crossed her face, and I wondered if she was thinking about him, the one man that still held her heart after all these years. Twenty-some years from now, would I be her?

"Gal, ain't ya got a book or somepin' to occupy your mind?" she said over her shoulder.

"No more reading. Or knitting or mending. I'm bored stiff." I plunked myself down in a chair at the wooden table in the center of the kitchen house. Many tears and laughter and hours of cooking and chatting had centered around the table with Mary Grace, Mammy, and me. Then when Whitney arrived, she'd joined us. My hand moved across the table with fondness for memories of times past.

"We all miss dem, angel gal. Et ain't gonna be de same widout de young'uns and Miss Whitney." Mammy pulled out a chair and sat down.

"Some things I wish would never change." I slumped forward, resting my elbow on the table to cup my cheek in my hand. My gaze floated out into the yard.

Mary Grace and Gray strolled toward the front yard, hand in hand. She pulled Gray's arm tight to her side as her chin tipped up and she regarded him with adoring eyes. Her light, carefree laughter was followed by his deep chuckle. A smile touched my lips. Though I felt I was imposing on a tender moment between husband and wife, I shamelessly watched them. I'd always admired their relationship. It was honest and genuine, the kind of marriage built on a solid foundation of trust and respect. Everything I'd wanted with Bowden. If people had control over who stole their hearts, I'd have picked a man less complicated.

"You got dat dreamy luk in your eyes. De one you git when you think of Mr. Armstrong. Any chance he's de reason for dat sadness leaking over your face?"

I lifted a finger to dab at my tears. "I do try to forget him. Honestly, I do. I've sent endless prayers up to heaven, begging God to remove him from my thoughts. But He's as sick of hearing about him as you all are. Why must I be so weak? Each time I see Bowden I want to recant my refusal of his proposal."

"Et will all work out." She patted my hand.

"I used to think so, too."

"Ef Mr. Armstrong sells his place lak whisper has et, my Mary Grace will be beside herself wid grief. Et ain't no secret dat Mr. Armstrong has a fondness for Gray. Ef he moves to Texas, I'm scared he plans to take him wid him."

My teeth pulled on the corner of my lip as I considered the truth of her words. "I can't see Bowden parting with him."

"'Less you talk to him," Mammy said.

"What could I do?"

"Purchase him." She squeezed my hand.

My eyes gravitated to the couple, who now stood in the yard locked in a kiss for all the plantation to see: the freedom of an affection forbidden in public for ladies and gentlemen. Again, I soaked in the beauty of their love.

Mammy was right, it'd break Mary Grace's heart to lose him. Would Bowden consider selling Gray to me? "I will speak to him about it," I said.

"Bless you."

"Don't be blessing me quite yet."

"Ef you jus' marry de man, both my gals git de men dey wants."

"If only it were that simple."

"I know what's in your heart. And et be honor and good. I don't lak seeing you upset, is all." Mammy bowed her head and peered at her clasped hands resting on the table.

I stood, and on my way out, I paused and rested a hand on her thick shoulder. "To think my own mother handpicked you to help raise me. If she only knew what a great mother she'd left in her place. How blessed am I?" I smiled down at her upturned face.

"Sweet angel gal." Tears pooled in her eyes and her hand covered mine. A hand that'd dried my tears and soothed away my fears every day of my life. She was a treasure beyond all mothers.

I left Mammy to her puttering around the kitchen house. With Sundays being the one day the slaves had off, Mammy, like Jimmy, could often be found at her usual post around the plantation. The pair were similar in so many ways. If I approved of arranged marriages, I'd have seen to it they'd jumped the broom years ago.

I passed Mary Grace and Gray on my way to the house. "Afternoon, Miss Willow." Gray encircled Mary Grace's waist with an arm.

"Afternoon, you two." I smiled.

"Pa!" A shadow followed the squeal, whipping by me to wiggle in between the couple.

"You got to go already?" Noah lifted big, adoring eyes to his pa.

Gray stroked the top of his six-year-old son's head. "Mr. Armstrong is expecting me back soon."

"You coming next Sunday, right?"

"Lak I always do."

"We go fishing 'gain?" He nodded for his pa.

"Are we going fishing again," Mary Grace corrected.

"What she said." He tilted his head at his mama, never letting his pleading eyes leave his pa's face.

The parents shared a smile.

"You've forgotten your manners." Mary Grace nodded at me.

"Oh, I'm sorry, Missus. How do you do?" Noah's eyes rolled from me to his mama, to see if he'd said what she requested of him.

"You did well, son," she said.

He beamed. She gave him a gentle push. "Now, run along and play."

Noah clutched his pa's legs, squeezing all his love and yearning for his pa into one massive hug, in case Gray were to forget his son's love between now and Sunday.

After the boy ran off, Gray said, "Dat boy got de strength of ten sons."

"That he does," I said before moving on to the house.

"De Lard shone favor on us by giving us dat boy," I heard Gray say.

It hadn't mattered that Noah wasn't born of Mary Grace's body; they loved him. In their love the boy found healing, and his real mama—who'd lost her life in the swamp massacre—faded from his memory.

ᏉᏇ CHAPTER ᏇᏉ
Sixty-Seven

Bowden

"MASA, COME QUICK!" A VOICE RANG OUT.
I lowered the newspaper I'd been reading and rose to my feet at the commotion.

A field slave raced into the front yard, gasping for breath. "Et's Gray, Masa."

"What about him?" I asked as I bolted across the piazza, my guts knotting.

"Someone laid a beating on him. He's barely breathing." His dark eyes were crazed with panic.

A domestic slave came out onto the porch, and I ordered her to grab my medical bag. My heart thundered in my ears as I charged down the steps. "How? He's at the Livingston Plantation."

The man mauled the legs of his trousers with his palms. "He should've bin back hours ago."

I took off running toward Gray's cabin without waiting to hear anything more. How could I have lost track of time? My heart pounding fiercely in my chest, I crossed the backyard with the slave on my heels.

At the cabin, I threw open the door, and Gray's pa's grief-stricken face turned to me. He knelt holding the hand of the still bloody form lying on the bed. Life had taken another blow at the father, and his shoulders slumped as endless tears soaked his timeworn cheeks.

With leaden footsteps, I moved to Gray's bedside and squeezed his pa's shoulder before turning my eyes to the man in the bed. His face was darkened with the blood pooling under his flesh, and his sharp jawline disappeared in the swelling distorting his face. The hand that hung over the side of the bed was deformed and crushed and looked like someone had taken a hammer to it. Multiple gashes from a blade had torn away the front of his shirt and the white and bloody masses oozing through the gaps of fabric and flesh ripped a groan from low in my chest. "No…" I swiped a hand over my face and dropped to my knees.

Gray's chest rose and fell with shallow breaths. I peeled back his shirt with trembling hands and swallowed the bile racing up my throat. Lacerations to his chest and stomach exposed his insides, and I knew that not even a miracle would save him.

"Cloths. Hot water. Get my bag!" I bellowed to the slaves hovering in the doorway. Blinking, I cut off the tears burning my eyes and frantically tried to tuck his innards back inside his body cavity.

Show mercy…please don't take him. I don't know how, but I promise I'll do right. Please help me save him, I blubbered like a helpless fool.

The door burst open, and a slave arrived with my bag.

I grabbed the bag as Gray's leg thrashed and his body stiffened before growing still. Placing an ear to his chest, I listened for a heartbeat, and the silence that followed sent a cold dread rushing over me. I rocked back on my heels and took in the image of the broken man kneeling beside me. His thin shoulders shook as grief wracked his body. Silent, painful tears trailed down the lines etched into his face from a life of sorrow.

The daunting voice reverberating in my head whispered, *Is he so different from you?* Together we knelt at the bedside, he a slave and I his master, both grieving over the loss of a great man…his son. Was the pain carving through his chest any less authentic and raw? A heaviness settled in the depths of my stomach, and the shame of who I was pulled my eyes from him.

I looked long and hard at the body of the man on the bed, and my jaw trembled as I thought on the one thing that'd burned inside of him. A vision that'd kept a smile on his face and pushed him through each day of oppression I'd forced on him. The hope that allowed him to look at me not as a master, but as a man who'd lost his way. He'd faced the hardships placed on him with bravery and aspiration. As he'd fought through the race we call life, he'd held freedom in his line of vision. And I'd kept that God-given right from him.

Who am I? Tears of guilt blinded me. The weight of all the wrongs I'd done in life slumped my shoulders and I wept as hard as the day I'd received the news of my parents' death.

A gentle hand capped my shoulder, and Gray's pa's voice was but a hollow whisper. "He's wid my Millie now."

Stumbling to my feet, I cleared my throat and wiped my face with my forearm. "I'll send for Mary Grace. After she's said her goodbyes, we'll prepare him for burial."

I turned and ushered the others from the cabin, leaving him to be with his son. As I stepped out on the stoop, several pairs of concerned eyes fell on me.

"Is he all right, Masa?" someone said.

"He's gone." I moved past them toward the yard, summoning them with a hand to follow.

In the middle of the circle of wide-eyed slaves, I asked, "Anyone know who did this?"

"No, Masa." A mutter arose.

"Who found him?"

"De blacksmith's boy," a woman said.

"Where is he now?"

"I'm here, Masa." The slaves stepped aside as a boy about ten years of age pushed his way to the front of the small gathering.

"Where did you find him?"

"Beside de privy."

"How did he get there in his condition?" I hadn't realized I'd said my thought aloud until the boy answered.

"I don't rightfully know, Masa, but I found dis lying on his chest." The boy held up a cloth.

Stepping toward him, I whipped it from his hand, and he stumbled back, trembling.

"You did good, boy," I said gruffly, pushing down the emotions stewing in me. Turning the cloth over in my hand to inspect it, my breathing caught as I recognized what I held.

So far the masked men had been untraceable, so why now would Silas be clumsy and leave behind a mask? Was he sending me a warning; and if so, why? With news spreading of my selling out and moving to Texas, I'd thought he'd remove me as his target. Had he discovered it was me who'd searched his place looking for something to pin on the bastard? There was no way I'd be leaving here without knowing who Silas Anderson really was and what his intentions were with Willow and Livingston.

I knotted the mask in my hand. "George," I called to a slave standing at the back of the cluster of slaves.

"Yes, Masa." The slave moved uncertainly forward.

"I need you to saddle a horse and head out to the Livingston Plantation and bring Gray's wife here."

"A horse, Masa?"

"Yes. A bloody horse!" I threw over my shoulder as I made my way to the house.

He hurried to keep up with me. "But ef someone sees a man lak me on a horse, dey'd think I stole et, and I'll end up lak Gray."

I spun around to face him and lashed him with the rage stewing in my chest. "And if you don't go, I'll whip your hide myself."

He staggered back, beads of sweat forming on his forehead to trickle down the corner of his eye. "Right away, Masa. I go, right away."

Dammit! I hooked my fingers through my hair. "Meet me at the house in ten minutes. I'll prepare your ticket."

He nodded and turned and broke into a full-out run in the direction of the stables.

On the front piazza, I met the slave with the ticket. "Be careful, and be aware of your surroundings," I said.

"Yes, Masa." He pulled his reins, and a cloud of dust stirred in the air as his horse charged down the lane toward Livingston.

"Be safe," I whispered after him.

"Masa, can I git you somepin'?" Abigail stepped out on the piazza, her face drawn with concern.

"Whiskey." I lowered myself down on the front step. Resting my elbows on my knees, I clasped my trembling hands and glanced out over the front fields at the human forms busy at work.

Early that morning I'd handed Gray his ticket to go spend his day off with his family, and he'd practically bounced with excitement as I'd drawn it up. After he'd left my study I'd watched him race down the lane; his feet had barely touched the ground in his eagerness to get to Livingston.

Never had I known a slave like him. Days when he'd reported back to me on matters around the plantation, I'd find myself wanting him to stay. I'd not wanted to admit it, but in him, I'd seen a commonality a master shouldn't find in a slave. He'd had wisdom and wit about him that I admired and respected.

Words Willow had spoken to me on the day I'd asked for her hand in marriage took precedence in my thoughts: "Men are not meant to be owned as one would cattle. What if they'd been the ones with the upper hand and we were the ones working the fields? What if I were the one summoned to the master's bed so he could use my body as he desired? And I was forced to bear his children. What then, Bowden?"

Until that day I'd never thought of it before, I'd been so used to doing things the way I'd always known. Like any other businessman, I'd wanted to make a profit. I'd never given much thought to the rights or wrongs in our ways. Yet Willow's convictions badgered my conscience more every day.

I dropped my head and squeezed my eyes shut. Inwardly, I laughed, mocking myself at my pathetic attempt to call on God. In my desperation, I'd begged him to save Gray, expecting him to hear me, but he'd turned a deaf ear to me. But why wouldn't he? I wasn't a praying man. Bitterness chewed through me as I opened my eyes.

A hand with a crystal glass of amber liquid entered my peripheral vision, and without turning, I snatched the glass and threw back the whiskey. The satisfying burn trickled down my throat and heated my belly. The blood drained from the knuckles of the hand gripping the glass.

"More, Masa?" Abigail had sensed my mood, and her question was timid.

I shook my head and waved her away.

Her footfalls faded and thoughts of losing Gray encumbered me.

"You will pay! Your spree of terrorizing folks is over." I set my glass on the steps with a clank and made my way down to the quarters.

Whatever it took, I'd pin Silas's crimes around his neck, and he'd be revealed for the thieving, murdering snake he was.

∾ CHAPTER ∾
Sixty-Eight

Willow

OUR ENCLOSED CARRIAGE JERKED SIDE TO SIDE, GROANING AND creaking as it tore up the lane of the Armstrong Plantation at a speed I was sure would topple us over. My fingers dug into the side panel to steady myself. Silent tears ran down my face and darkened the bodice of my dress. For Mary Grace's sake, I tried to control the anger ripping through me. The inside skin of my lip was raw and stinging from the gnawing of my teeth.

Across from me, Mammy sat with her eyes closed; her lips moved without words, as runnels of tears curved over her plump cheeks and became lost in the head rag of her weeping daughter.

Mary Grace hid her face in the side of Mammy's bosom, and her hands beat at her mother's lap as her wails echoed throughout the carriage. "Why, why?"

Ben sat beside me on the seat with his hand interlocked with mine, and I clung to the strength the warmth of his fingers provided.

Leaning my head against the carriage wall, I closed my eyes to escape the agony going on around me.

I hadn't realized our carriage had come to a stop until Ben's voice parted the barrier in my mind. "We're here."

The footman opened the door, and Ben stepped out and

turned to help Mary Grace and Mammy before offering me a hand.

Gray's pa and Bowden came to greet us, and Mary Grace walked into the outstretched arms of her husband's father. After a tearful embrace, they headed for the quarters with Mammy trailing behind them.

Bowden had held Gray in high regard and the magnitude of his feelings was palpable as he watched them walk away. He'd always seemed unbreakable, but now he stood vulnerable and unsure of himself. He turned and I saw the red threads lining his anguished eyes from past tears shed. "Thanks for bringing her."

I inclined my head in a gesture of acknowledgment but hung back, feeling helpless and tongue-tied.

"How did this happen?" Ben asked.

"Come." Bowden twisted on his heels and strode toward the house.

We followed him inside and down the corridor to a room at the far end of the house.

He stepped to the side of the doorway and extended a hand, inviting us inside. "Please."

Bowden strode to the desk, picked up a piece of cloth, and held it up to reveal what appeared to be a mask. "Someone went to the trouble of bringing Gray back here and left this behind." Hardness crept into Bowden's eyes, and bone-shaking chills coursed through me at the transformation in him. Dark and deadly determination consumed him as he seated himself on the edge of the desk, crossing his arms.

Ben stepped forward and took the cloth; inspecting it, he said, "Looks like the mask worn by the men who held up our carriage."

"The men being Silas and his men," I said with conviction. "Until now his moves have been flawless, leaving no real proof to link the robberies back to him. So why leave evidence behind now? Do you think he's threatening you?" I turned my attention from the mask in Ben's hand to Bowden.

"Maybe. He killed my most trusted slave and what else can I think besides it was a direct strike at me?" His tone was tightly controlled.

"It would appear so. But why? You've made it clear you're leaving. What threat can you possibly hold now?" Ben said.

Bowden's brow furrowed. "It doesn't make any sense. The man's unreadable."

"We have good reason to suspect it belongs to the men responsible for the attacks on folks, but the mask isn't any real evidence. Before we gather a posse, we need to know what else he has planned." Bowden uncrossed his arms, and his palms gripped the edge of the desk.

"What do you intend to do?" Ben said.

"Outsmart him."

A kernel of fear somersaulted in the pit of my stomach and my hands twisted in the folds of my skirt. "How?"

"I haven't figured it out yet, but I will, and he'll pay for all he's done. If I have to hog-tie the bastard myself and drag him to the constable and the lynch mob with his crimes nailed to his empty chest, I will. Or I'll take my last breath trying."

I clambered to my feet. "You...you mustn't. We must use wisdom and not do anything rash. We all feel the loss of Gray and want nothing more than for the ones responsible to pay, whoever they may be."

The sting of Bowden's laugh made indignation flare in my chest, and I glared at him through pooling eyes.

Catching himself in the misery transforming him, he ceased his laughter and grew serious. "I'd be saddled up and gone already if that was my intent. But I won't lie: the thought crossed my mind. I wanted to go charging into his place and snap his murdering neck, but then he'd have the upper hand and know we were onto him."

"What if someone left the mask because they wanted Silas to get caught?" Ben, who'd remained quiet for most of the conversation, said.

"Who'd do that?" Bowden said as we turned to him.

"Someone within his gang. Three men attacked us on the road; one was a larger fellow, and he followed the orders of the leader without much hesitation."

"Caesar." I breathed the name, repressing a shudder. "Why would he risk his life to help us?"

A blanket of thoughtful silence swathed the room. All I could hear was the pounding of my heart.

"Sometimes…" Bowden's anguish-filled voice cut the silence. "A man can only see so much before it changes him…"

CHAPTER
Sixty-Nine

"WE'LL BE BACK BEFORE THE SUN SETS," BEN SAID TO Tillie some days later as I descended the staircase dressed in my riding attire. To lift my spirits from the slump I'd fallen into, Ben had suggested an afternoon ride.

Moments later, saddled up, we rode across the field and away from Livingston. We passed Whitney and Knox's homestead and the yearning for her company heaved a sigh from me. I pulled alongside Ben as we slowed our horses to a trot. "Why do people have to get married? Can't they just be content with the way things are?" I pouted.

Ben chuckled. "Most ladies dream of their wedding day."

"She promised she'd never get married and leave me. And she, of all people, I believed spoke the truth. She and I were supposed to grow old together at Livingston. I really should be angry at Knox, seeing as he is the one responsible for melting her frosty heart."

"Here I was, hoping you'd grow old with a husband and give me some grandchildren." Ben craned his neck to look at me.

I blushed. "There was a time I thought children wouldn't be part of my future—"

"Sailor wouldn't have anything to do with your change of heart, would he?"

I thought of the beautiful, chubby boy I loved more with

each passing day. "He's special."

He shook his head in disapproval. "The love you hold in your heart for the boy is dangerous. But no amount of warnings from me and those around you has stopped your affections from growing."

"He needed me…" I pleaded.

"He needed a mother. Any woman in the quarters would have cared for the boy." His tone was gentle but firm.

"I know, but Jethro trusted I'd do right by him. He deserves to be loved—"

"And the fact that his knees never hit the floor to crawl isn't loved enough?" he said with raised brows.

"Again, I concede your point."

He pulled his mount to a stop and looked at me. "But it won't change what's already in your heart."

I smiled. Choosing not to answer, I tugged on my reins to lead my horse down a narrow opening in the woods. He cursed and his horse fell into single file behind mine. We wove our horses in and out of fallen trees and brush until the wooded area parted and expanded into a sun-drenched meadow. I reined my horse to a stop, and Ben moved his mount in beside mine.

"It's beautiful, isn't it?" I said.

He mumbled his agreement and we sat in silence, engrossed in the beauty.

"Willow?" Ben's voice was quiet, as if in thought.

"Mmm…"

"I think you should get away for a while."

I twisted to look at him and read the intensity in his eyes.

"You've had too much on your mind for too long. It'd do you good to release some of the burden and worries you carry, which are a lot for a young woman. Also, I think it'd be wise—"

"If I wasn't in the mix of whatever you and Bowden are up

to," I finished for him.

He brushed some flies from his horse's mane with his hand. "Yes."

Most days, running away was all I wanted. With Whitney married and soon to be preoccupied with the responsibilities of her own home, and Bowden leaving and taking with him what was left of my heart, the thought had often entered my mind. I dreamed of running off to England to find Callie, but with all the uncertainties about Silas, I couldn't go. Lately, out of self-pity and a bushel full of regrets, I'd resolved that happiness wasn't part of my future.

"I'll think about it."

At the far end of the meadow, a red buck stepped out. His head erect and ears attentive, he cautiously scanned the surroundings before lowering his head. We watched quietly as he fed on the tall grass until I said, "Do you think you'll ever marry?"

Taken aback by the direct question, he turned bewildered eyes on me before he expelled a long breath. "I suppose if the right woman ever came along and I found things in common with her, I might consider marrying for companionship."

"But not for love?"

"Maybe. I don't know what the future holds. But it's hard for me to imagine loving anyone like I did your mother. It seems unfair to marry a woman without letting her know that my heart will only truly belong to another. Why do you ask?"

"I'd like to see you happy. You've spent your whole life protecting me and not enjoying even the smallest things in life. It's time for you to take care of you. I'm not a child anymore; I don't need you to hover in the background waiting for me to break."

"What if I'm simply enjoying the time I never got with you?"

"I, too, enjoy our time together—immensely, in fact. When Father was harsh, I'd run to my room crying, and I'd dream of a father like you."

"Speaking of happiness, what about you? Don't you think it is time you secure some for yourself?"

I shrugged and returned my gaze to the meadow. Could I marry out of convenience? A lifetime spent as lonely as I felt now seemed dreary and long.

A reflection of the sun on metal or glass drew my eyes to the left. I leaned forward in my saddle and squinted to get a better look.

"Do you see that?" I pointed.

Ben turned his head to the cluster of trees at the far end of the meadow and shielded his eyes with a hand. Without waiting for his reply, I nudged my mount in the direction of the trees. Ben's mount fell into position behind mine.

As we drew near, I dismounted when I spotted the object hanging from the limb of a tree. Still holding the reins, I froze as I took in the ground at the base of the tree. A makeshift cross made out of two branches and twigs marked a grave smoothed over time. The cross was lopsided, as if it'd been made in a hurry and hadn't been sturdy enough to hold up to the elements.

I cast a glance at Ben as he dropped to the ground. His jaw locked, he swept his eyes over the woods before he crept closer to the burial. I grabbed his arm as we trudged onward.

At the tree, fear strummed every nerve in me as Ben reached up and grasped the two slave tags entwined with what appeared to be a locket. Vomit rose in my throat as he turned them over in his gloved hand and the knowledge of who they belonged to dropped in my stomach.

"It's them," I said.

"Who?"

"The Widow, Ruth, and William."

"You can't be sure without checking these tags with the

town," he said, for my sake. He'd never stop trying to protect me. Did he think I was so fragile?

"I gave this locket to Mrs. Jenson one year as a Christmas gift."

"Are you certain?"

I reached for the locket. Removing my glove, I used my fingernail to open it. Inside, the image had faded of the painted bunting bird I'd cut from a bird book. Mrs. Jenson, a lover of birds, had watched and studied all the different species and would often pass on her knowledge to me. And as a nine-year-old, I'd thought the locket with the cut-out was a splendid gift. I recalled how she'd gathered me into her arms and kissed the top of my head, saying over and over, "You're a darling girl, young Willow." She'd stepped back and handed the locket to Ruth and lifted her once-blond tresses so Ruth could put it around her neck. "I'll treasure this forever." Tears had dampened her gray-blue eyes.

I turned to the marked grave and dread and horror filled me as I took in the broad extent of what lay before me. The past year of niggling and suspicions came to rest on the cold hard facts. There wasn't a doubt in my mind that Silas Anderson had murdered the widow and her slaves and laid claim to her property. An icy chill scurried up and down my spine and raised even the roots of the hair on my scalp. "He wanted her property so bad that he was willing to commit murder," I said without taking my eyes off the grave.

Ben bent in front of the grave, balancing on his heels. "And again, the evidence is left that could lead back to him. There's no way he'd leave this for anyone to find if he wanted the story he'd concocted to remain intact."

"Maybe he thought no one would pass this way." My words seemed feeble even to myself. I wanted nothing more than for all of it to be part of a horrible nightmare.

Could our theory about Caesar warning us be true?

"But to build a cross to mark a grave is done out of reverence. Something murderers don't do."

"We need to bring Mr. Sterling here. This proves Silas is guilty of murder." I strode toward my horse. Glancing over my shoulder, I noticed he hadn't moved. "Come on; what are you waiting for?"

"We can't bring this to the constable and the posse until we are certain." He stood and turned to me. "Silas murders the widow and her slaves with the motive to be closer to Livingston and you. We believe he intends to win you over and obtain your fortune, but I believe there's more to this story than simple greed."

"Like what?"

"I'm not certain." He helped me up on my horse before mounting his own. His eyes shifted over the meadow, taking in every inch of it as if memorizing our surroundings. "Something tells me there's a greater plan in the works, and we can't let Silas know we're onto him until we figure out what that plan is."

Nausea rumbled in my stomach and fear of what exactly Silas's plan was terrified me to the very core. "If we hadn't paused to take in the view, I'd never have noticed the reflection of those in the sunlight." I looked at the tags and locket he clutched in his hands. "And we'd never have stumbled onto the grave."

"Charles said he spotted someone watching him." His shoulders sagged with an invisible load that rested on his shoulders.

My heart drummed in my chest. "Y-you think Silas could be the man?"

Ben nodded grimly. "I don't like this at all. I've got a feeling his plan has been in the works long before his arrival in town. The man moves in next door. He proves to not be a lover of slavery, which he thinks will win favor in your eyes. Bowden meets with an accident that could've very well ended his life. Then you and Bowden drift further apart, and Silas comes asking to court you. It has troubled me for a while, but until now there's never been any solid information to solidify my questions. If we intend to make him pay for his crimes and figure out the grand scheme he has planned, we need more information."

"So you and Bowden keep saying. How do you suppose we go about that? And whose life does he mold in the palm of his hand in the meantime while we try to figure this all out?"

"The question we need to be asking ourselves is who stands in his way?" He kicked his heels into his mount's sides, and the horse charged off the way we'd come.

His question controlled my thoughts the entire ride home, and my nerves pinged by the time we got there. Who was next on Silas's list and when would he strike next?

Back at Livingston, I dropped to the carriage stone and handed my reins to a stable boy, mumbled a thank-you, and hurried after Ben into the house.

"Send someone to fetch Jones immediately, and find James," Ben said, and strode down the corridor to the study.

"Yes, Masa."

"Close the door," Ben said when I followed him into the study.

I obeyed and then took a seat in an armchair.

Ben tossed the locket and tags onto the desk before resting his hands on his hips. His posture stiff, he turned and chased the floorboards. I sat nervously watching him, and each scuff of his boots made my heartbeat quicken. Engrossed in his mood and the worry lining his face, I jumped when a knock struck the door minutes later.

"Jones, come in," Ben said without waiting to see who it was.

Jones's head peeked around the door. "You asked for us?"

"James is with you?"

"I'm here, Masa." Jimmy stepped into the room.

"I want you to go to the Armstrong Plantation and tell Mr. Armstrong I need to speak with him. And for God's sakes, be careful," Ben said in an authoritative tone.

"Sho' thing, Masa." Reading the urgency in Ben's face, Jimmy turned and ran down the corridor.

After he was gone, Jones asked, "What's the issue, boss?"

"Willow and I happened upon a marked grave not far from here, between the Jenson plantation and our property line."

"I don't recall no family plots in these woods." Jones's brow rippled in puzzlement.

"There isn't. The earth has settled around the grave, and if it were not for Willow's keen eyes, we'd never have found it." Ben handed Jones the locket and tags. "The locket belongs to the widow woman, and we believe the tags are those of her slaves."

"Anderson?" Jones's posture stiffened.

"We've reason to believe he killed the widow for her land and didn't want to leave behind any witnesses."

Jones's confusion grew. "She didn't own but a small piece of property, and had nothing of real value."

"He needed the land as a way of being closer to Livingston and Willow," Ben said.

Jones eyed me, enlightenment reflected on his face. "That's what Mr. Armstrong's been suspecting."

"When have you been speaking to Bowden?" I said.

"Off and on since Mr. Hendricks passed away. When you returned from the North and you," he said to Ben, "were across the ocean, Mr. Armstrong asked me to keep an eye out for you until Mr. Hendricks's return."

"That was him I saw you talking to down at the dock the

night I went to fetch Henry from the quarters?" I said.

"Reckon so. He told me not to tell you because you'd bring down the wrath of God on him if you got to thinking he thought you couldn't take care of yourself."

Warmth swirled in my chest with the realization of just how far Bowden would go to protect me, even with the difference in our views.

Hours later, Bowden, Jones, Ben, and I had formulated a plan to out Silas Anderson. We all knew the risk involved, and though I felt my part was being reined in by Bowden and Ben's attempts to protect me, I'd do as instructed to ensure nothing went awry.

CHAPTER
Seventy

O UR PLAN, IF WE PULLED IT OFF, WOULD PIN SILAS TO THE masked men and the attacks on the townsfolk, along with the murders of the widow and her slaves.

"Outsmart him at his own game," Bowden had said.

"Mr. Anderson, I'm so happy you could join us for a luncheon." I ascended the front steps a week later when Silas rode into the yard.

Today I'd paid extra attention to my appearance. Dressed in a butter-yellow afternoon frock, I'd had Tillie pull my corset so tight it pinched my flesh, but smoothed me from my waist to my bustline. The neck scooped daringly low, and the off-the-shoulder style revealed more skin than I'd ever been comfortable with. My hair swept to the side and cascaded down over one bare shoulder. I was every bit the alluring bait to capture the unsuspecting Mr. Anderson.

"Miss Hendricks, I was delighted, yet surprised, to receive your invitation." He dropped to the ground with a thud, and the repugnant smile he provided never carried past his lips.

"I suppose you would be, after my dreadful behavior in town." I lowered my lashes to brush my cheeks, overcome with feigned shame. "I was beside myself with worry over a friend I'd run into in the general store. You may recall her from the Abbottses' Christmas banquet: Josephine?"

"I've seen her and the Carter woman together."

I released a long sigh and lifted my eyes to look at him with a hand placed to my breast. "I'm afraid she's terribly unhappy, and seeing her so upset and not herself was too much for me to bear."

"No need to explain yourself, Miss Hendricks. I do hope, for your sake and hers, she'll pull herself together."

"I do hope so," I said with a cheerful smile. "Enough about trivial things. Please come and join me on the veranda." I placed a hand in the curve of his elbow. The warmth of his body so close to mine roiled my stomach.

"Will your uncle be joining us?" He glanced around.

"Of course; it'd only be proper. You don't mind, do you?" I raised a brow and slowed my steps.

He patted my hand and peered down at me with a smile that'd typically take even my breath away, had I not known the crimes tallying up against him.

"Certainly not," he said. "You're a lady of quality, and one must always do what's right to avoid casting unnecessary shadows on one's reputation." Darkness flitted in his eyes, and I wondered if he was thinking of the methods he'd taken to go undiscovered thus far.

On the veranda, I led him to the white linen-draped table spread with various cheeses, breads, and smoked meats. After we were seated, I carried the conversation for what seemed like forever, wondering what was taking Ben so long.

"May I?" I picked up the pitcher of cider in the center of the table.

Silas nodded, his eyes never leaving my face. Not once during our chatting had I caught his eyes lower to my breast, and I questioned Ben's insistence that I wear a gown that made me feel like a streetwalker.

"Good afternoon." Ben's voice squeaked as he stumbled out

onto the veranda. As he drew near, I could smell the whiskey on him.

What in heaven's name was he thinking?

"Mr. Hendricks." Silas rose to his feet.

"It's a fine day, isn't it?" Ben said, grasping Silas's out-stretched hand.

"That it is, sir."

Ben dropped into a seat next to me and wasted no time getting down to the task at hand. "Willow said you made mention of courting her." Ben stabbed a piece of smoked pork and dropped it on his own plate without offering any to our guest.

"I-I...why, yes." A line of confusion creased Silas's forehead.

"Yet you haven't come asking?"

"She didn't seem fond of the idea." Silas gulped and adjusted himself to sit up taller.

Ben removed his napkin from the table, his hand hitting the pitcher of cider and upending it. I leaped to my feet and grabbed for a napkin and frantically tried to soak up the liquid. I didn't know if I was more shocked at Ben's blundering of the plan or the cold penetrating the seven layers of my attire. It took everything in me to still the anger bubbling in my chest. It was unlike him to act like such a fool.

"Willow, darling, please forgive me for my clumsiness. Do go and get that taken care of." Ben laid a hand on my wrist to stop my wiping of my gown.

I stared at him in bewilderment. *Go take care of it?* No. We had to continue with the plan we'd confirmed not but a few days ago. The exact plan we'd run over every detail of this morning. Had he gone mad?

"Run along now, dear, before the stain gets worse." Ben dismissed me with his eyes before directing a drunken smile on Silas.

Ready to chew off my tongue with the rage I struggled to

hold back, I excused myself and went inside. I paused in the foyer when I heard Ben say, "Now to take care of matters that sometimes women have no business being a part of. As you may have noticed, my niece is a bit stubborn and lacks the sensibility to think for herself. Women need to be taken in hand sometimes. It's our duty as men to think for them."

I moved tight against the wall, out of sight to listen in on their conversation. What was Ben up to? This wasn't part of the plan.

"Yes, sir," Silas replied in an even tone. "They do need us menfolk to keep them in line."

Ben chuckled. "Willow has always been a stubborn child. I fear her father spoiled her, trying to make up for the lack of a mother in her life. He was a difficult man. Always left the girl alone with no real parents to guide her while he ran off on his ships. I hated the man most of the time. He had the whole world at his disposal, yet he chose to leave all this behind to live a life far away."

I placed a hand to my breast. Tears sprang to my eyes. The hatred in Ben's slurred words sent a chill through me. Was it so? Did he hate my father?

Silas coughed.

"Don't think poorly of me. I did love my brother, if one can ever truly love something. I do, however, think he was a complete fool," Ben said.

"He seemed to do all right for himself," Silas replied.

"More than one man should attain, don't you agree?"

This had to be a ploy to trick Silas. Yes. That was it. But why not inform me of the change of plans? Between the wall and the drape, I peeked out at the pair on the veranda.

"I suppose so." Silas had leaned back in his chair and was assessing Ben.

"There's no denying Willow's his daughter. Greed runs deep in her veins." Bitterness lined Ben's words.

"I wouldn't have thought that of her." Silas sounded guarded.

Does he suspect something is off? I hope you know what you're doing.

"Why do you suppose she hasn't allowed me to take over this place and run it? With the little help you have at your place, surely you can understand the hardship of running a plantation of this measure. I tried to play the loving, doting uncle, but I grow tired of waiting for her to relinquish her control and I've come to believe she never will. Likely afraid I'd take her money."

"I've reason to believe she may not be far off." Silas's eyes narrowed.

Ben dipped back his head, and his sinister laugh unnerved me. "That's where you're wrong. Sure, I'd take a percentage of my brother's estate, but then I'd set sail to England. Found myself a woman over there, and I'd rather be tossing in the hay with a bar wench than being stuck here in this country, playing father to my brother's orphan."

Silas's shoulders relaxed as Ben tugged at the fishing line he'd baited. That conniving trickster! I'd been replaced as the bait and Ben had conjured up a scheme far cleverer. A grin parted my lips.

"That's where you come in," Ben was saying when I returned my focus to the men.

"Me?" Silas leaned forward, intrigued.

"Yes. You don't suppose I demanded Willow apologize for her ill manners in town and had her dress up like a prized Negro temptress fit for a master's bed for nothing, did you?"

"I apologize, but I'm confused—"

"I know my niece has turned your head. And I can see why;

she's a beauty like her ma. Since Jones and I visited you at your place, I got to thinking, maybe you and I could strike a deal."

"What sort of deal?" Silas said.

"You marry the girl and all of this will become yours. It's a winning solution for both of us. I'm relieved of my burden of her and can go off to my lady—with one condition, of course."

"And what's that?"

"You set me up with some of the money to take care of my living expenses—money that greedy bastard should've left me to start with—and I'll gladly hand over my niece and all of this."

"How do you figure you'll get her to agree to marry me?"

A snort came from Ben. "Oh, you underestimate me, my friend. Why, I've got a few secrets on the girl."

"What secrets?" Silas's voice elevated, his interest piqued.

Ben's laugh echoed, dark and cunning. "That I can't tell you, for if I did, I'd hold no blackmail over the girl, which would then even the playing field between you and I. You can't expect me to show you all my cards, can you, Mr. Anderson?"

"I suppose not." Silas repetitively twisted the utensil beside his plate as he studied Ben.

"Tillie!"

Ben's bellow made me jump, and my head struck the wall. I bit down on my lip to stifle a cry.

"Where's that damn nigger?" Ben raged.

Tillie hurried by me with a tray of brandy and snifters, her eyes never lifting, but I saw her take a sideways glance at the hem of my gown. She moved on without a word.

"Here I am, Masa," Tillie said, disappearing outside.

"Fill my glass and then go and hurry my niece along. We've got plans to make. Maybe with that loud-mouth Northern girl off on her wedding journey, we can seal the deal before her return. What do you say, Mr. Anderson?"

"I-I'm not opposed to the idea."

"You'd better be more assured of yourself than that. I can't have no yellow-bellied coward messing up my plans."

Silas's mouth twisted in irritation. "You go too far with your insult, Mr. Hendricks."

"Forgive me; I didn't mean to offend, but if we're to be partners I need to make sure you have some grit to you."

"I assure you I possess more grit than maybe even you can handle."

Ben chuckled and leaned forward to slap him on the back. "Good. Now to figure out how we'll present the plan to my niece."

"Come on, Miss Willow, we need to git you outta dat dress," Tillie whispered, and I pulled away from the wall and followed her upstairs, where I demanded to be informed of when I'd been eliminated from the plan.

CHAPTER
Seventy-One

"YOU HAVE A LOT OF EXPLAINING TO DO," I SAID AS WE walked back inside the house after Silas's departure. Laugh lines creased the corners of his eyes. "I guessed as much."

Once settled on the settee in the library, I unloaded the questions I had bombarded Tillie with, but she'd refused to answer on strict orders from Ben.

"Why the change of plans?" I glanced from him to Tillie, who stood waiting by the end of the sofa, after Ben had requested she follow us when we'd passed her in the corridor.

"A man like Silas, who has planned out every move so thoroughly, was unlikely to fall for a dramatic change in your behavior. Most are aware of the fiery and stubborn Willow Hendricks, and if you were to suddenly become a devoted woman looking to please a man that would seem suspicious."

"Yet your change in behavior doesn't?"

"It was a chance I had to take. I put a stake in the past rumors of the townsfolk that I'd run off with your mother to prove I may be a man with no moral integrity. A man with no honor, who'd steal his own brother's wife, would be capable of stealing his niece's inheritance."

"But why leave me on the outside of your ambitious plan?"

"Bowden suggested—"

"Bowden? Why, of course! What did he have to do with this?"

"He was behind the blindsiding of you."

"Was he now!" I fumed.

"And I have to agree with him, it worked better than even I expected."

"Bravo; you pulled it off swimmingly." I clapped my hands. "You've truly missed your calling in life, Uncle. You should be playing on Broadway and selling out theaters around the world."

Ben laughed at my sarcasm. "Don't get your nose bent out of joint over something that was a success. You were yourself and, when you did catch on, you played your part brilliantly. I knew I could count on your smarts to pull through once you grasped what was going on. But your shock, along with the flames shooting out of your eyes, is what sold the whole plan."

I released a deep breath before a smile tugged at my lips. "Your performance was outstanding."

He grinned and half bowed in his seat. "Why, thank you."

"What is next? Or am I on the outs with this part of the plan, too?"

"Quite the opposite, in fact. It's your time to shine, as you will be front and center," he said.

"Meaning?"

"That you, my dear, will be joining me and my new partner in a carriage ride tomorrow. Where I'll suggest an arranged marriage between you and Mr. Anderson. Early morning, Jones will ride out and get the constable and gather the posse. While we are enjoying a pleasant afternoon and have Silas away from his place, Bowden, Mr. Sterling, and his men will take care of Caesar and Collins while Tillie searches the place."

My gaze swung to Tillie. "No. I don't want her involved. We've risked her life once already."

"She's the one who has spent the most amount of time around the homestead, and our best chance of finding all the nooks and crannies in the place."

"But—"

"She's safer now than when you sent her in alone," he reminded me. "And she's agreed that she wants to help."

"Is that so, Tillie?" I asked.

"Yes, Missus," she said in her quiet manner. "Mr. Anderson can't be going around killing folkses and thievin'. A bad man lak him can't be good for dis plantation, and de good et's doing for de folkses here. He's a danger to evvyone of us and after what he did to Gray…" Her voice broke, and her hands curled at her sides.

"You're right that he needs to pay for Gray. The lynch mob will see he's held accountable for his actions," I said.

A colored man's death would be on the short list of the posse's concerns. The only repercussion Silas would pay for Gray's murder was a fine for damaging another's property. But what would secure a rope around his neck would be us proving he was responsible for the death of Mrs. Jenson, and the robberies.

We'd considered rounding up the neighboring planters and menfolk from town and cornering Silas. But the bloodbath that was sure to happen wouldn't give us the answers we sought. Was he the man who'd been following my father, and if so, was his goal to marry me to obtain all my family owned? Or had he contrived a scheme that went much deeper?

❧ CHAPTER ❧
Seventy-Two

Tillie

M R. ARMSTRONG HAULED ME UP BEHIND HIM ON HIS MOUNT late the next morn. With my legs sprawled wide over the creature's hindquarters, I looked at my hands, not sure where to put them.

"Mr. Armstrong, I don't care for horses much. Et be all right ef I put my arms 'round you?"

"I don't plan on coming back for you if you fall off. So I reckon you'd better hang on," he said in a strained voice.

There had been a time when I'd have considered him disgusted by a colored girl hanging onto him, but lately I'd noticed a difference in the man. His eyes used to go over the heads of the slaves who attended to the Hendrickses' household, like we were the furniture filling up the place. Lately his feet had taken long pauses, like he was studying us, as though we're the artifacts and pretty artwork that gives the big house so much intrigue to the guests that visit. If I dared look into his eyes, I'd guess I might find a whole lot of puzzlement.

Recently, Mr. Armstrong's conversations with Masa Hendricks and Miss Willow have his mind catching and wandering away until they have to bring him back. I'd always liked to hear the man talk when he came to visit; he had a nice sound to his voice. Miss Willow said it was because he's from that wild place they call Texas. A place where cowboys and ranchers with hundreds of cattle roam the fields and outnumber the slaves.

"Ride out." Mr. Sterling's call made me jump and come back to what was going on around me.

Mary Grace was standing on the front veranda of the big house when I'd come out. While the constable had been with his two men and their horses out back at the water trough, I'd overheard Mr. Armstrong promise her that he'd get justice for Gray. The deadly tone in her reply lifted my eyes. Darkness clouded Mary Grace's face, a look that seemed to be shadowing all the white folks around the plantation. The look yanked my heart to my knees.

"Hang on." Mr. Armstrong clicked his tongue. He spurred his horse, and it broke into a gallop and fell into line behind the constable's gang as we cut across the field toward Mr. Anderson's plantation.

All his thieving and murdering ways had caught up to Mr. Anderson. Masa Hendricks and Miss Willow had left an hour ago to lure the fox from his den. I'd bet if someone could outsmart a fox, it'd be Miss Willow. After the visit with Mr. Anderson on the veranda, you'd think her uncle be her real pappy, with how he pulled a fast one over Mr. Anderson. Over these last months, I'd begun to wonder if maybe the chattering of folks may be true about the dead Masa Hendricks's wife and his brother. Not that it mattered much, because I liked Masa Hendricks real well.

The horse eased to a walk as we moved from the open fields and into the woods. Mr. Armstrong lifted his arm to protect us both from the lash of the branches. I buried my face into the back of his shirt and clung tight to his waist to keep from tumbling off as the horse leaped over fallen trees. Mr. Armstrong's muscles were taut and firm under my fingers, and the scent of his freshly laundered shirt centered my tumbling mind on the safety of home.

My heart thumped against my bony chest. Only the Lord was going to keep us from ending up as fish food at the bottom of the river or in a dark hole somewhere with nothing but our drawers on. Surely the thieving man would leave us those, wouldn't he?

A shudder scurried through me from my tight-fitting shoes right up to the itch under my head rag, and I started talking to the Lord.

Lard, don't let anything happen to us. Please keep our clothes on, and my brain focused on the important task at hand. Amen. Oh...and Lard, please watch out for Miss Willow and Masa Hendricks. Amen again.

All too soon, Mr. Sterling raised a hand in the air, and the men reined their horses to a stop. I knew it was time, and all I wanted to do was jump down and bolt for home. But the only thing doing any jumping was my nerves.

When Masa Hendricks told me about the plan, my knees took to knocking like when I saw Miss Whitney coming. That girl scared me right out of my drawers. Most days, that'd be all right with me. I never had to wear the dreadful things until I moved to the big house. Days in Carolina got hot, and there's nothing like a gentle cooling breeze to air things up under all those layers Miss Willow makes me wear now. The sweat runs down my legs and drops to the ground, leaving a trail behind me like I've gone and peed myself.

Mr. Armstrong dismounted and reached up and with one arm whipped me to the ground like I weighed nothing. The solid ground felt good under my feet, but it didn't stop my innards from trying to come up my throat.

The constable and his men come to stand with us. I scurried

back in the shadows behind Mr. Armstrong. I'm not used to being in the company of men alone, and thoughts of what happened to Mary Grace out in these woods snatched at my mind. A whole other kind of panic slithered up my back and over my shoulders and down—

"Tillie!" Mr. Armstrong's voice stopped my runaway mind.

"I'm listening, sir."

"We'll take care of Caesar and Collins. When we get there, you go straight inside. You got it?"

"Yes, sir." I bobbed my head.

"If Anderson gets a notion something's up, he could return sooner than expected," Mr. Armstrong said.

"And we'll be ready." Mr. Sterling's feet shifted on the ground. "The good folks of Charleston will be happy to know they can sleep at night, once this criminal's done away with. I hope your and Mr. Hendricks's suspicions will prove to be right."

Mr. Armstrong widened his stance, and he rested all his weight on his heels. "Do you have another plan? Anderson's responsible for all the mishaps around these parts, and folks have yet to bring the masked men in."

The constable rocked in his boots like he was considering what Mr. Armstrong was saying. But they tied the horses up, and we moved forward. We crept through the trees, making sure to stay low. Every branch that snapped under the men's feet sent my eyes to scan the woods. Each snatch of my skirts by the underbrush sucked the wetness from my pores. I imagined for a moment the fear and panic the freedom seekers went through as they raced across rivers and through swamps in search of the promised land, hiding from the bloodhounds and slave traders.

Ahead, the trees thinned, and Mr. Anderson's homestead came into view. We paused to stake the place out. I spotted Caesar first. He walked across the work yard with a load of lumber over his shoulder. The man they called Collins had to be the other man coming out of the barn, the man I'd seen ride up to the house back when I'd been hired by Mr. Anderson.

"You go around that way and slip in on the north side of the house." Mr. Armstrong gave me a nudge.

I hesitated as panic rooted my feet to the ground.

"Girl, you can't get cold feet now. Go!" Mr. Armstrong's voice sounded agitated.

I zigzagged through the trees to the river and circled around to the other side of the house. I looked across the work yard to where Mr. Armstrong and the others were, and from my position, I couldn't see any sign of them.

I tilted my head to the heavens. *You watching me, right, Lard?*

Not waiting for a reply because sometimes the Lord takes his good old time answering, I ran to the side of the house. I pushed out a breath as I lay snug against the wall like the slaves' clothes after Preacher John dips them in the river.

You got to do dis. Dey're counting on you. I tried to stoke some courage in myself. Swallowing to coat my dry tongue, I poked my head around the corner of the house. I spotted Mr. Armstrong and the other men skulking from the woods.

I didn't wait to see no more. I dashed around the house and up the front steps and into the house. The licking my heart was taking on my ribs grew as the smell of Mr. Anderson's recently smoked cigar tickled my nose.

Masa Hendricks said not to put myself in any unnecessary danger, and Miss Willow had laughed at him. She hadn't been herself since she came back from their ride in the woods the other day. Worry had kept her feet from staying still. Under her gown, her foot had tapped repetitively on the floorboards. Plumb scared. Now I aimed to put her faith in me to good use. I started at the rear of the house and made way to the front.

Outside, I heard the surprised voice of a man. "What in the—"

His words were cut off, and I heard a cry of pain. The racket that followed after made me move faster.

"Get in and get out," Masa Ben had said.

Finding nothing in Mr. Anderson's chambers, I moved down the small corridor to the study. I dug around in the papers on the desk, and my trembling hands halted midair at the pounding of footsteps coming up the steps. I ran to the doorway to make sure it was the right men coming in the house.

"You find anything?" Mr. Armstrong asked as the door crashed open.

I let out a breath. "Not yet, sir."

"Does the place have a study or library?" Mr. Sterling asked.

"That way." I pointed to the door to my right.

"I'll take the study. You and the slave take the parlor." The constable's boots shimmied past me.

Mr. Armstrong darted for the parlor, and I hurried after him. His strides leaped across the hallway into the room without hesitation. Outside the wide doorway, I stopped at the movement of the third board in the hall under my feet. I dropped my eyes and lifted my dress a smidgen to view the plank under my feet. The board had some give to it, but it wasn't like the ones surrounding it.

Dropping to my knees, I ran my fingers along the boards. One board seemed tighter than the rest and something about it didn't seem right. I hauled myself to my feet and went in search of something to wedge in the gap. Finding a butter knife in the small warming kitchen, I returned to the board. I used the palm of my hand to hit the back of the blade to jam it in the crack before putting some pressure behind it. My heart knocked rapidly as the board gave way.

Lifting the board, I peered down into the compartment below. Inside the narrow space, no bigger than a small bag of sugar, lay coins, papers, jewels, a wedding band, and a pocket watch, along with newspaper clippings amongst other rich folks' belongings.

The Charleston Mercury
Official Account of Last Hour and Death of Mr. Hendricks,
Charleston, South Carolina, October 15, 1851.
Gentlemen: Last eve, at the age of 60 years, Mr. Charles Hendricks expired.
Our town unites in great sadness over the loss of a great man.

I flipped through the other documents and newspaper pieces.

"Mister…" I called to Mr. Armstrong.

No answer came. The papers rattled between my trembling fingers.

"Mr. Armstrong," I said louder.

The slamming of drawers and rustling of books inside the room stopped. "What is it? You find something?"

"Yes, sir." I held up the papers, and he raced toward me. He ripped the clippings from my hand, and his eyes fell to the hole in the floor. "Mr. Sterling, get out here, and make it quick."

I scrambled to my feet and stood back as the men scooped the things from the hole. Mr. Armstrong took extra interest in the gold watch.

"This watch is the one the robbers took from Mr. Hendricks," he said grimly.

"How can you be certain?" Mr. Sterling said.

"Look at the engraving."

"To the keeper of my heart, Olivia," the constable read.

"Olivia, as in Charles Hendricks's wife?"

"I'd say so," Mr. Armstrong said.

"What's the brother doing with the watch?"

"Willow must've given it to him after her father passed."

The constable's body relaxed. "Let's get these things collected. I reckon we got the culprits responsible. Now we wait for Anderson's return."

The men got to their feet and headed for the door. On their way out, I felt a hand on my shoulder.

"You did good, girl. Let's get you home before Anderson returns," Mr. Armstrong said.

"Now evvybody is safe, right?" My heart dared hope.

"Thanks to your find. How'd you know about the trap door?"

"Dat floor had some give in et."

"I hadn't noticed."

"Ef you excuse me for saying, sir, you and Mr. Sterling warn't exactly taking et easy. More lak charging 'bout de place, lak de animals in de corral had bin let loose." Something in me drew my head up and I looked him in the eye.

A glimmer played in his pretty eyes, and heat like when I caught sight of Pete from the quarters swirled up from my belly and over my face before I dropped my head.

He's a masa and Miss Willow's gentleman, whether she lak et or not. Now, don't you go acting lak a silly filly over his simple kindness, I scolded myself before following the nice man outside.

CHAPTER
Seventy-Three

Willow

THE LUSH COUNTRYSIDE APPEARED BLEAK AND UNMOVING AS WE rode along in our open black carriage. During the last tortuous hours spent in Silas's presence, I'd struggled to keep my thoughts from wandering to what might or might not be going on at the widow's farm. Thankfully, Ben carried most of the conversation. His ingenious sham marriage arrangement with the monster who sat across from me allowed me to sulk over my unhappiness with the situation for most of the ride.

Our carriage turned the last bend en route to the widow's plantation, and I repressed a shudder. The worry of something going wrong had haunted at me all afternoon.

"We can avoid an extravagant wedding and be married quickly," Silas said.

"Have you forgotten who I am?" My grip tightened on my parasol. "Folks will expect nothing but the best from the Hendrickses. A wedding will take months of planning."

"She may be right in this one." Ben encircled my shoulders with an arm.

I cringed from his touch and pressed my body against the side of the carriage. Convincing Silas of the animosity my uncle and I bore toward each other was essential to the success of Ben's and my ruse.

Silas lapped up the apparent dislike between us. "Upon our marriage, you will avoid all contact with the Barry woman," he said.

"I think not," I retorted before I could catch myself.

The look I'd witnessed on the boardwalk sheathed his face, and a mystifying flicker blazed in his eyes before his expression became vacant. "You have much to learn, Olivia."

A chill wave coursed over me and I heard Ben suck in a sharp breath. Evidently, Silas had fallen prey to the endless rumors of my wayward mother.

"Pardon me?" I said after a few moments had passed.

No reply came.

"Mr. Anderson!" Ben snapped his fingers to pull Silas from his daze.

Silas shook his head and his brow knitted in puzzlement. "Did you say something?"

"You called me Olivia. That was my mother's name." My voice sounded foreign and strained.

Silas fixed his gaze on me. "No, my dear. You must have misheard."

"I assure you I did not," I said as the carriage veered up the drive. "It's illogical to think you would've known my mother. You wouldn't have been but a boy when she was alive. Besides, you mentioned you were from Kentucky."

"That's absurd. Of course I didn't know your mother, though I would've loved to meet the woman who'd created the divine perfection that sits before me." He bestowed upon me a dazzling smile that ended at the curves of his mouth. "You're stressed and hearing things. Isn't that correct, Mr. Hendricks?"

"Yes. I heard no mention of the name." Ben smiled convincingly.

Silas relaxed against the brown velvet seat and extended his arms across the back of it. The instantaneous change to his demeanor was chilling to observe.

The carriage came to a stop and Silas, not waiting for the driver to jump down, opened the door and stepped out. I resisted the urge to glance around for the men who lay in wait. Closing the door behind him, Silas eyed Ben before he cloaked me in the powerful warning of his gaze. "We'll move forward with preparations for our marriage first thing tomorrow, and you will cooperate. Understood?"

I glared at him before turning to stare at the woods.

"Don't mind my niece's rudeness," Ben said. "She'll learn when she should and shouldn't speak soon enough."

"And that she will," Silas said.

"Good day, Mr. Anderson." I needed to put as much distance between me and the evil standing before me as possible, or I'd come unhitched on him and these past days would be for naught. "Driver, please take us home." I moved to sit in the seat Silas had vacated.

The driver had circled the carriage back around and down the drive when Silas's bellow sounded. "Collins! Caesar! Where are you?"

Rage flashed in Ben's eyes and his fist balled on the seat as he stared off into the trees. We reached the road and the view of the homestead disappeared. Ben instructed the driver to stop and we climbed out.

"Promptly, now, back to Livingston," Ben said to the driver.

The driver slapped the reins and the horses continued on. Ben and I dashed for the cover of the trees. Gathering my gown in my hands, I threaded through the trees behind Ben as we doubled back to the homestead. We reached Mr. Sterling and his men as Silas's voice rung out again.

Silas stormed out onto the porch. "Caesar, you imbecile,

where are you?"

As he marched toward the outbuildings, Bowden stepped from behind the barn and into plain sight. Taken by surprise, Silas came to a halt. "W-what are you doing here?"

"Came to take you in and even a score."

All eyes turned to the men who stood a hundred paces in front of us. No one dared breathe.

Silas's laugh sounded taut and unsure. "And what score is that?

"Willow."

"What about her?"

"You think you can marry my lady?"

"Oh, so this is what this is about? Your ego is bruised," Silas said. "How could you possibly know about me marrying the girl?"

"The overseer at the Livingston Plantation reports back to me, for a sum, on the happenings at the place. Cut a deal with him after the scoundrel uncle of hers showed up."

"Why do you still concern yourself with her? She's proven to be a superficial being with her dismissal of you after your misfortune. Furthermore, you've sold out. And Miss Hendricks would never leave her precious Livingston behind to follow you into Indian territory. She's too refined for the frontier life."

"With the relocation of the Indians to the reservations, things are settling. Or do you not keep up with the news?" Bowden said. "But that's neither here nor there, now. You won't be marrying Willow or any other woman after folks find out who you really are."

"What do you think you know?"

"You killed my slave and took a swing at me in which you failed. Which is the least of your worries, considering I now know you and your men are indeed responsible for the robberies of the good folks of Charleston and surrounding areas. I need only to spread the word, and a lynch mob will come for you."

"You have no proof."

"No?" Bowden laughed and held out a hand, and a bright object unrolled in his fingers and dangled in midair. "This here pocket watch belonged to Mr. Benjamin Hendricks and was taken from him when he and his family were attacked by the masked men. The first time I came searching your place, you rode in, and I had to abandon my mission. But this time a little carriage ride—in which you and the slimy Mr. Hendricks planned to force Willow into marrying you, no doubt—kept you occupied so I could search the place. And to my surprise, I located a hidden compartment in the floor in the hallway. You can only imagine my satisfaction when I found all the evidence I needed within."

Silas glanced around.

"Don't bother looking for them; they aren't coming to back you up this time. A blow to the back of the head took care of Collins and, had I not been in a hurry, I'd have tied him up to keep him from running off. And the slave Caesar…I ended his life without a second thought. His life for my slave's life." Bowden shrugged nonchalantly.

Anger underlined Silas's tone. "What makes you think I had anything to do with that?"

"You know of his death?"

Silas's voice caught and he quickly said, "People talk."

"Yet no one was told of his death."

"Why do you care about that nigger so much, anyhow?" Silas inched toward Bowden, who circled him, giving himself enough distance to avoid his reach.

"What does it matter to you what I do or don't do with my property?"

Silas circled. "It doesn't."

"The better question is, why did you kill him?" Bowden lunged at him, throwing a baited punch and purposely missing.

Silas chuckled and his shoulders hunched. "I gathered you were weak, but that was a deplorable attempt."

"I won't miss next time," Bowden said.

In a flash, Silas's fist connected with Bowden's face, and he stumbled back. He staggered with a hand to his face, but quickly regained his footing. My heart catapulted into the back of my throat with the second connection of Silas's fist. Bowden delivered two swift punches to Silas's middle, and he yelped but never lost his balance. The men circled each other while Ben, the other men, and I hid in the trees, watching the scene unfold.

No one breathed a word but tension stiffened the bodies of all who lay in wait, hoping Silas would deliver all accounts of his guilt into our hands.

A crack as bone met bone, and Bowden went down on his knee. He scrambled to get up as Silas landed another hook to his chin and Bowden snapped backward, his back nearly touching his heels for a moment. Silas took advantage of the human knot before him and planted his boot hard into Bowden's chest. He sprawled on the ground.

Silas centered his boot in the middle of Bowden's chest and held him down. "You see, Armstrong, if you expect to make a threat, you must be certain you cut them off at the knees. Your nigger overheard something he shouldn't have, and I gutted him so he wouldn't come running to you. A waste of a good slave, seeing as you've come looking anyhow. You've no one to blame but yourself."

"You'll never see the light of day again. You worthless—" Bowden sputtered in rage "—murdering son-of-a—"

"Silence!" Silas craned his neck and lifted the heel of his palm to his temple and struck himself.

I frowned at the gesture and cast a look at Ben, whose brow was furrowed. He shifted in place. I turned my focus back to the yard.

"Not now." Silas shook his head as if to dispel a buzzing fly. "Silence, I said." His voice cracked with remote vulnerability.

"Worthless," Bowden repeated.

"Don't say that, Pa. I'm...not," Silas cried. "No...not you! Get out of my head...witch." He lifted his hands and covered the sides of his head.

"He's plumb crazy," I whispered.

"Witch?" Bowden's voiced hitched with confusion.

Silas never removed his hold on Bowden but continued to act eccentrically and speak in broken statements. "It's all your fault. You and Pa brought the curse upon our family. You killed the Hendricks woman. We should've burned the witch alive instead of snapping her neck."

Mother! Fear curdled in my stomach with the realization. Ben grabbed my arm as I teetered.

"I'll kill him," Ben whispered through clenched teeth.

"Caesar, where are you," Silas cried, sounding desperate. "You dumb nigger. Show yourself."

"He's dead, I told you," Bowden said as he twisted to remove himself from Silas's hold.

Silas's head snapped back and then dropped forward as if coming out of a trance. "I don't believe you."

"Check behind the barn. I painted it with his blood. We are even now, with the death of your prized mule. But rest assured, it was he who revealed to me your treasures under the floor before I ended him."

"I should've ended him when he wanted to squeal about the Hendricks woman, instead of taking his tongue." Silas's voice boomed. "You won't be leaving here alive. I should've got rid of you from the start."

Had Caesar been there when my mother was murdered? Did he try to tell someone of what he'd witnessed? She'd died years ago. They'd have only been boys at the time. Had Silas's pa killed my mother? But why? Silas spoke of another person, but who was he? The questions in my head consumed me, and I missed the movement from Bowden signaling for the men to move in.

"Stay," Ben ordered me before stepping from the woods.

Mr. Sterling, rope in hand, and one of his men followed after Ben. Crouched low, they moved into position flanking Silas, using an outbuilding as their shield. I saw Mr. Sterling remove his pistol from his holster and nod at the men and Ben. They walked into the yard.

"All right, Anderson. It is over," Mr. Sterling said.

Silas spun around in surprise at the approach of the men. "Ahh, so you didn't come alone. I underestimated you, Armstrong."

"It appears you misjudged a lot," Ben said. "To think you believed I'd sell out my niece for money."

"Better men have fallen for less." Silas shrugged and locked his eyes on the woods where we stood. "Come out, come out, wherever you are."

My heart thundered.

"You murdered her!" Ben pounced on Silas and threw him to the ground and sent fist after fist at his face and torso. Finally, exhausted, Ben rocked back on his heels.

Silas's sadistic laugh bewildered me, but it was what happened next that buckled my knees. His voice changed to that of an Irishman with a heavy accent. "Yes! And she wiggled and twisted for life like your brother did beneath the carriage as the underbrush around it turned into an inferno."

364 | NAOMI FINLEY

Father...what was he saying? I leaned on a tree for support. What asylum had Silas escaped from?

I moved from the trees and shook free of the hand of the man who reached for me. I heard his heavy treads behind me as I hurried closer.

Bowden had risen to his feet and hovered over Silas.

"I saw the fire and met Jones and his men as they brought him in." Ben's voice was hollow, as if he were recalling the night, and a daunting tone echoed in his next words. "It wasn't an accident...nor was Bowden's. You needed to be rid of them to get to Willow."

"You would've been next if you hadn't convinced me of your willingness to help me take her fortune," Silas said matter-of-factly. "Well done."

"And after you achieved her fortune, what then?" Bowden growled.

"Kill her, and end the curse Olivia placed on my family once and for all!" he screamed. "No, don't talk. We mustn't tell them any more." His voice altered from the Irishman to that of another. This one was more childlike and frightened.

"The man's insane!" Mr. Sterling swiped a hand over his face. "Get him up! You get the horses," he told his man, and he took off toward the barn.

Bowden and Ben pulled Silas to his feet as I stepped into the circle. Silas's head flopped side to side, and he grinned at them like someone who'd floated away from the present time. They turned him around, and Mr. Sterling bound his hands behind his back.

The man returned with the horses, and Bowden and Ben lifted Silas up onto the horse. He appeared harmless in his current crazed state of mind.

"Mount up. We'll see to it he meets his fate tonight." Mr.

Sterling swung up on his horse and turned sad eyes on me. "I'm sorry you had to hear this. Your mother's disappearance has always troubled me. Now we know. And your father...he was my friend."

Ben's arm slipped around my shoulder, and I slumped into him, burying my face into the curve of his shoulder, and wept.

"I'll ride with them. You'd best take her home," Bowden said. "She's dealt with enough for one day."

"Yes," Ben said.

After the tramp of horses' hooves faded, Ben pulled me from his side and lifted my chin so I'd look at him. His face reflected the pain and horror of Silas's revelation.

"His pa? Where is he now?" I said.

"I don't know. Tomorrow I'll go to town and place an advertisement in every paper offering a reward for anyone with information on the Anderson men."

CHAPTER
Seventy-Four

THE NEWS OF SILAS'S ESCAPE FROM THE POSSE RIPPLED FEAR through the country folk and tensions were high. Ben doubled the guards at the gates and the entrances to the house and quadrupled the bounty on the fugitive's head. Citizens placed advertisements in newspapers across the country for his capture. Vigilantes and bounty hunters spread from one border of South Carolina to the other in search of him. Far and wide the news traveled, and the sheriff of Charleston and those of nearby towns made it a priority to discover were Silas the drifter had come from.

People fabricated stories, and the Guardian became Silas Anderson, the serial killer who'd roamed the outskirts of Charleston stealing slaves and murdering them to satisfy his appetite for blood.

The lynching mob hung Collins for his involvement in the deaths related to the robberies. Caesar would've suffered the same fate if Mr. Sterling and his men hadn't backed Bowden up on his insistence that Caesar had been as much a victim as we were in all of the crimes. And without a voice or the ability to read and write, he'd done the only thing he could to warn us all. Bowden went as far as to deem Caesar a hero, but the other men had scoffed at the title. Caesar had been listed for auction, and when I informed Caroline Smith of the cruelty done to him at the hands of Silas she arranged to have her source attend the auction and purchase him.

Together Caroline and the source secured safe passage for him to the city of Hamilton in the Province of Canada.

In early January, Mr. Sterling showed up with information that'd shed some light on the unanswered questions on Silas Anderson.

"Name's Reuben McCoy. From Jamestown, Virginia." He leaned over the neck of his horse and held out a wanted poster to Ben.

I moved in to take a look. The shaded sketch of a bearded man with shoulder-length hair looked dissimilar to the man we'd come to know as Silas.

"He wasn't from Kentucky," I said.

"No. He was born to a Martha and Horace McCoy. The family owned a small plantation in Virginia and had two sons. Horace was a local drunk and frequented the saloons and eventually was banned from all establishments for starting brawls and reported abuse to the whores. The man moved his wife and two sons to James Island.

"Folks said the family kept to themselves. Their homestead was isolated and off the beaten path. A trapper who roamed those parts of the woods said the mother up and vanished one day. Town says the husband never reported her missing. Horace and his eldest son were seen in town but the younger boy, Reuben...folks never would've known he existed if it weren't for their wagon rolling into town the day they'd arrived.

"Horace continued his past behavior and was a regular at the saloons in town and was rumored to have mentioned on occasion a curse on his family. Was said to have stated 'The witch is the reason for the money drying up and my land being nothing but powder.' No one knows who he spoke of, but he believed her to be the reason for his turn of bad luck."

"Any idea where he is now?" Ben asked.

I noticed dark circles from sleepless nights had settled under Mr. Sterling's eyes. "In a grave. It seems the McCoy homestead burned to the ground a few years back and the remains of a man were found inside."

"Only one?" His revelations did nothing to soothe my concerns that Silas…Reuben…lay in wait for the opportunity to come back and finish what he'd started. I rubbed my arms to quell my shivering.

A grimace twisted Mr. Sterling's face. "A neighbor said that after the land proved to be unyielding, the brother took off to find work. But he was never seen in those parts again. Horace had sold off their slaves to keep food in their bellies. The most bizarre thing is the alias Reuben was using. It belonged to a Negro planter not far from their homestead. The Negro and his wife were found dead. Their deaths were grotesque and appeared to be done by wild animals. Yet the Negroes' bodies were desecrated and their valuables, along with their few slaves, gone."

My stomach went hollow and I said in a shaky voice, "How he escaped you all is beyond me."

Mr. Sterling averted his eyes. "Should've used chains instead of rope. Crazy one moment and a mastermind the next. We will get him, and I, for one, won't rest until he's caught. He's moved to the top of the list of most wanted men across the country."

"Yet he still wanders free and is a threat to our family and others. His family murdered my brother's wife, and he's responsible for Charles's death. He made his intentions clear with coming after Willow." Ben pulled me into the curve of his arm.

"What he did to your family has taken on a whole other aspect that has folks around here riled up. Your family's well respected, and until he pays for what he's done to you all, folks won't rest. Even as we speak, the story grows. I've never been one for idle gossip, but this time it may work to your advantage." Sterling laid kind eyes on me. "I know she loved you. Never made any sense why she'd leave. After what we've come to know of the sort of man Reuben is, I doubt we'll ever have her body to lay to rest properly."

"Thank you for caring, Mr. Sterling. You've been a valued friend to my family and we won't forget your kindness," I said.

"Don't mention it. Only wish there was more I could do," he said before he rode off.

In fact, my mother's body had been secretly laid to rest by my father in the family cemetery in a grave marked Katherine Shaw. When father had found her, he'd buried her and used her middle name to mark the grave. The slave woman he'd found hanging with her, he'd buried in the slave cemetery with her given name, Ellie.

"Do you think Reuben McCoy will ever be brought to justice?" I said to Ben as he led me back inside the house.

"You put enough money on a man's head, and someone will deliver him to you." His fingers gripped my shoulder.

Many nights I didn't sleep, for fear of waking up and finding Reuben standing over me. Nights when I did sleep, my dreams were filled with images of Reuben and two faceless men who stood back laughing as my mother clawed at the rope around her neck. Then her face would turn to mine and I'd sit straight up in bed with my heart battering my chest wall. And the next night it'd happen again.

Inside, I mounted the first step to head upstairs to my bedchamber and turned to face Ben. Since the night Reuben had revealed he'd murdered my mother and father, he'd become consumed with finding the ones responsible. I'd often find him lost in thought, and his smiles were staged for my benefit.

"Maybe it's time I take that trip to England," I said.

He kissed my forehead before wandering down the hall to the study, where he'd spend the rest of the afternoon and late into the evening. "Maybe," his reply echoed after him.

CHAPTER
Seventy-Five

Bowden

THE THURSDAY BEFORE MY DEPARTURE, I RODE TOWARD Livingston. Tuesday I'd catch a train to Texas to meet the bank about a property I'd been considering since my visit this past summer. In my desperation to be rid of my plantation and forget Willow, I'd sold the place for significantly less than the property was worth. The new owner, Mr. Barlow, had said he and his wife would be keeping a small staff, and they'd acquire their own when they arrived in South Carolina. Mr. Barlow had gone on to inform me that though slavery was abolished in England in 1833, he'd never shown favor to the barbaric trade.

The man had sent my plan cruising down the Cooper River on a one-way ticket by leaving me with fifty-three slaves. I'd made the decision to sell all the slaves and keep only my trusted servants. The dream of starting a new life in Texas had become my focus until Gray's death. A muscle twitched in my jaw at the memory of his butchered body lying on the bed. Only a deranged lunatic could perform such brutality on another man, and Reuben McCoy had proven to be such a man. The fact he remained at large and could turn up at any moment to exact his warped vendetta against Willow and her family plagued me.

In the dead of night last night, I'd had an epiphany. What

was I doing? I couldn't leave without trying one last time to hook the fool woman into marrying me.

"The worse she can say is no." I patted the neck of my horse as I rode into Livingston.

Coming to a stop in front of the main house, I dismounted, and James, the slave I'd heard Willow affectionately refer to as Jimmy, rushed into the yard to take my horse.

He bowed his head. "Morning, Mr. Armstrong, sir."

"Are Mr. Hendricks and Willow around?"

"Miss Willow has gone to see Missus Tucker, but Masa Hendricks is inside, I do believe."

"I see." I removed my hat and tucked it in the crook of my arm before turning to look up at the house, swallowing back the nerves that had been playing in my gut all morning. "I'll show myself in." My feet remained planted.

"You all right, sir?"

"Yes. It's just…" I twisted to look at the man. "I've come to seek Mr. Hendricks's approval on marrying his niece."

A yelp came from James and he shot a fist at the skies. A wide grin lifted the tips of his ears. "Now dat's de most sense I've heard in a long time. De Missus loves you a whole lot."

"And I, her. But she isn't an easy woman."

"Aww, she's easy 'nuf, but dere ain't no changing what she thinks in dat purty head of hers."

"That was a realization I've come to terms with. A journey of discovery I had to make on my own…" I kicked at a stone with the tip of my boot.

"Sometimes in life, et's de hard lessons dat affect us de most and make us look at things differently."

"Unfortunately, so," I said, eyeing the man. "I can see why she respects your opinion."

He reddened and ducked his head. "Miss Willow is a lot to

handle, but she's a fine woman."

"A woman worth nabbing, do you agree?"

An odd but pleasant chuckle came from him. "Dat she be, Mr. Armstrong, dat she be."

I left him and mounted the front steps to the house, and Mary Grace came out to greet me. The months of hardship and grief hollowed her eyes and jutted her cheekbones. My pulse sped up, and for lack of better words, I said, "I've come to speak with Mr. Hendricks."

"I'll…I'll get him," her voice quavered, and she turned to go inside.

"Wait."

She froze.

"How are the children?"

Her body stiffened. "They are fine, sir."

"I wish…I miss him too," I managed to say. "I…I'd do anything to have him back. I should've taken him away from here myself."

She turned slowly and raised tear-filled eyes to me. "What happened to him isn't your fault. Gray spoke highly of you, and you did right by him."

"Not good enough. He was a man beyond men, and he'll be remembered as such."

"Thank you, sir. I'll let Mr. Hendricks know you're here."

I nodded, and she disappeared inside. Turning away, I choked back the tears collecting in my throat and walked the length of the veranda to wait.

"Afternoon; what can I do for you?" Mr. Hendricks's gaunt appearance took me by surprise.

"I've come to ask you a question."

"Let's talk in the library," he said and without waiting for a reply, turned and walked back into the house. I followed him.

In the library, he closed the door behind us, moved about the room, and came to stand in front of the fireplace, resting his arm on the marble mantel.

My eyes roved over the endless assortment of books on the floor-to-ceiling mahogany shelves, then to the paintings, one of Willow and her father and the other of her mother. I studied her mother with reverence and thought of the tragic way her life had ended, and the pain of learning the gory details Reuben had shared with Mr. Hendricks and Willow.

"I loved her, you know." Mr. Hendricks's voice broke through my pondering, and I craned my neck to look at him. "She was the love of my life." His eyes softened as he thought of her. "She was a remarkable woman and one I've spent a lifetime trying to force from my mind."

Shortly after her father's death, a grief-stricken Willow had told me of her parentage, and I'd held her in my arms and sworn to never tell another.

"I know you are set on placing roots in Texas, but I'd hate to see you and Willow make the same mistakes we did. She'll never leave this place. When we found out Olivia was pregnant with Willow, I tried to get her to marry me and go someplace where no one knew us. But this place became ingrained into who Olivia was, and she wouldn't leave her father or the folks in the quarters."

"Like her daughter," I said.

"My daughter loves you, and I don't want her growing old pining after the Texan who stole her heart. It's about time some happiness came to this family, and you and Willow could be a new beginning. You aren't the man you were but a few months ago. Sometimes death has that effect on people. It has a way of making you evaluate who you are and what really matters in life, doesn't it?"

"I reckon so. Shame it has to resort to that." I swallowed hard before continuing. "You see, the thing is…I came here to ask your permission to marry Willow—"

"It's about time!"

I grinned before becoming solemn. "I'll love her and treasure her each day I draw breath. And protect her from her enemies and herself, with your permission, sir."

"Gladly." He smiled broadly as he strode across the room and held out his hand, which I shook vigorously.

I blew out a breath. "Much obliged, sir. Now, if it's all right with you, I'd like to marry tomorrow."

His brow lifted. "So soon?"

"Your daughter has a history of running. If she agrees when I ask her, I plan to seal the commitment then and there before she changes her mind." I laughed.

He slapped my back in merriment. "I concede your point."

Later that afternoon, my head overseer entered the house and paused in the hallway outside the study. "Sir, I've gathered them as you've requested."

"Thank you." I picked up the envelope on the corner of the desk and crossed the room. "I appreciate your dedication to my grandfather and to me. I hope this will take care of your needs until you can secure employment elsewhere."

The overseer's eyes grew round at the hefty sum within. "You sure you want to go to Texas? You've got a fine business for yourself, right here."

"With the plantation sold, I've got no choice but to find somewhere else to put down roots."

"Well, it's been an honor, sir. Take care of yourself."

"You as well," I said, following him to the door and stepping out on the piazza.

The house staff and the folks from the quarters stood in the front yard. All fifty-three sets of eyes rested on me. Distress and uncertainty covered their faces.

The overseer mounted his horse, and with a tip of his hat, he and his men rode out. After their dust had settled, I lowered my eyes to the folks in front of me.

Friends and families huddled together, and tears liberally flowed, as the anxiety of being separated consumed their thoughts. A lump stuck in my throat at a sight that merely a year ago wouldn't have concerned me as it did now.

I expelled the emotions clenching my chest with a cough. "It's no secret that I've sold this plantation."

Murmurs and wails rose, and a tremor like a hurricane wind whipped through them. A woman dropped to her knees and pleaded, "Please, Masa, don't take me from my babies. I can't...I won't survive..." She sobbed into clasped hands.

I put up a hand to calm the anxious chatter. "Hear me out."

A silence stretched out over the yard, and they waited for me to speak.

"Too often people are born into a way of life and grow up believing what they've always been told with little consideration of the rights or wrongs of it. Sometimes these wrongs and injustices are brought to your attention, but you're too blinded... or don't wish to see for yourself because it's the way it's always been. An excuse I'm ashamed to say I hid behind for far too long. Gray..." Again, emotions swelled in me as my eyes fell on his pa.

"He was a good man, Masa," a woman said.

"He was the best." My eyes remained on his pa. "Never have I known a better man."

His pa's eyes dampened and he inclined his head in appreciation.

"Gray had but one dream…and that was to be free." I looked out over the faces of the folks who had given years of their lives to serve my family and me. The folks who'd helped us earn my fortune. "Freedom that was taken from him and freedom that he'd earned back tenfold, but laws bound me from giving him something that was rightfully his.

"Who am I to tell another person that he doesn't have the right to wake in the morning when his body tells him it's ready to? Who am I to tell a husband he can't hold his wife in his arms at night because I've sold her to another master? Or that he can't see his children grow each day. Who am I…" A great ache seemed to shatter my chest. "…I'm no one.

"Gray was my friend, and I loved him like a brother. Society and laws say I'm not allowed to have such feelings. And why? Because he's a black man?" My voice rose with the passion that had awakened in me. "I love my country, but I will not be part of this madness any longer."

"What are you gonna do, Masa?" Concerned voices rang out.

"If Miss Hendricks doesn't marry me today, I'm fixing to go back to Texas and take up ranching. On my return, I'll secure passage for us all to make the move. Starting over won't be easy and if I could give you *all* your freedom, I would."

"All we ever know is planting."

"You can learn as well as another man, woman, or child."

Whispers ran through them yet again.

I pointed to a man. "You—what do you do?"

"I'm a blacksmith."

"And you?" I waved a finger at a man not but eighteen years. "Why, I'm a field hand, Masa."

I descended the steps. "So you're a farmer?"

A grin twisted the boy's mouth and his shoulders lifted. "I guess, of sorts."

"What about you, Abigail?

"I'm a cook, Masa."

"You make the best soupikandia around." I cupped the back of her neck and placed my lips to her forehead. Pulling back, I rubbed away the tear cascading down her cheek with a thumb before coming to stand in front of another woman. "And you?"

"I'm a seamstress."

I gently clasped her arthritic fingers. "And our store has sold some of the finest linens and clothing this side of Charleston."

A gleam of pride brightened her weary eyes.

"You?" I moved on to the next person.

"A cooper."

"What about you."

"A boatman."

"Carpenter."

"Shoemaker."

A thunder of cries arose.

"See?" I jutted my hands toward the heavens. "You all have skills and are better at them than most white men. But we've led you to believe you're incapable of fending for yourselves. If I can't convince Miss Hendricks to do me the honor of being my wife, we'll be leaving for Texas at the end of the month. If you choose to go find your families, I'll not hunt you, but I do caution you that if you leave, you risk the chance of getting captured and sold off to God knows where. By the time the new owners arrive, we need to be gone. Please think about what I've said and report back to me with your thoughts."

After the yard emptied, I turned and lumbered up the steps.

"Masa?" a man said.

I turned to find Gray's pa. "What is it?"

"Ef things don't go lak you be wanting…I thought maybe you'd consider selling me to de Livingston Plantation. You see, Masa, Mary Grace and de chillum are all I got left. And I figured dat I'd lak to spend de rest of de years I got left wid dem."

"Very well, I'll speak to Mr. Hendricks and Miss Hendricks on the matter."

"Bless you, Masa."

I waved a hand at him and turned back to go inside.

"Masa?"

I paused and spun to face him.

"You honor my boy. Gives me peace, knowing your caring for him stirred dis change in you. Makes me think…maybe he didn't die for nothin'."

Tears faded the man below from my view. "I…I made God a promise that if he saved Gray, I'd change." I heaved a sigh. "When he didn't, I was angry at Him and myself. Then one day, I woke to feel different. I sat on this piazza for most of the day and looked at all I owned, yet inside, I was empty and lost. None of it matters without the ones you love. Losing Gray removed my blinders and lit a flame in me to make my wrongs right. I don't have it all figured out, but one day at a time is all I can do."

"Dat's all we can ever do," he said with a shrug before shuffling off.

CHAPTER
Seventy-Six

Willow

THE FOOTMAN GRIPPED MY FINGERS IN HIS, LATE THE NEXT morning as I stepped from the carriage at the Armstrong Plantation. Dark clouds sprawled across the rumbling sky.

Ben had informed me on my return from Whitney's that Bowden had stopped by to see me. I'd questioned Ben on the reasoning behind his visit, but he'd said he had an appointment in town and left me to ponder on what Bowden would've wanted. I took it upon myself to ride over and find out for myself.

Knox had mentioned Bowden would be leaving for Texas soon. Though I'd numbed my heart to his going, my stomach twisted with anxiety and my heart raced at seeing him.

"Is Mr. Armstrong home?" I asked the woman sweeping the front veranda.

"Yes, Miss Hendricks. He's 'round somewhere." A gleam shone in her eyes. "You might want to check down by de cemetery. He goes dere often."

"Thank you," I said.

Overhead the sky cracked, and sprinkles of rain spotted my gown. Gathering the sides of my skirt, I hurried my steps to the cemetery that sat isolated on a hill guarded by an ancient oak tree.

Reaching the top, I saw Bowden standing inside the black wrought-iron fence enclosing the small family plot. He didn't turn when I opened the gate and entered. Or when I came to stand beside him. He gave me a sideways glance but remained quiet, studying the grave he stood in front of.

The gravestones were engraved with the names of the family who owned the plantation before him. One bore the Armstrong name and it was that of Bowden's grandfather. The stone Bowden stood in front of had an image of a weeping willow carved into it along with the words:

In Memory of Gray
Husband of Mary Grace
Died Nov. 5, 1853
at 32
May you soar with newfound wings

My throat thickened and my lashes cut through sudden tears flowing down my cheeks. Not long ago we'd gathered here and said our final goodbyes to Gray, and my heart had been too broken at the time to grasp the significance of what Bowden had done.

"Bowden…"

"Hmm," he said, never turning.

My heart thudded against my breast. "You honor him in ways that'd never be accepted if others were to find out."

"If only I'd done so in life." He choked back the emotions pulling at his face.

"It's what you do now that matters. By honoring him with your life," I said.

He turned, and his eyes brimmed with unshed tears. "For too long I've claimed human lives as if they were possessions to be owned. Too stubborn to listen to what was in my own heart. I've been a fool. In my blindness I was ready to set out for Texas without you, rather than open my eyes to what was right in front of me. I love you, Willow Hendricks, and as I told you before, there'll never be another woman for me. And with that, I have a proposal…"

"Proposal?" I held my breath.

"As you may know, the new owners of this place will be arriving in the spring. And I now have no plantation, but have fifty-three lives on my hands. A responsibility I no longer want, yet laws forbid me from setting them free. That leaves me with only a few choices. Allow the ones who want to chance their freedom on their own to leave and take the others with me, or…"

I waited. The heavens released.

He cupped my trembling shoulders in his hands. "Or you do the honor of being my wife, and we join forces to make a difference in the lives of the ones who want to stay."

The burdens and pain of the past years rolled into a jumbled mess of emotions and burst in me. I buried my face in my hands and sobbed. Bowden gathered me in his arms and pulled me close. My hands slipped around him, and my fingers dug into the fabric of his rain-soaked shirt. His heart drummed against my ear, and the strength of his arms swathed me in a blanket of safety and love.

Moments later, regaining my composure, I pushed back, my hands resting on his chest. "The man who stands before me is all I've ever wanted. There's a fire in you to fight for what's right, and this is the man I want to spend my life with. I love you, Bowden Armstrong, more than I've ever loved anything in life. If you leave, I will become a spinster and die a million times over."

"Is that so?" He threw back his head and laughed.

"I will die. I promise you!" I said, growing angry.

His expression grew serious, and his thumbs stroked the

curves of my shoulders. "Are you sure about this?"

"More than I've ever been. But you must know I can never leave Livingston."

"I've always known that."

"You must think about what this means to you. Will you stay and help me run Livingston as my husband?"

"What about Ben? Livingston already has a man of the house. I'm not sure there's room for two of us."

"Ben's heart is in medicine. He doesn't wish to run Livingston, but does want to remain there. If you're willing to accept my secrets, then yes, I'll be your wife."

"I accept you for all you are and all that's yours. I'll spend my life proving to you my love." He dipped his head, and I lifted my face to meet his kiss.

Lost in a kiss and entangled in each other's arms, the world faded around us. The passion of years of longing molded our bodies together until I broke away, breathless. I blushed at the desire rushing through me.

Bowden grinned at my embarrassment. "No backing out?"

I smiled. "Promise."

"Good, because Ben should be at the house by now. We're heading to the registry office before you change your mind."

Without warning, he swooped in and flipped me over his shoulder, and he hurried to the gate, which he kicked open with his boot.

"Bowden Armstrong, you put me down." I laughed, striking his back with my fist.

"You got a thing for running, and I need to make sure I get you in the carriage." His voice echoed from behind the flouncing fabric of my skirts as we made our descent from the hill. "You'll be mine before this day is over."

"Not if you have to hog-tie me to get there," I said as he set my feet back on solid ground.

"Let's not waste time."

He clasped my hand in his and broke into a run. I laughed as he pulled me forward, slipping on the wet grass as we hurried toward our future.

Epilogue

Silas

"WATCH WHERE YOU'RE GOING!" I YELLED AT THE numbskull German scum driving the wagon like it was his first day.

Baltimore, Maryland, reeked of the haze of chemicals pumping from the factories and the immigrant scum lining the harbor and streets. I threaded through the wagons and carriages to the tavern house.

I'd escaped South Carolina with barely the clothes on my back. I'd made my way north by hiding in wagons and on cargo trains and sleeping in barns and under bridges to avoid the bounty hunters that waited to ambush me from every corner in the towns I passed through.

That witch will pay! There was only one way to kill a witch. And I'd take great pleasure in seeing her fry on a post. I'd bathe in the ecstasy of her screams and the stench of her flesh as it melted from her bones. My heart fluttered, and a smile eased the taut muscles in my face.

Entering the establishment, my nose twitched at the repulsive scent of cheap cigars and unwashed bodies. I removed a handkerchief from my pocket and shielded my nose. Scanning the room, I spotted him seated at a table in a darkened corner by the far wall.

A buxom tavern wench with flaming red hair and wearing a pink ruffled dress welded her body against mine. The bodice of her dress cut into her hefty mounds. She'd doused herself in a whiskey keg of rouge and the essence of rose. The scent, mixed with the stale tobacco on her breath, made me gasp.

She batted her lashes at me. "Hello, handsome. Do you care to have a go at Miss Mary? Men say I fulfill their greatest fantasies." She stroked my arm with her breast, and the heat radiating from her body convulsed my stomach.

I leaned down and for her ears only said, "Move away from me, or you'll end up in the bottom of the ocean with the rest of my victims."

Her pale blue eyes grew wide, and she pivoted and charged off.

I smirked and continued toward the man I'd come to find.

He sat hunched over the table, his badly burned hands gripping a pint of ale. The bottom of the mug seemed to compel his thoughts, and he never glanced up as I towered over him. I pulled out a chair in front of him and dropped into it. Removing my hat, I tossed it on the table and leaned back in the chair, studying my brother.

"What secrets does that pint hold?" I asked dryly as he lifted his head.

"I see you made it." His eyes narrowed. "Run out of Charleston with your tail between your legs. Still in one piece, but a failure, nonetheless." He pushed back his hat and scratched at the bandana partially masking his forehead—a habit for him that he remained unaware of. The cloth moved slightly and revealed the edges of the gnarly pink letters engraved in his forehead.

My brother leaned in, his eyes checking for listening ears before he said in a low voice, "We've no choice but to lie low, now that you've got a bounty on your head that even I'd consider turning you in for."

I gritted my teeth and leaned forward, slamming my fist on the table. The thunder of my fist ricocheted throughout the tavern and turned heads our way. "I swear to you, we'll have our revenge, Rufus."

Dear Readers,

When I decided to write a series set in the antebellum era, I began with a simple plot for *A Slave of the Shadows*. Surprisingly, what started out as a trilogy quickly became a five book series. My goal in writing historical fiction was not to convey all the data I've collected researching, but instead scatter historical facts throughout the story to enlighten you by offering new insights into the period. By purposefully placing you within the pages of my novel I hope to inspire, entertain, and create a reading experience offering you an escape from the burdens of everyday life.

With this in mind, I want to share my personal journey into the story's development. Like Willow, the relationship I had with my father was not great. I resonate strongly with this character because I was raised to believe a woman's role was to obey and keep silent. Throughout my life, I longed to be accepted by my father for being a strong woman. When I was younger I refused to be silenced about the wrongs I'd witnessed, and as a result I spent most of my life searching for his approval. When he died suddenly six years ago, I felt robbed of reaching a place of peace in our relationship. This grieved me because I loved my father. Sadly, a healthy relationship with him was never part of life's plan.

About twelve years ago, an ex-military man named Jimmy walked into our lives and became a friend of my family. He had a shy disposition, with a unique and endearing laugh we adored. Jimmy chose to spend time with a few connections from his military days, as his family members were not part of his life. He refused to let others get close to him because of past hurts, so at first he denied the bond my family tried to form with him. Eventually, we won his trust and he became an important part of our lives.

Over time Jimmy became very special to our family and we cherished him. He would often show up at our place on Sunday mornings around 7a.m. offering a coffee and a smile. He had a beautiful spirit and viewed the world with an open mind. This man taught me to strive to be a better person. One of the many endearing things about Jimmy was he could never say my name correctly. He called me "Yomi," and this was the inspiration for the character Jimmy referring to Willow as "Miss Willie."

In 2012, Jimmy was diagnosed with prostate cancer. We hoped he would recover after surgery, but instead we found out the disease was in his liver. Our friend underwent another operation, but sadly the cancer moved to his lungs. At this point, things were looking grave, but he refused to give us permission to contact his family to inform them about his illness.

Jimmy also resisted a care nurse coming into his home because of his fear of doctors and his ornery disposition. As time went on, he depended on my husband and I to drive him to his appointments and run other errands. It still makes me chuckle when I think about him instructing the medical supply delivery service to throw his colostomy bags over the fence instead of bringing them to the door. He reminded me of Max Goldman from the film *Grumpy Old Men*.

Jimmy and I spent endless hours chatting during the three years we cared for him before he passed on June 15, 2015. He sometimes spoke about his daughter and he kept a small image of her hanging on his living room wall taken when she was one. Jimmy was estranged from his wife and had not seen his daughter since she was six. All too quickly the day came when he wanted to chat about his will. At first I didn't want to talk about it—the thought of losing the man I'd come to love like a father was too heartbreaking. I comforted myself with the hope his health might improve.

My optimism was dashed when Jimmy made the choice to stop his chemo and radiation treatments in December 2014. At his request, I went over his will and I learned his daughter was the first person named on the document. The details of her whereabouts were scant, consisting of her first name and last known location only. He knew her mother's first name, but he couldn't remember her maiden name. Jimmy insisted he didn't want to see his daughter. I suspect the fear of her rejection crippled him. All my husband and I could do was respect his final wishes, ensuring his daughter was notified and received the money he was leaving her after he passed.

By the time we decided to take action to find this girl, Jimmy's cancer had moved to his brain. Both the illness and drugs were now affecting his mind. I knew if we were going to honor his will, I had to pick his memory for anything he might still recall to help our quest. Unfortunately, he blocked most of the details about his past as a coping mechanism. Thirty years had gone by since he had contact with anyone who might offer some direction, nonetheless, I was determined to find her.

The urgency to locate this woman kept me awake at night. I searched social media sites to obituaries and high school class lists to marriage records, but I came up empty-handed. I even spoke to a private investigator who insisted it was impossible to locate Jimmy's daughter or her mother with so few facts. I was devastated, and felt overcome with grief and sadness. All I wanted to do was to give our dear friend the gift of peace knowing we tracked down his daughter before he passed. Despite the complicated nature of the circumstances, I refused to lay down and accept defeat.

Thankfully my search was revived in May when we were sitting in Jimmy's living room and he suddenly remembered his wife's maiden name. Armed with this piece of information, I went on the search again, and in June I tracked down his daughter's uncle on Facebook. Searching through his list of friends I found Jimmy's wife. As I scrolled through her list of friends, a familiar face popped up. Chills ran through me. The woman's similarities to Jimmy were uncanny. I stared at the screen blinded by tears and full of confidence I finally found his daughter.

The next morning I drove to Jimmy's house to deliver the news. He was beyond thrilled. I showed him her picture, and he marveled about "what a looker she was." Each day he would ask me to see her photo.

Though it pained me, I respected his wishes and only contacted his daughter after he passed. She flew to my hometown. When I saw her, I knew with complete certainty she was Jimmy's daughter. She was the portrait of Jimmy and their similarities were eerie. Upon inviting her into my house she instinctively sat in *his chair* at our supper table. During this visit I also took her to his home and shared our memories of her father, recounting what an important man he was to us. Jimmy had profoundly impacted my life: he healed my soul and filled a void of the father I always longed for.

I wish I could write a happier ending to Jimmy's relationship story with his daughter the way I could for my fictional characters Jimmy and Ruby. Instead, all I can do is focus on how blessed my family was to have this amazing man in our lives. In the end we needed him, just as much as he needed us, and we will cherish each moment we spent with him.

As you can see from these personal connections, I love to build my stories around real life experiences and emotions. My hope in sharing this information is to give you a glimpse of the richness behind my characters reflecting pieces of my own life story.

Sincerely,
Naomi

Available March 2019
Preorder Now

RUBY'S STORY

Coming May 2019

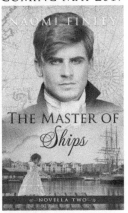

CHARLES'S STORY

Coming July 2019

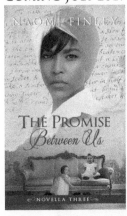

MAMMY'S STORY

Coming September 2019

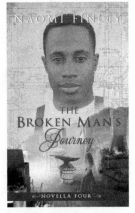

JIMMY'S STORY

COMING 2020

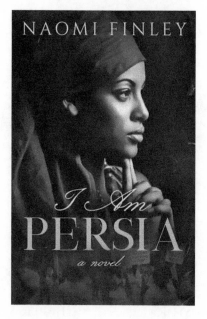

COMING LATE 2020 OR EARLY 2021

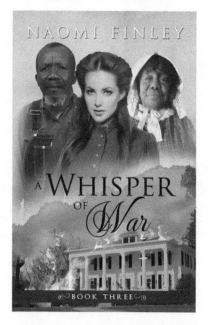

ACKNOWLEDGEMENTS

A Guardian of Slaves may never have come into fruition this past year without a team of supportive people behind me. First, I want to offer a special thank you to my editors: Marg Gilks, Jena Parsons, and Jennifer Dinsmore. Marg, your insight and appreciation of my work encouraged me to continue doing what I love. Your mentoring and guidance through each manuscript motivated a desire in me to make you proud. Victoria Cooper, you shine as both a gifted designer and a person. I am continually captivated by how you take my ideas and transform them into beautiful works of art. From the time you first read my novel you believed in my abilities as a writer, and our chats bloomed beyond conversations about artwork to upcoming books. You truly are a gem. To my husband, whose faith in me makes all of this possible—thank you for every walk, vacation, and drive you spent discussing plot lines to exhaustion with me. You are my sustaining rock and quiver. To my children (my heart), family, and friends, I sincerely appreciate your forgiveness and understanding when I disappeared for days on end to hide out and write. And last, to my incredible readers for sending an outpouring of treasured feedback through your emails. Your kindness and support are the force behind what I do each day. Thank you for waiting for me to complete *A Guardian of Slaves*. I hope you enjoy it!

ABOUT
the Author

Naomi is a bestselling and award-winning author living in Northern Alberta. She loves to travel and her suitcase is always on standby awaiting her next adventure. Naomi's affinity for the Deep South and its history was cultivated during her childhood living in a Tennessee plantation house with six sisters. Her fascination with history and the resiliency of the human spirit to overcome obstacles are major inspirations for her writing and she is passionately devoted to creativity. In addition to writing fiction, her interests include interior design, cooking new recipes, and hosting dinner parties. Naomi is married to her high school sweetheart and she has two teenage children and two dogs named Ginger and Snaps.

Sign up for my newsletter: authornaomifinley.com/contact

CPSIA information can be obtained
at www.ICGtesting.com
Printed in the USA
LVHW110204260419
615486LV00011B/29/P

9 781989 165140